Getting Started with Adobe Target

a Gentle Introduction for Web Analysts

FLORENT BUISSON

EDITED BY BETHANY WINKEL

Getting Started with Adobe® Target: a Gentle Introduction for Web Analysts

by Florent Buisson (author) and Bethany Winkel (editor)
Visual design by AtriTeX

Published by Implicit Knowledge, LLC, 8 The Green Suite B, Dover, DE 19901.

ISBN: 979-8-218-68639-0

Table of contents

PART I: Basic Activities in Adobe Target

PART II: Premium activities

PART III: Transversal Topics

Introduction

Adobe Target is an experimentation and optimization solution that is part of the Adobe Experience Cloud and is used by large companies such as Macy's. It offers a lot of capabilities, but it can be intimidating for new users. I have used Adobe Target extensively in my role as Experimentation and Optimization Principal for a large e-commerce company. When I began I was told, "Here's the tool we're using; now it's your job to manage it." This is the book I wish I'd had back then!

Audience

This book is intended for web analysts and marketers who use Adobe Target on a regular basis. It assumes that someone else will handle the software engineering aspects involved, but I'll touch on them from time to time so that you have at least a minimal understanding of what they're doing.

This book is not a prep guide for Adobe Target certifications, but I certainly hope it will help you if you want to get certified. Think of it as an introduction to help you get your bearings before studying for a specific certification.

Partnership with MiaProva

I wanted this book to be very visual, so that you could see directly where to look and where to click in the Adobe Target user interface. This would not have been possible without my partnership with Brian Hawkins at MiaProva, who graciously allowed me to take screenshots of the website and the Target interface. MiaProva is an innovative Optimization Management Platform that pioneers value-based testing, promotes innovation through rigorous testing methodologies, and integrates cutting-edge technology to ensure scalable and excellent testing operations. With customizable alerts and notifications, MiaProva empowers organizations to uphold high standards of performance and responsiveness throughout their testing processes. MiaProva ensures that learnings are always preserved and promoted across the organization so others can benefit and extract value. MiaProva has deep integrations with Adobe Target, Adobe Analytics, Adobe Experience Platform, GA4, BigQuery, Slack, Teams, JIRA, and Adobe Workfront. Check out https://www.miaprova.com/ to learn more.

Contents of the book

This book is broken down into three parts.

Part I will walk you through projects of increasing complexity so that you can familiarize yourself progressively with Adobe Target:

1. Initial setup and AA testing
2. Canary release and debugging
3. Scheduling and progressive rollout
4. Experimentation and AB testing
5. Multivariate testing (MVT) for higher velocity
6. Experience targeting (XT)

Part II will cover two additional activities that are available only with premium subscriptions:

1. Personalization
2. Recommendations

Part III will cover a series of transversal topics that will deepen your understanding of the tool and help you handle common issues and specific use cases:

1. Review of audiences and visitor profiles
2. Case study in audiences and visitor profiles: filtering out paid traffic in e-commerce
3. Debugging from the browser
4. Interactions between activities
5. Server-side and hybrid implementation
6. Single-page applications (SPA)
7. Administration

Finally, there are the appendices. In many books, these are an afterthought and turn out to be somewhat of a broken promise, like that room you've always wanted to turn into a home office that instead ends up containing all the junk you don't know where else to put. This is not the case here. Due to Adobe Target's complex genealogy and layer upon layer of features, I have taken great care with the glossary (i.e., dictionary of technical terms used in the book) and index, and I hope that you'll find them to be very helpful whenever you want to check the meaning of some Adobe lingo or see how a feature works.

A1.Glossary

A2. Index

PART I:
BASIC ACTIVITIES IN ADOBE TARGET

Chapter 1.1: Initial Setup and A/A Testing

Introduction

In this first chapter, after explaining the basics of web optimization and experimentation, we'll see how to set up Adobe Target for the very first time. If Adobe Target is already in use in your organization, you can skip that section and jump to the next one. That section will have you run your first activity, an A/A test.

Web optimization and experimentation explained in less than 500 words

Let's start with the basics of how the internet works. The internet is based on three programming languages: HTML, CSS, and JavaScript (JS). HTML determines the content of a page and its logical structure, while CSS makes that content look pretty by adding formatting and colors. Finally, JavaScript is what makes internet pages actually "do" things.

If we used only HTML, the internet would be like traditional black-and-white books or the first generation of ebooks. With the addition of CSS, it would be like glossy undergrad introductory books, with text sleekly formatted in multiple columns around photos, graphics, and call-out boxes. It is JavaScript that separates the internet from printed materials. JS is what allows you to click on buttons, enables a page to call you by name, and lets a site display the information that is most relevant to you.

Typically, web optimization and experimentation uses the power of JavaScript to deliver different experiences on a website in real time. Despite a bewildering variety of configurations, it relies on the most simple of programming concepts: the IF/THEN instruction. For example, *if* a randomly generated number is lower than a given threshold, *then* show the visitor this content (otherwise show them the default content). *If* a visitor comes from paid search, *then* show them this content. *If* a visitor is using an Apple device and content B has been performing the best for Apple users, *then* show them content B. And so on.

This use of IF/THEN is often called a *feature flag* in programming. Think of it like the lifeguard flag on a beach: if the flag is green you can go swimming; if it's red you can't. Here, depending on what the flag says, a feature either will or will not be activated and displayed to the visitor. Adobe Target has a particular name for feature flags, because of its roots in marketing optimization: the *mbox*, which stands for *marketing box*.

To provide speedy interactivity without having to send request after request to the website server, your browser executes JS directly on its own. In fact, the ability for web browsers to execute JS locally (a.k.a. ***client side***) has been a major factor in its popularity, and it remains the dominant modality for optimization and experimentation. However, with the increasing complexity of websites, we've seen a movement towards having more of the computation being executed on the website's server (a.k.a ***server side***), using either JS or a different programming language such as Python or Java.

Thus, depending on how your website is built, you may have to use Adobe Target on the client side (its primary mode) or on the server side; for the latter Adobe provides ***Software Development Kits (SDKs)*** for Python, Java, and other programming languages.

Client-side initial setup (for illustrative purposes only)

Setting up Adobe Target on your website requires adding some JS code to it. There are currently two options for doing this:

- the Target Web SDK, which relies on a JS script, or **snippet**, named *at.js*
- the Adobe Experience Platform Web SDK, which relies on *alloy.js*

While this task should be handled by your engineering team, I find it helpful to visualize how it works, namely by loading the required script in the <script> section of the page. For example:

```
<script src="<url to at.js>" async></script>
```

(Note that in this instance, the at.js script is loaded asynchronously, which can reduce the time it takes your page to render but may cause flickering.)

The Target Web SDK can also be handled from the AEP Tags application.

Activity setup

We'll now get to the first type of activity we'll cover, an A/A test. You can think of it as a dress rehearsal for an A/B test: it allows you to confirm that everything is working as expected without causing any real damage if anything goes wrong. This will also provide an opportunity to become familiar with Adobe Target's three-step guided workflow to create activities: (1) Experience, (2) Targeting, (3) Goals & Settings.

For a typical A/B test, the logic is as follows whenever a new visitor comes to the website:

```
Generate a random number x between 0 and 1
IF x is less than 0.5 THEN show the visitor the "control" experience A
IF x is more than 0.5 THEN show the visitor the "treatment" experience B
```

With a default setup, if anything goes wrong (i.e., the random number generator was not called, failed, or didn't send the value of x in time) then the control experience A is shown.

An A/A test follows a similar logic, except that the treatment group also sees experience A:

```
Generate a random number x between 0 and 1
IF x is less than 0.5 THEN show the visitor the "control" experience A
IF x is more than 0.5 THEN show the visitor the "treatment" experience A
```

This means that you don't create a second experience to test, and all visitors will see the same thing: namely, the website as it currently exists. You're simply asking Adobe Target to generate a random number and assign an experimental group to visitors. If everything goes as planned, your data should show that approximately half of the visitors are tagged as part of the control group and the other half are tagged as part of the treatment group.

Setting up the mbox

With Adobe Target, mboxes play an important role in the implementation of experimentation and optimization on your website. Many bugs and painful mistakes can be traced back to calling the wrong mbox or having a typo in its name. In this first chapter, we'll keep things as simple as possible: one test (*activity*) running in one place (**location**) through one mbox. But this convenient one-to-one correspondence will fall apart in the following chapters, so don't get too attached to it.

For the very first A/A test that you run, you'll want to place an empty mbox on a page with a limited but reasonable amount of traffic, such as the site's fifth or tenth most visited page. The website that we'll use, www.miaprova.com, does not have many pages, so we'll use the page containing its privacy policy, https://www.miaprova.com/privacy. The mbox for our first A/A test will thus be "aa1_privacy", indicating which test it will be used for and on which page it is located.

Creating the activity

Optimization and experimentation projects in Adobe Target are called *activities*, which is the first tab in the user interface.

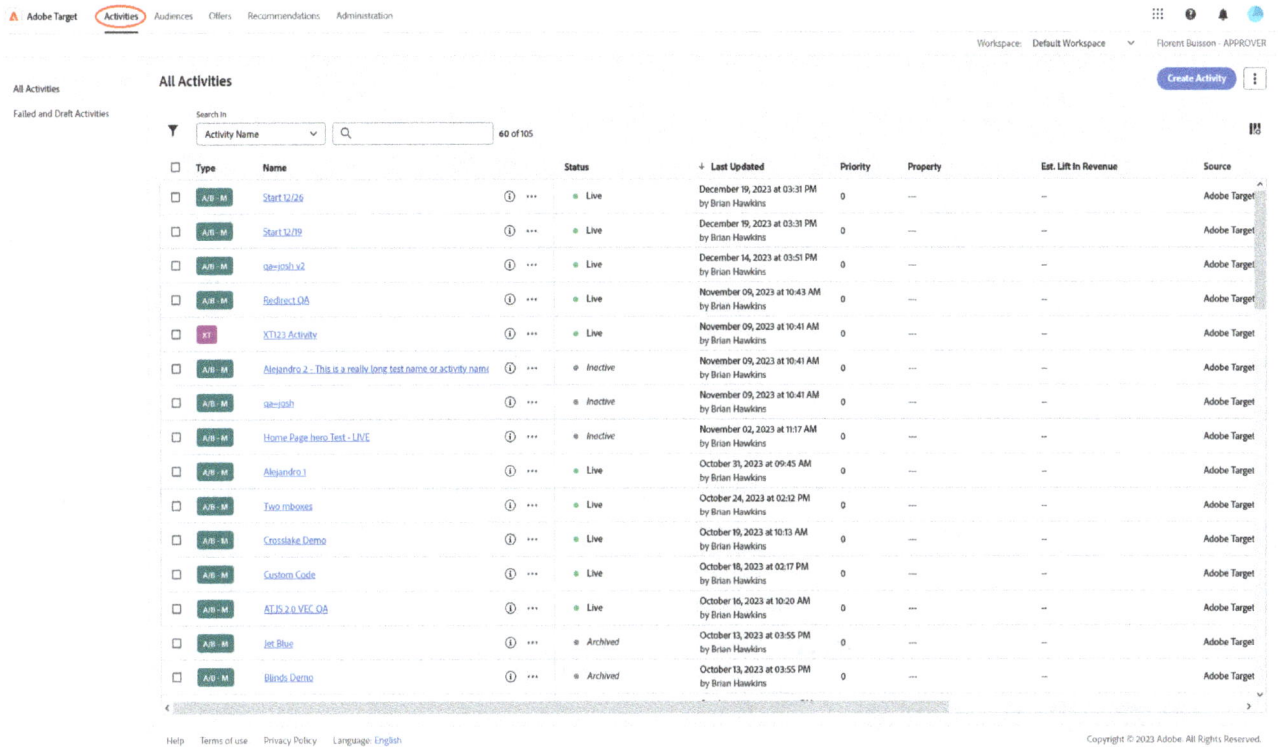

When you click on the *Create Activity* button, a drop-down list appears. Select *A/B Test* (even though you are actually creating an A/A test).

- A pop-up then appears, asking you to select a few configuration settings. The following are the most common, though depending on your situation, some may be missing or slightly different:
- **Type.** This asks whether you want to create an activity for a website, a mobile application, an email server or other possibilities such as an API. We'll leave the default *Web* as is.
- **Choose Experience Composer.** Here you choose the interface you want to use to set up your activity. We'll go with *Form* for this first activity.
- **Choose Workspace.** If your account has access to several workspaces, select the one you wish to use.
- **Choose Property.** If your account has access to several properties, you'll select the relevant one here.

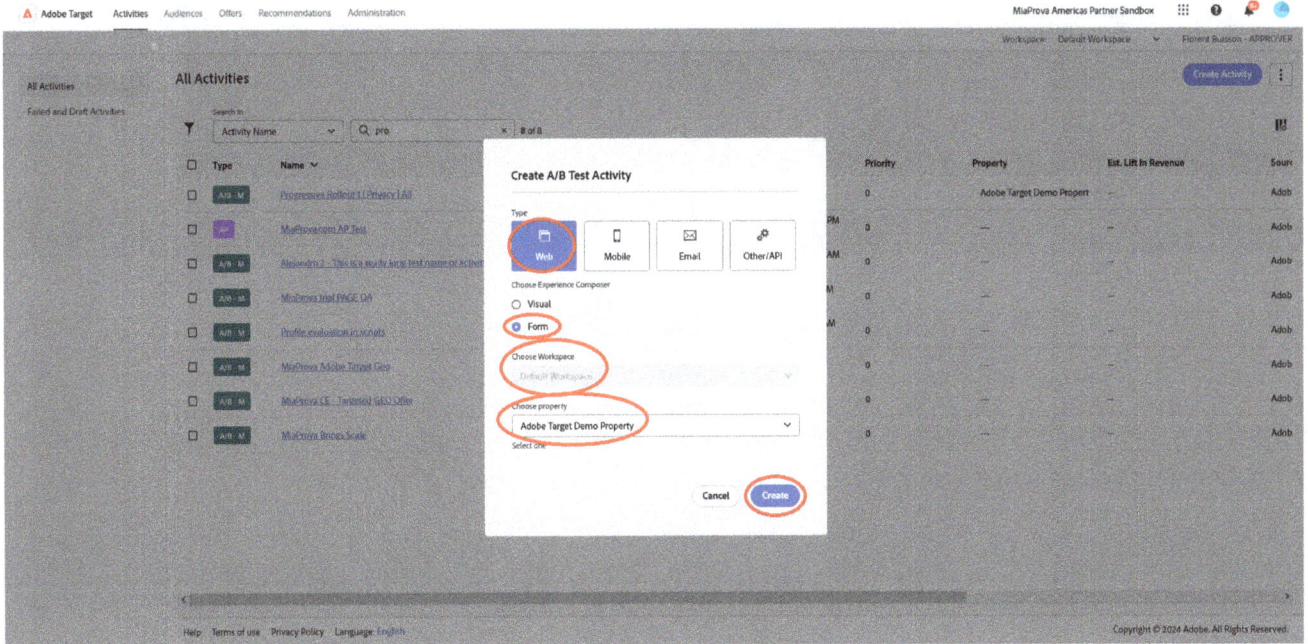

Clicking *Create* opens the Experiences screen. As you can see in the progression path in the second title bar, this is the first step of Adobe Target's three-step guided workflow.

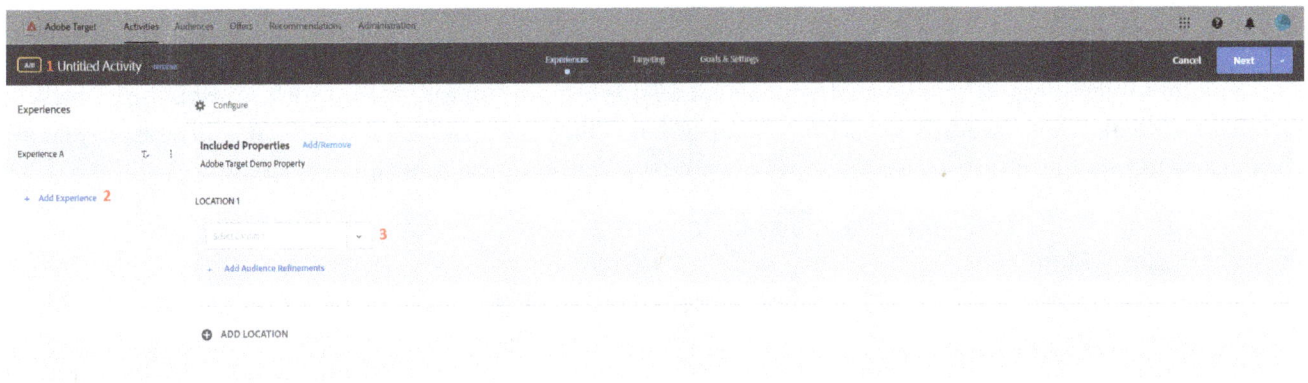

Let's look at the steps one by one:

1. We need to give our activity a **name**. For this very first one, the name you pick doesn't matter, but at some point you'll need to get a system that will scale up as you run more and more tests. I personally like "Test number | location of test | audience." Since this is our first A/A test, on the Privacy page, for all visitors, the name would be "AA 1 | Privacy | All." Which system you use really doesn't matter as long as other people can easily follow along.

2. We need to add **a second experience**. Here again, the naming system itself doesn't matter as much as consistency. Consistency is especially important if other people, such as software engineers, need to be involved in the implementation of tests. The default convention in Adobe Target is "Experience A / Experience B / …," which is perfectly fine for our purposes here, especially given that the two experiences will be identical. If you like more science-y names, an alternative convention is "Control / Treatment 1 / Treatment 2 / …."

3. We need to indicate the **location(s)** of the test. This is simply the name of the mbox that has been set up previously for this test.

Here's what the screen then looks like.

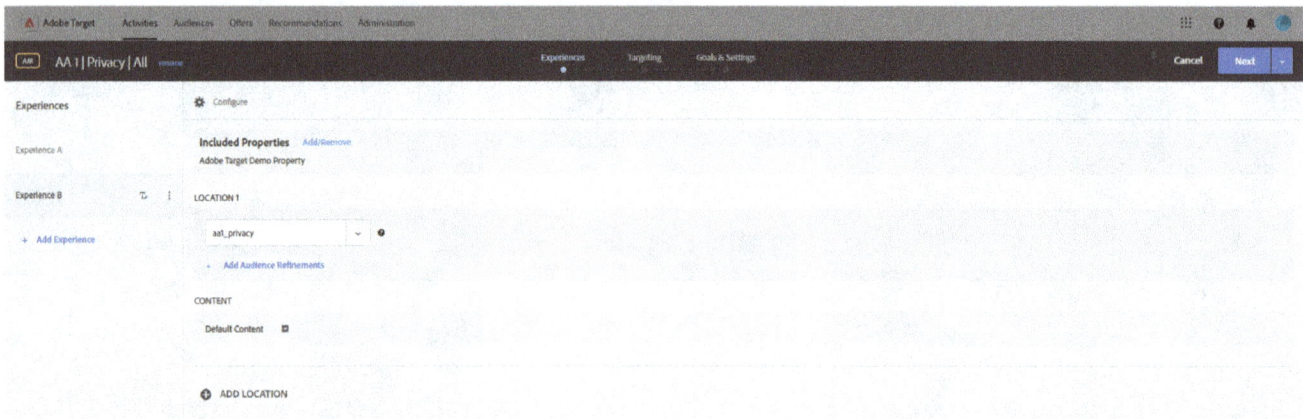

Clicking *Next* takes us to the second step of the workflow, the Targeting screen.

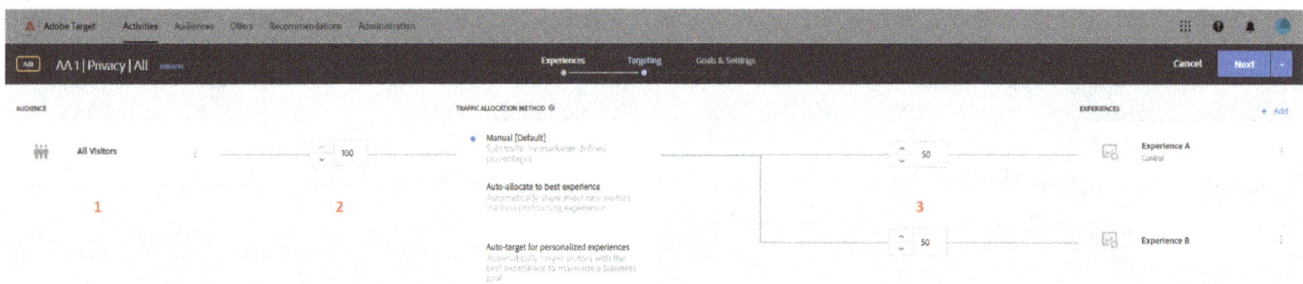

We're not actually going to change anything here, but this is an opportunity to start familiarizing ourselves with this screen. There are three essential components connected by lines; these lines flow from left to right, showing that each subsequent piece is a restriction or refinement of the previous:

1. First of all, the **audience** area allows us to restrict a test to certain visitors only. For this one, *All Visitors* will do.
2. The **traffic** selector allows us to determine what part of the audience we just selected should be included in the test, expressed in percentage points. The default is 100%, indicating that every visitor in your audience will be part of the test once it's activated. If we set the value lower than that, visitors who are not randomly selected to be part of the test (that is, 25% of visitors if you chose 75%, and so on) will just see the current (default) experience and not be included in the test analyses.
3. The **traffic allocation selectors** allow us to split the traffic between the different experiences. (Don't worry about the Traffic Allocation Method widget, it is automatically set to *Manual,* and we'll discuss the other two options later in the book.) The default 50%-50% split works for us in the present case. Please note that the traffic allocation selectors should always add up to 100, regardless of the fraction of the audience included in the traffic for the test. For instance, if we included only 10% of the audience in the test in the previous step, a 50/50 allocation would translate to 5% of the total audience being allocated to each of the two experiences.

Clicking *Next* takes us to the third step and final screen, Goals & Settings. We're not going to make any meaningful change in this screen, but before we can move forward, Adobe Target requires that we set our ***Goal Metric***.

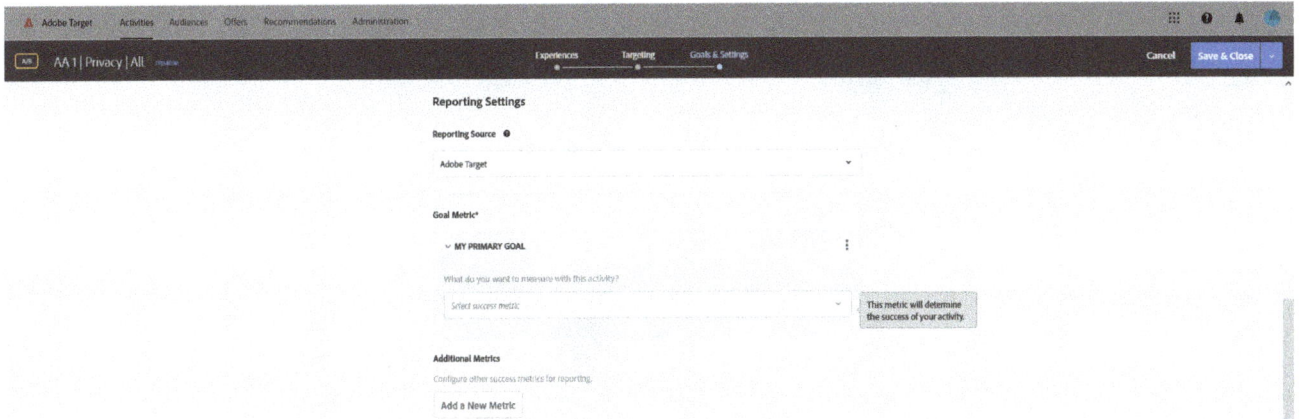

Let's put down that our primary goal is *Conversion*, based on the activity *Clicked an mbox*, using the mbox name for our test. We'll leave alone the *Audiences for Reporting* section for now.

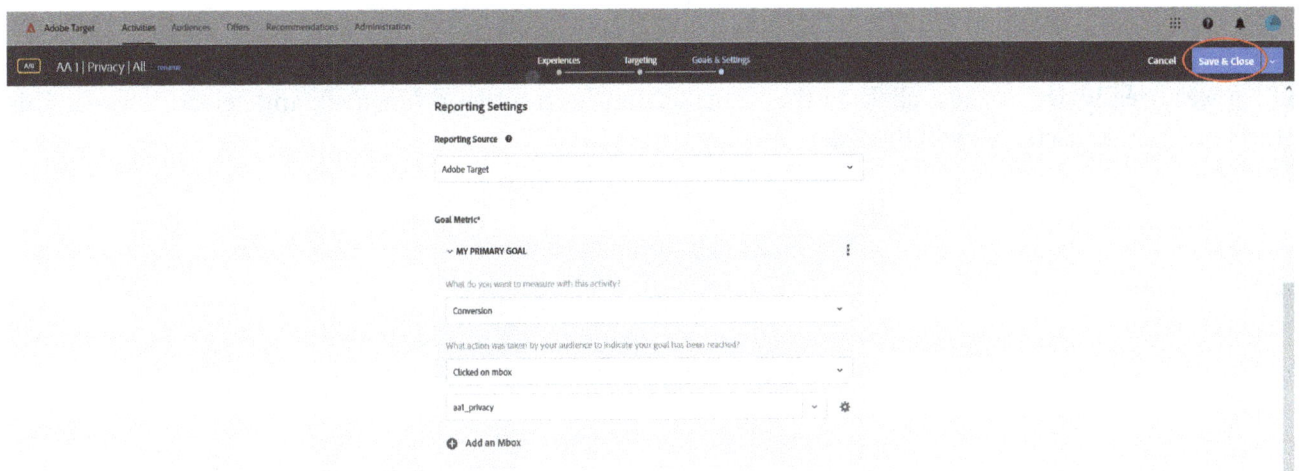

Clicking *Save & Close* creates our activity and automatically takes us to the summary screen. Note that at this point, nothing is happening on our website or being tracked in the data. The test is ready to go, but we still need to activate it.

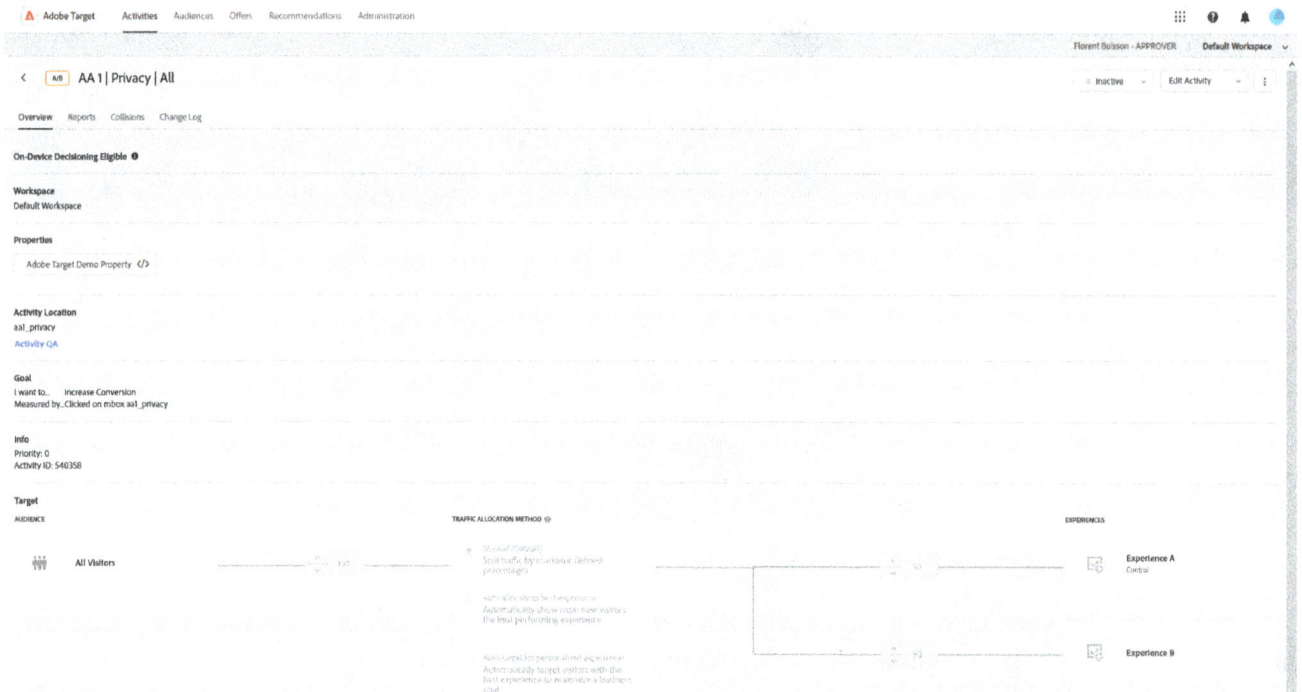

Once we're ready, we can just click on the status button (currently on *Inactive*), and select *Activate*. This starts our test, and visitors will then start flowing through.

The status button changes to *Live*. Let's then click on the < arrow on the left of the test name.

This brings us back to the overall *Activities* tab, where our test is now visible.

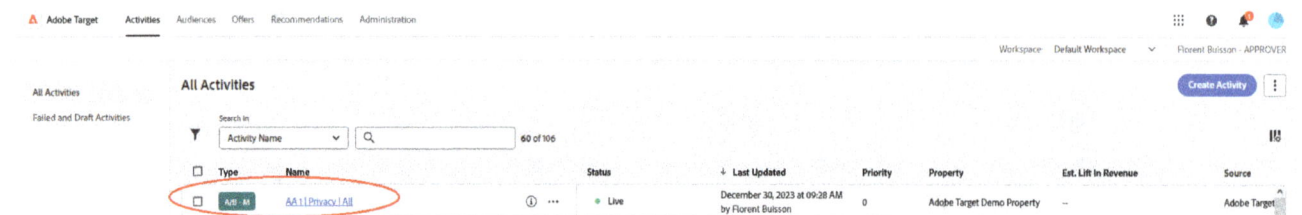

Reporting

Once your test is active, you can navigate to the corresponding page of the website on a few different browsers, ideally after clearing your cookies and on different devices—for instance your laptop and your mobile phone. For this test, no news is good news: everything should look the same as before.

Reporting with Target as data source

Adobe Target offers a simple reporting interface, which will allow you to get a high-level view of how an activity is faring in real time. You can access it from an activity's summary page, under the Reports tab.

The amount of information displayed depends on your activity setup. For example, if you don't have Adobe Analytics installed, the data source for the activity will be Adobe Target, as in the picture above. In this case you'll see only minimal reporting for each experience. Information includes:

- **Name of each experience.** If your activity has a control, it's indicated under the corresponding experience name, and if there is a winning experience, it will have a star before its name.
- **Number of unique visitors and their share of the total for the activity**, expressed as a percentage. The goal is that over time this second number will get pretty close to your traffic allocation.
- **Conversion rate and total number of conversions.**
- **Lift relative to the control group** (calculated as (conversion rate for the experience - conversion rate for the control experience) / (conversion rate for the control experience)).
- **Degree of confidence** in the lift, which is defined here as one p-value per lift statistic. The p-value is the probability of observing a lift as large as or larger than the lift observed in the activity if there is no true difference in the underlying conversion rates.

Note: if you haven't correctly set the data source and primary success metric before starting the activity, you won't be able to visualize that data in the report screen, and you'll have to get the relevant data from your database.

Getting back to our A/A test for a minute: At this point we haven't done the necessary setup to restrict the activity to new visitors only, which means that all visitors are eligible to enter the activity, regardless of their visit number. By default, all analyses are also done at the visitor level, which is usually what we want. For the sake of completeness, let's see how to switch to visit-level metrics and analyses.

We can set this up by clicking on the gear icon in the middle of the Reports screen.

This opens a Settings pop-up, where we can set the counting methodology to *Visits* instead of *Visitors*.

Reporting with Adobe Analytics as data source

If you have set the Analytics for Target (A4T) integration between Adobe Target and Adobe Analytics, the Reports tab offers richer information. In particular, you'll be able to visualize different metrics by clicking on the *Report metric* button.

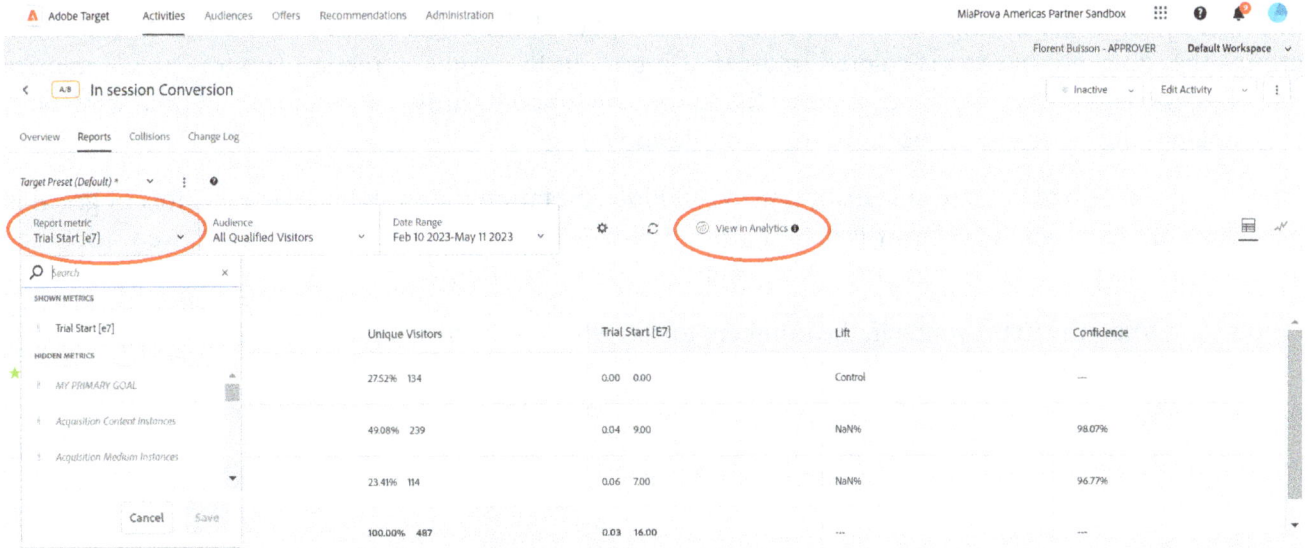

Notice as well on the right the *View in Analytics* link which has appeared. Clicking it gets you to an Adobe Analytics dashboard with automatically generated content for this activity.

Validation

When running an A/A test, we need to confirm two things.

First, the number of visits in the two groups should be "close enough" to the proportions set up for the activity. If they diverge too much, we have what is called a **Sample Ratio Mismatch**, which suggests that there is something wrong with our implementation. The formulas for that are outside of the scope of this book, so I'll refer you to any good statistics or experimentation book (such as *Trustworthy Online Controlled Experiments: A Practical Guide to A/B Testing*, Kohavi et al.).

Second, key business metrics should also be "close enough" between groups in that the observed differences should not be statistically significant. Fortunately, Adobe Target provides useful visualizations in those circumstances. If the conversion rates are too close to each other for the degree of uncertainty in the numbers (formally, their **standard errors**), then the table with the results displays their confidence intervals.

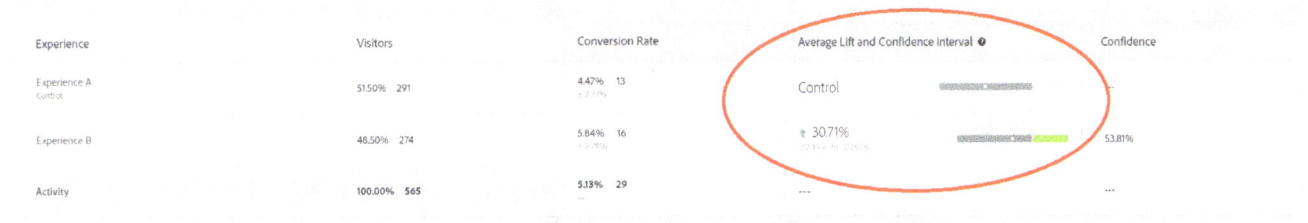

The first part of the circled column shows *Control* for the control group row and the average lift compared to the control group for the other rows. The second part of the column displays visually the confidence interval (CI) of the primary metric for the control group; for the other groups, it displays the CIs for both that group and the control group, which allows us to visually determine if and how much they overlap.

The confidence interval for the control group is always colored in gray, as is the part of the confidence intervals for the other groups that overlap with it. The part of the confidence intervals for the treatment groups that does not overlap is colored in green if it goes in the "right" direction (up for "good" metrics like click-through, down for "bad" metrics like bounce rate) and red if it goes in the "wrong" direction. (Fortunately, the latter doesn't occur in the example above).

However good or bad you are at statistics, the visual interpretation for an A/B test is easy: lots of green is good; lots of red is bad; lots of gray is neutral. In the case of an A/A test on the other hand, we want to see as much gray as possible! Things are looking pretty good in this example.

If you want to do the math yourself, the numbers for the 95% confidence interval are also displayed under each of the conversion rates.

Experience	Visitors	Conversion Rate	Average Lift and Confidence Interval		Confidence
Experience A Control	51.50% 291	4.47% 13 +/- 2.37%	Control		...
Experience B	48.50% 274	5.84% 16 +/- 2.94%	↑ 30.71% -0.10% to 73.01%		53.81%
Activity	-	5.13% 29	...		...

For Experience A (control), the value is +/- 2.37%, meaning that the lower bound of the 95% confidence interval for the conversion rate is 4.47% - 2.37% = 2.10% and the upper bound of the confidence interval is 4.47% + 2.37% = 6.84%.

Concluding the test

Once we are ready to conclude the test, we can click on the three-dot menu button in the line for the test and select *Deactivate*. (The other two options are *Copy*, which allows us to create a new activity using this one as a starting point, and *Edit*, which allows us to start editing the activity without having to go through its summary page first.)

After a couple of seconds, the test is now displayed as inactive.

If we click on the three-dot menu button for the test, we'll now be presented with slightly different action buttons.

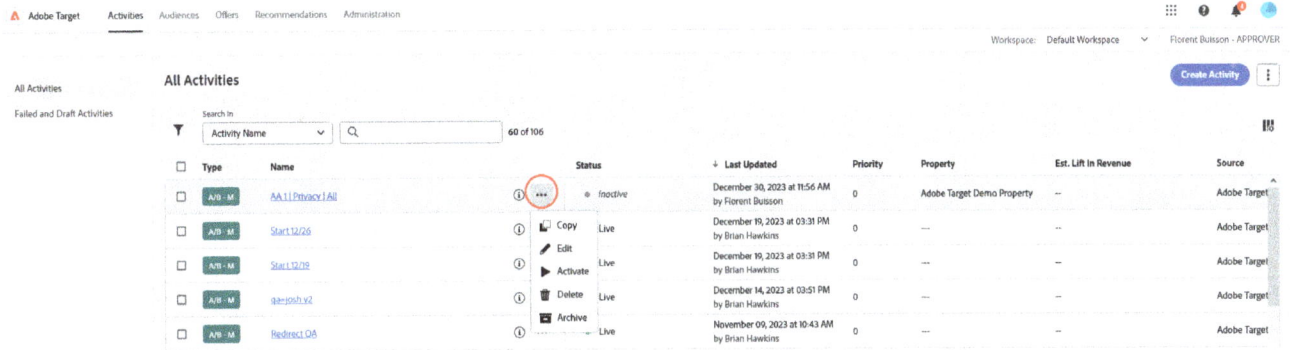

The first two buttons are the same as when the test was live: *Copy* and *Edit*. The third button is now *Activate*, and we also have the options to *Delete* or *Archive* the test, which can only be done when it's inactive.

To recap, an activity can have the following status:

- **Live or Active.** The activity is currently running on the website, and external visitors are being routed to it according to the activity configuration.
- **Inactive or Paused.** The activity is not running on the website for external visitors, but if the mbox has been set up, internal users such as the Quality Assurance (QA) team can access it for validation and debugging purposes.
- **Scheduled.** The activity has been created with a scheduled start date in the future.
- **Ended.** The activity was created with a scheduled end date that it has now reached.
- **Archived.** The activity is not accessible to anyone on the website and by default is not displayed in the list of activities (although it can still be accessed with the corresponding filter).
- **Deleted.** The activity and all references to it have ceased to exist.

When an activity is archived, you can still access its summary by selecting the appropriate filter (this is handy if you want to copy an old test). To do so, click on the *Show filters* button, symbolized by a funnel.

Then, under the *Status* category, select *Archived*. From there, find the activity you want to access.

That's it! You've had your first encounter with Adobe Target's user interface, and you've run your first activity, an A/A test.

Chapter 1.2: Canary Release and Debugging

You may have heard of the 80/20 rule, also known as the Pareto Principle. While it is often unduly applied or misused, it unfortunately applies pretty well to experimentation: Most (perhaps not precisely 80%) of your time will be taken up by a few (around 20%) of the tests—those that are more complex or that go wrong in some way.

This makes debugging an important part of running experiments. More generally, feature flags are often used to validate new features in production by making them available on the "real" website (as opposed to local, sandbox environments that external visitors will never see), but only for certain users such as the QA team. This is sometimes called a "canary release," in reference to the birds historically used to detect gas leaks in coal mines.

In this chapter, we'll also see how to use Target's global mbox and take a first look at audiences in Adobe Target by creating an activity for mobile visitors only, that is, visitors using a web browser on a mobile phone.

Activity setup

Local versus global mbox

In the previous chapter, we used a dedicated mbox specific to our activity. With this traditional approach, the website makes an individual call to Adobe Target each time a user reaches a new activity on the page. Over the last few years, however, Adobe has been implementing and promoting a new approach based on a *global mbox*. With this new setup, your website makes a single network call to Adobe Target when opening a new page and retrieves the relevant information for all the activities on the page at once.

In terms of latency and payload, there are pros and cons to using a global mbox; it comes down to a matter of fetching information "just in case" versus "just in time." For our purposes, we'll simply note that while some companies still use the traditional setup, the global mbox is now the more common choice for organizations getting started with Adobe Target.

Let's now see what using a global mbox looks like in practice.

Setting up the feature

The A/A test in the previous chapter didn't have any new content because the two experiences, control and treatment, were supposed to be the same. Let's now add some content—for instance, a button on the Privacy page of the website whose call-to-action we want to vary. In Adobe Target jargon, each version of the content inside the mbox is called an *offer*. Thus, "Call us" might be the Control offer and "Call now" might be the Treatment offer.

Instead of wrapping this new content in a dedicated mbox, the engineer will use the `getOffers()` and `applyOffers()` functions in the relevant place in the code for the Privacy page.

Setting up the activity in Adobe Target

As in the previous chapter, setting up the activity starts within the Activities tab. We could set up the activity by once again clicking on the *Create Activity* button and selecting *A/B test*. However, to make things a bit faster and easier, we'll instead copy the activity from the previous chapter.

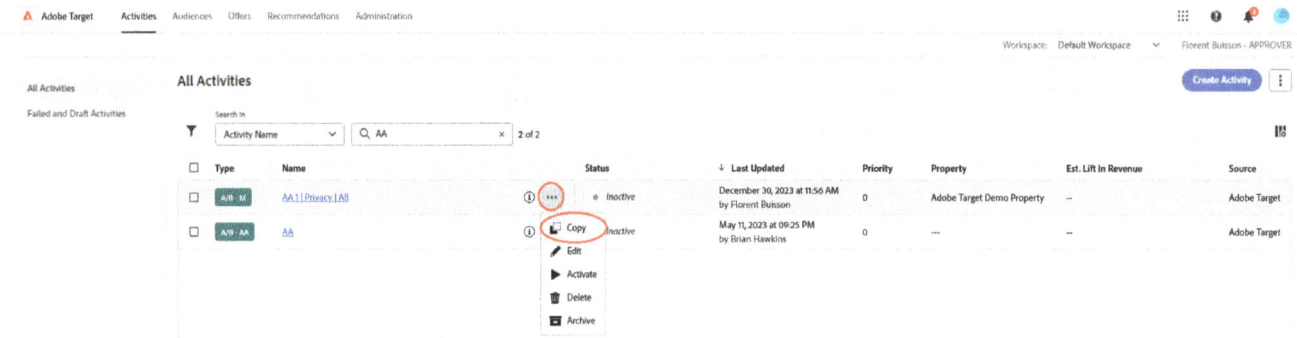

Since the previous values have been automatically copied, we need to update the name of the activity to "Canary 1 | Privacy | Mobile" and the name of the mbox to the name of the global mbox, by default target-global-mbox.

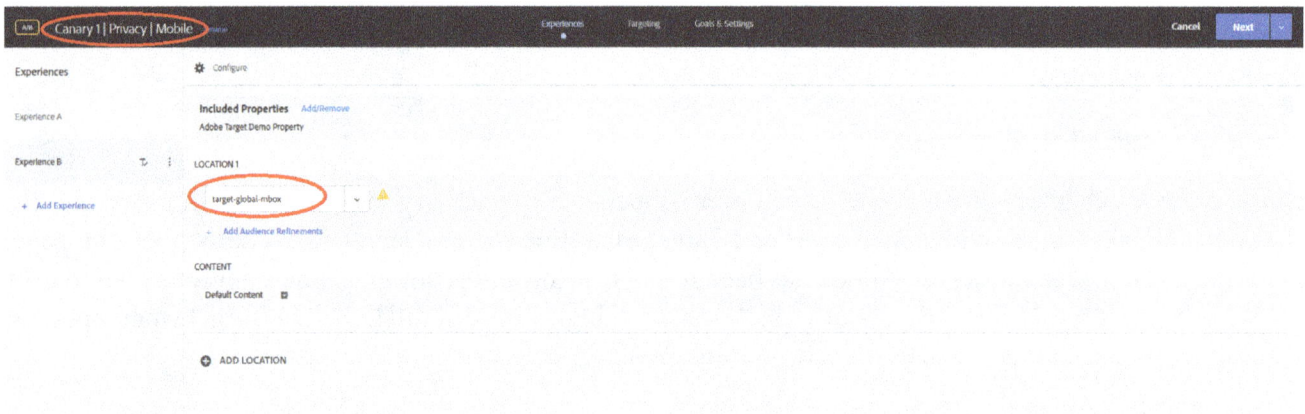

When we assign an activity to the global mbox, an orange warning triangle appears to the right of the mbox name, to helpfully remind us that we should probably add some restrictions to our activity. Let's click on "+ Add Audience Refinements" right under the mbox name.

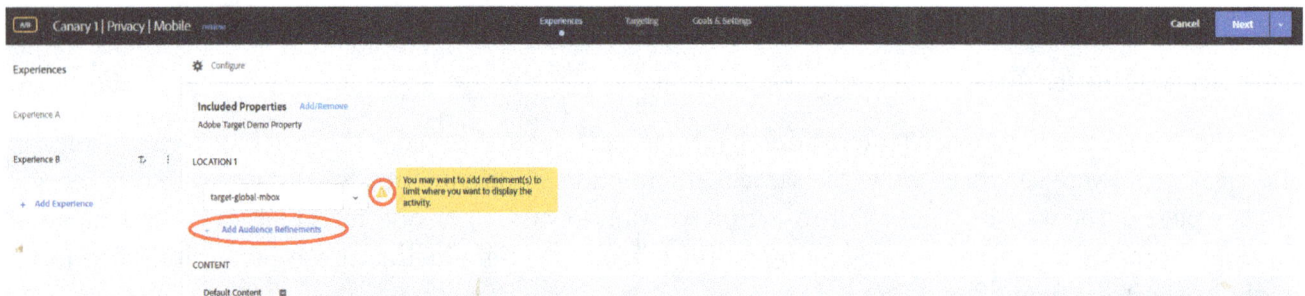

This opens the Add audiences pop-up window, where we can create a new audience or search for one that has already been defined. If the audience already exists, we can add it simply by checking the box in front of it and clicking Assign Audience.

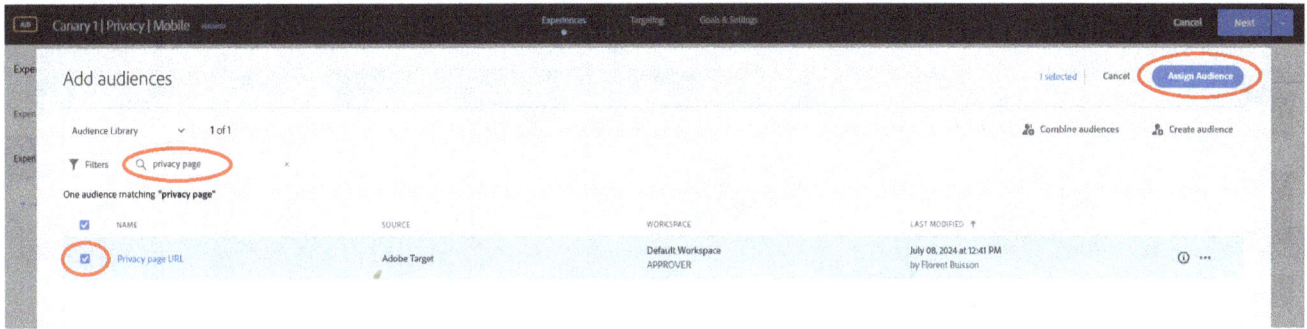

The audience refinement now appears on the Experiences page and we can click *Next*.

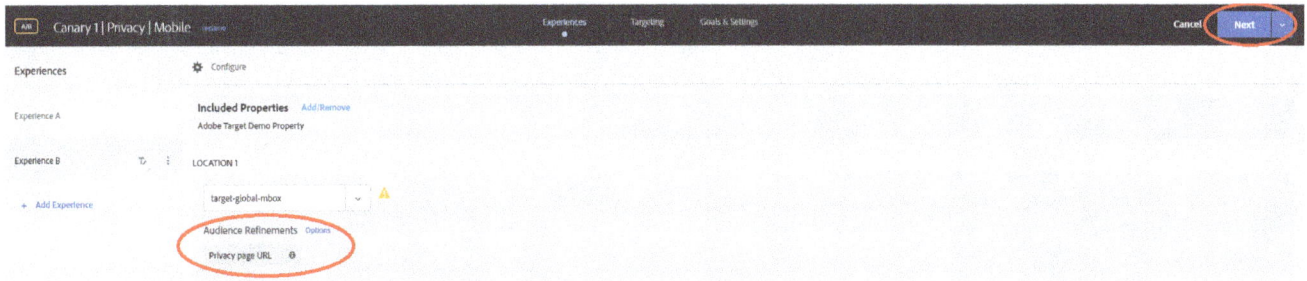

Creating an audience for the activity

We're now in the Targeting stage. Let's click on the three-dot icon in the Audience area to open the drop-down option *Replace Audience*.

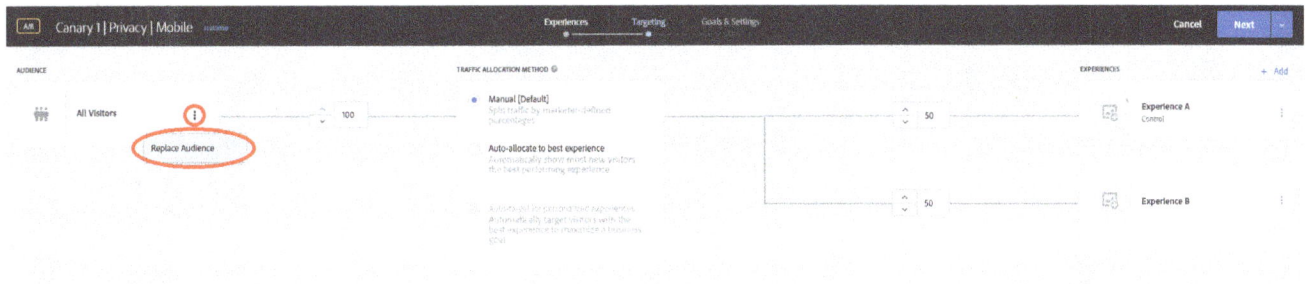

This opens up the same pop-up window Add audiences as in the Experiences screen. This obviously begs the question: which one of the two should you use to enter audience restrictions? As far as I can tell it's up to you, the main difference is that audiences assigned in the Targeting screen will be displayed in the activity summary screen when we're done. Let's assume a mobile phone audience hasn't been created yet, so we'll click *Create audience*.

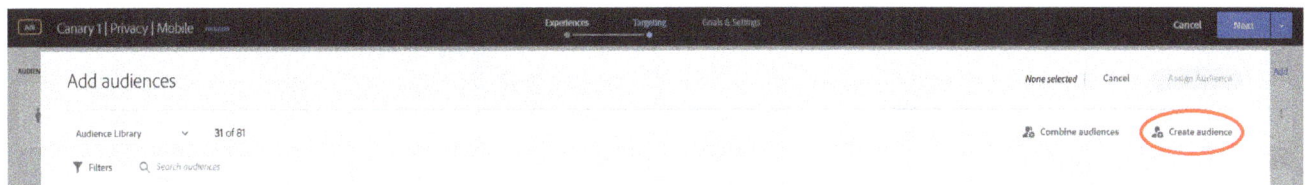

In the following Create Audience pop-up, we can see a list of attributes on the left, including *Mobile*.

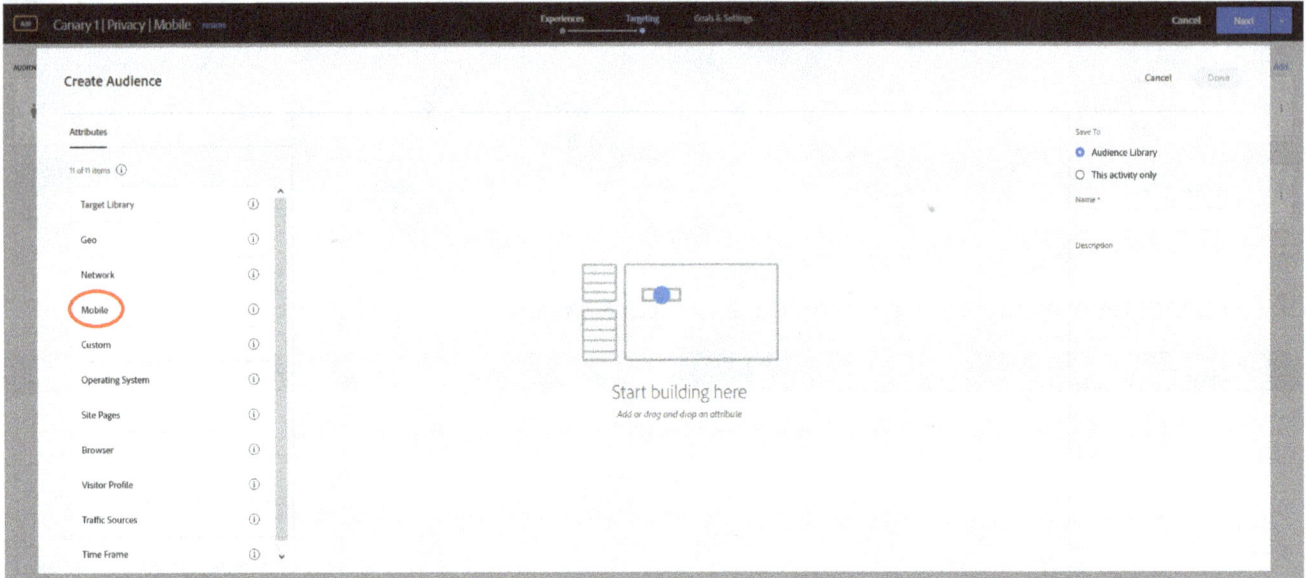

Let's drag and drop *Mobile* into the middle of the screen. This creates an Include container.

Containers allow us to include, exclude, or combine criteria to form audiences. We can then click on *Select* and then *Is Mobile Phone* to get the criterion we want.

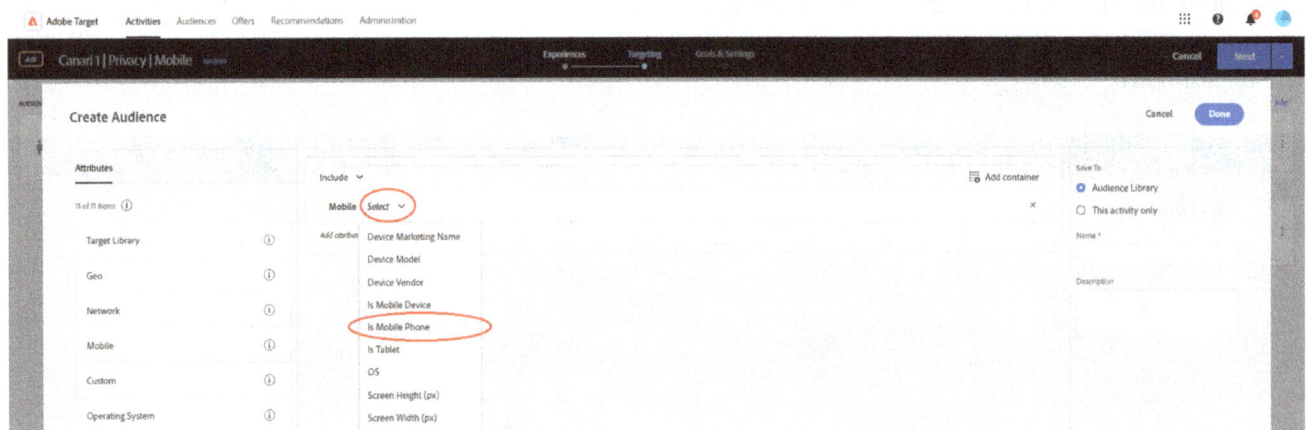

We'll set that criterion to *true*.

We'll name the audience "Mobile Phone" and save it in the Audience Library (the default setting) so that it's available for future activities, before clicking *Done*.

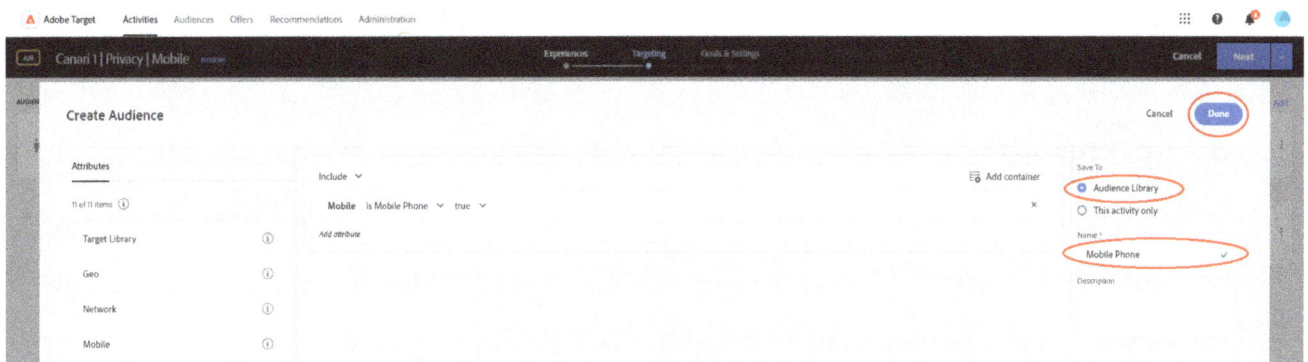

This returns us to the Add Audiences screen, where we now see our newly created audience listed.

Assigning an audience to the activity

Once you have created an audience (or found an existing one), you can assign it to your activity by highlighting it and clicking *Assign Audiences* in the top right corner.

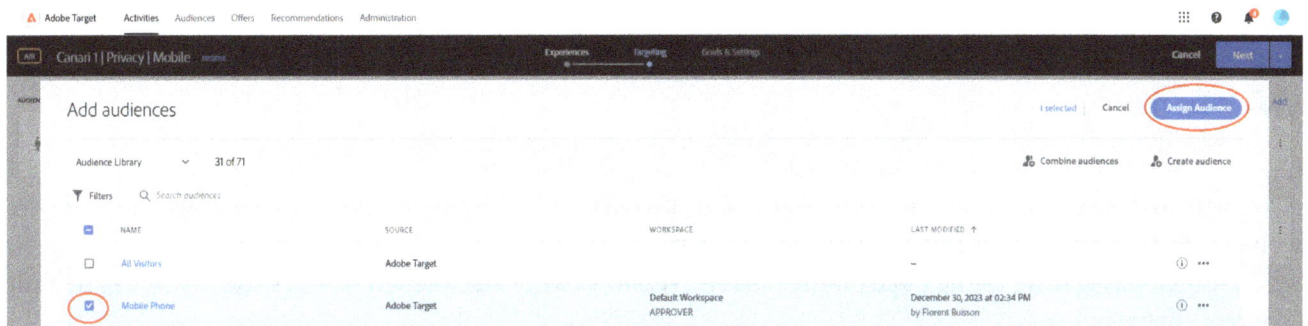

Once we're back to the Targeting step of creating the activity, we can check that the audience has been correctly assigned.

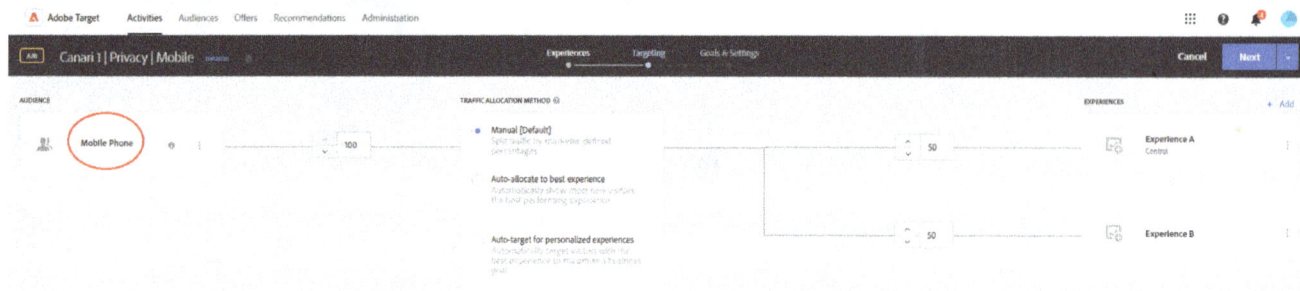

Clicking on *Next* takes us to the Goals & Settings step. We can simply keep the parameters from the previous activity, but note that if the primary goal metric involves the activity's mbox, we'll need to update its name. Finally, we'll *Save & Close*, which brings up the summary screen.

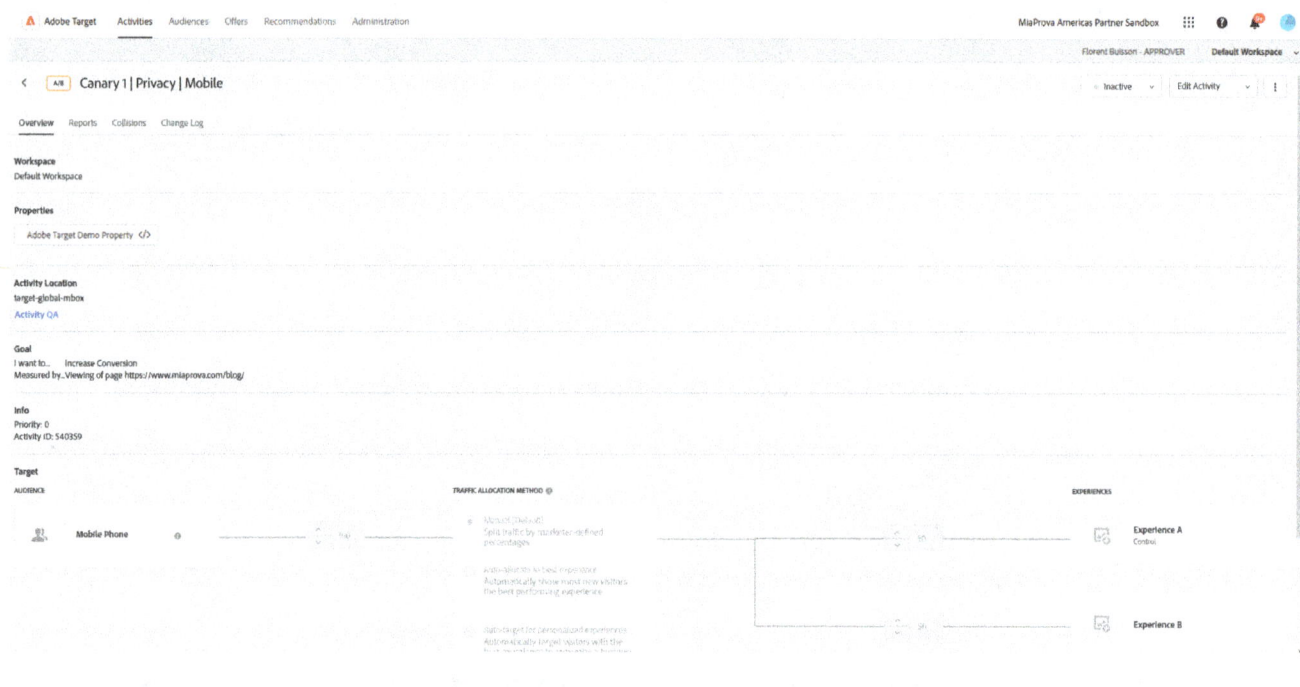

QA mode

Once an activity has been created in Adobe Target and its current status is Inactive or Live (but not Archived or Ended), you can use QA parameters to see what a specific experience looks like on the website. For instance, you can see what the treatment experience is like before activating an A/B test, whereas just navigating to the page on the current version of the website will always show you the default (control) experience.

Generating QA parameters

You can open the QA screen by clicking *Activity QA* in the summary page of a test.

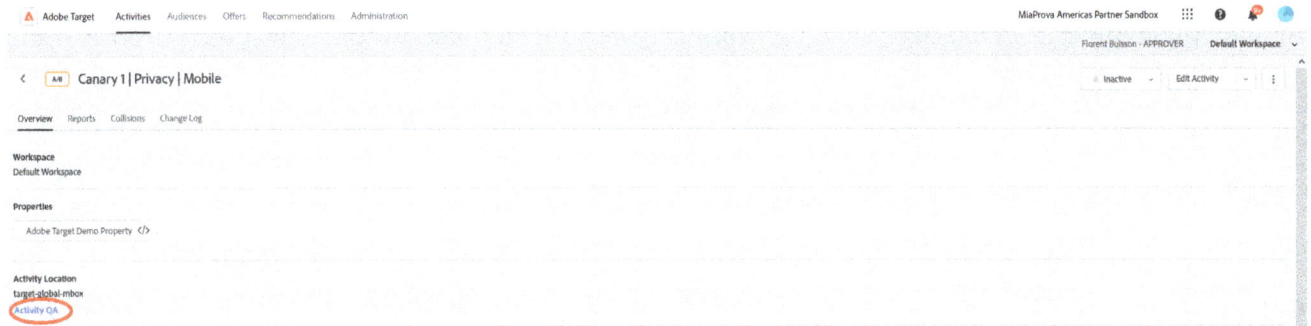

The QA screen shows information about the activity followed by QA URLs. The latter section is the one we'll be working with.

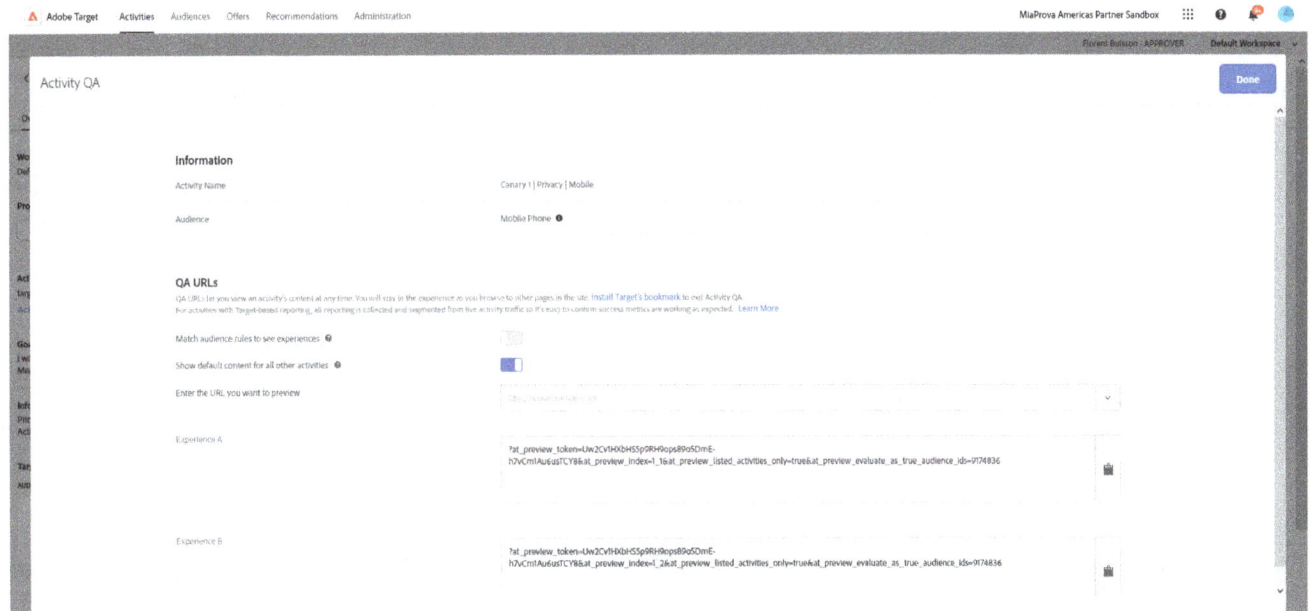

First are two toggle buttons: *Match audience rules to see experiences* and *Show default content for all other activities*. We'll leave both of them in their respective default settings of inactive and active.

The first button determines what happens when you use a QA URL while not fulfilling the conditions for a visitor to be entered in the test. Here for instance, the activity was set to only admit visitors using a mobile phone; all other visitors are routed to the default experience.

If you use the QA URL for the treatment experience on a computer browser, then:

- If the button is active, you'll be routed to the default experience like any other computer visitor.
- If the button is inactive, you'll be shown the treatment experience no matter what.

The button is inactive by default, because that's generally what you want. If you only need to verify that the experience looks as expected, you don't want to have to run through hoops before getting to the page. For instance, if you're working on a test that will be applied only to SEO traffic, having to go through a search engine like DuckDuckGo before getting back to your site can be cumbersome, impractical, and costly. In some cases, it might even be impossible for you to emulate the audience conditions on your computer (e.g., visitors from a certain state with a certain purchase history).

On the other hand, if you need to verify that the assignment and routing itself is working correctly, you should toggle this button to active, because bypassing the audience rules would defeat the purpose of the verification.

Of course, if the content of the new experience only renders well on mobile browsers, you should use or emulate a mobile browser. If you mistakenly use a desktop browser, seeing a poorly rendered experience offers a better clue to what you did wrong than seeing the default experience.

The second button determines what happens if you encounter another test while using the QA URL—for instance, if you already have a test running on the page. If you toggle the button to inactive, you may be assigned to the treatment experience of the preexisting test, depending on its audience rules, its traffic allocation, and the luck of the draw. This makes the QA process less predictably deterministic. Hence, this option defaults to active, meaning you're always assigned to the default (control) experience of preexisting tests.

There are, however, specific situations where it makes sense to toggle the button to inactive so that you can see the treatment of other activities. For instance this may be desirable if you are routing 100% of traffic to the winning treatment of a test while waiting for it to be implemented as the new default.

Lower on the QA screen, we'll find the text box labeled *Enter the URL you want to preview*, where we will—you guessed it—enter the URL of the page where our mbox is located. As soon as we're done typing, the strings in the two boxes labeled Experience A and Experience B immediately update (you might have to click outside of the text entry box to trigger the update). We can then copy the string under Experience B by clicking the clipboard icon to the right of it:

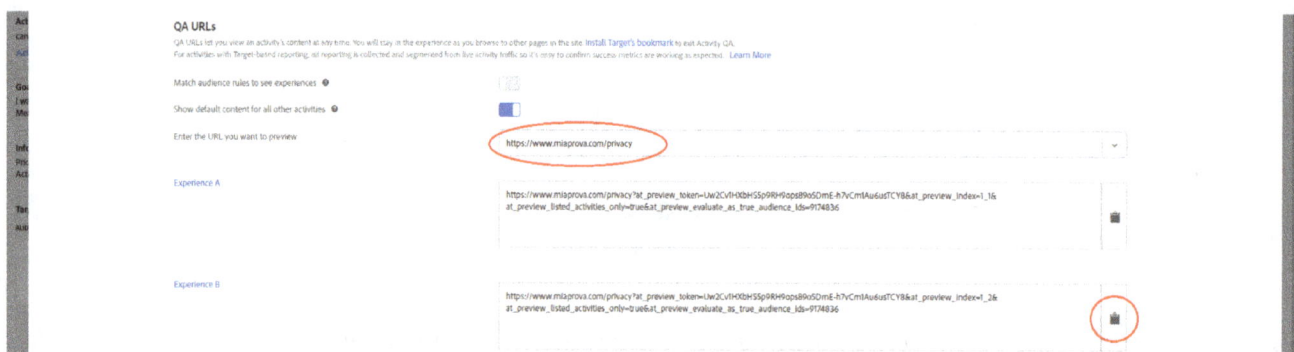

You can then go to any browser and simply paste the string into the navigation bar.

Browsing in QA mode

Adobe Target relies on cookies to store information and persist it between visits, so we always need to make sure that we have a virgin browser with no prior cookies stored when we want to enter QA mode. "Private" or "incognito" browsing mode usually does the trick, but not always; if you suspect there's some stale information stored somewhere, it's better to open a browser in normal mode and erase all of its history before navigating to your site. On my work laptop, I reserve a specific browser for QA mode only, to prevent inadvertently erasing information or passwords I would like to preserve.

Remember that our experience is for mobile audiences only. Therefore, we need to emulate a mobile browser on our computer. You can do so with a keyboard shortcut (Ctrl + Shift + M in Firefox, for instance) or by opening the developer console with Ctrl + Shift + I and then selecting the mobile device emulation icon. This modifies the page display on the left and adds a menu bar to select a specific device.

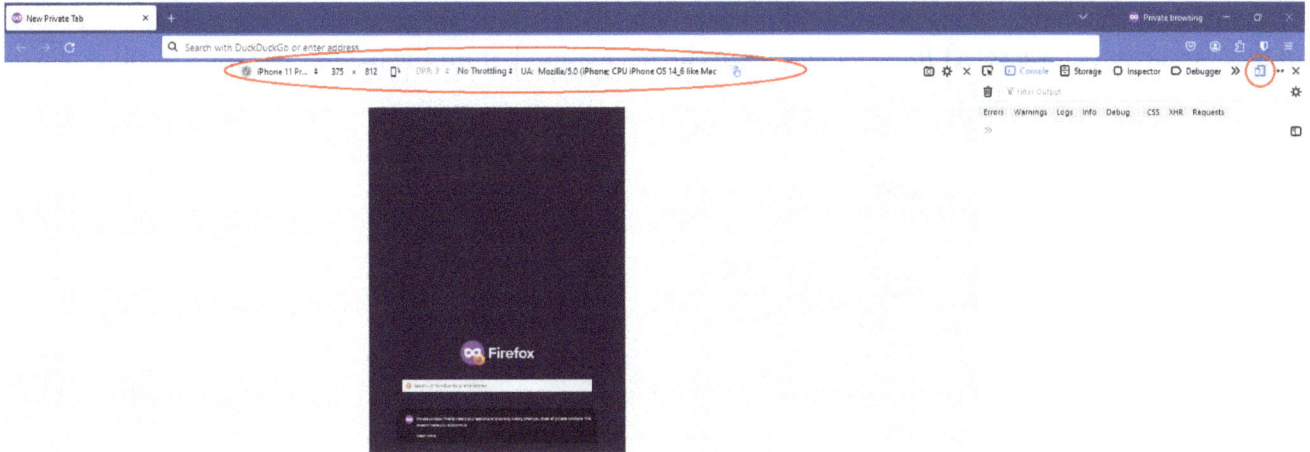

We can then enter our QA URL in the address bar. Once the page loads, you'll notice that there's a message box inserted at the top of the page.

QA Mode Enabled

This QA Mode session will **expire in 1 hour**. If you wish to extend the session, append `persist=true` to the URL. If you choose to persist, you must delete your cookies to disable QA mode.

Current QA Mode Data Fields:
Persist?: false
Adobe Target Data: %Engine.QAMode.AdobeTarget{activity_index: "1", evaluate_as_true_audience_ids: ["2256155"], experience_index: "2", listed_activities_only: "true", token: "zaisY5a6zNwjOwNyCkaSkEQCglbNEyUoD-Z7lhzvCgc"}

The only thing we need to pay attention to at this point is the *experience_index* field, which should be equal to "2" if you're debugging the treatment experience (or the first of multiple treatment experiences). You can now scroll down and confirm that everything looks as expected on the page.

You can also freely navigate to other pages on your site or even go outside of the site and come back. As long as you're within the duration of the QA Mode session indicated at the top of the previous message box and you don't erase your cookies, you'll stay within the treatment experience.

Trace mode

While QA mode allows us to get into a specific experience of the test regardless of the test's status or traffic allocation, it provides only limited information. We can identify when something is wrong, but it doesn't tell us what. Trace mode allows us to look under the hood of Adobe Target and check for ourselves whether an mbox sends the expected request and parameters to the Adobe servers.

There are two ways to display traces. The first one is to use the Adobe Experience Cloud Debugger, as we'll see in part III, chapter 3. The second one, which I'll explain now, is to generate trace mode parameters from the Adobe Target interface.

Generating trace mode parameters

Trace mode is enabled by going into the Administration tab of Adobe Target. After selecting *Administration* in the top menu (1), we select *Implementation* in the navigation bar on the left (2) and then scroll down to the *Debugger tools* section (3).

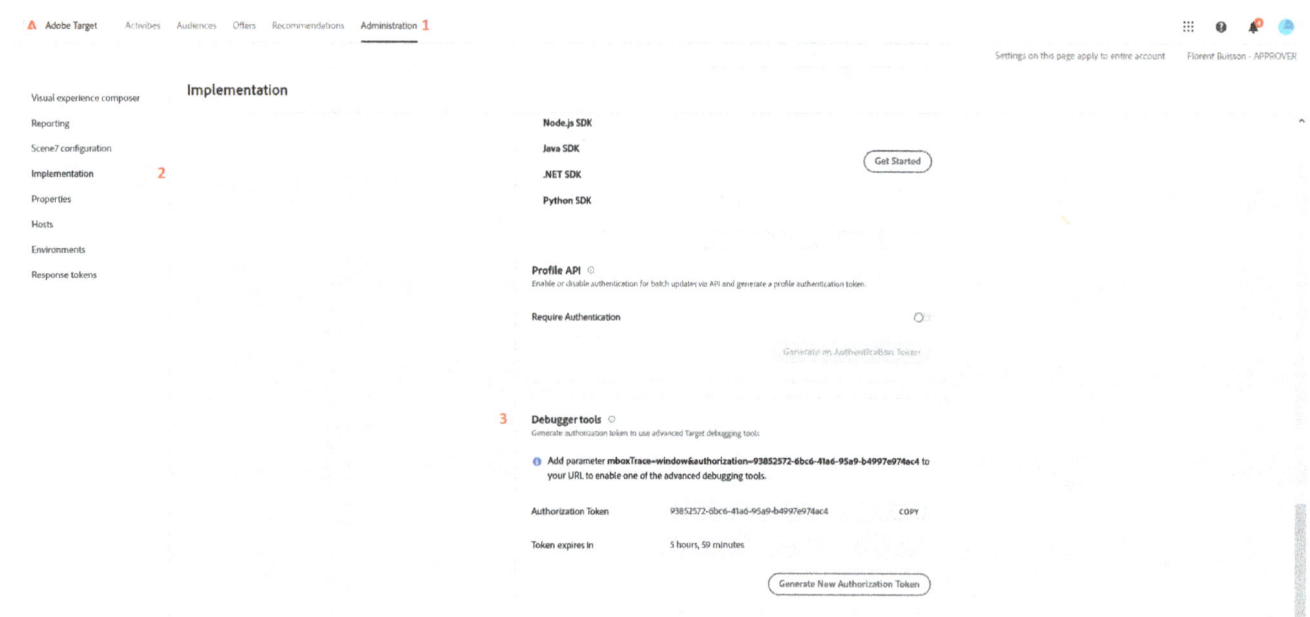

Let's then click *Generate New Authorization Token* (1). Doing so may open a scarily worded confirmation pop-up, but don't be intimidated by that; just confirm. The string for the authorization token (2) will be replaced by a new one, and the *Copy* button at the right of it will now become active. By default, a new token will expire after six hours, and you can check its remaining lifetime in the next field (3).

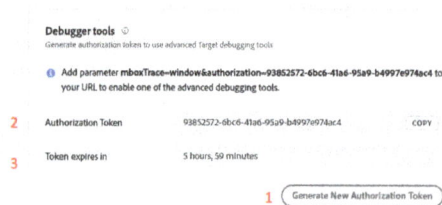

Once you have the authorization token, you can append it at the end of the URL for the page on your website where the mbox for the activity is located.

- If the activity is live, you can just pass the token as follows: *www.miaprova.com/ privacy?adobeTargetTrace=[authorization_token]*. Please note that the variable name in the query is not the same as the one suggested in the Adobe Target interface; that one may or may not work depending on the version of the mbox.js or at.js script you're using.

- If the activity is not live, you'll need to take the QA parameters that we saw in the previous section and add them before or after the *adobeTargetTrace*. Note that the first parameter you're passing should be preceded by a question mark, and then parameters are separated by ampersands (&). For example:

*https://www.miaprova.com/privacy?**at_preview_
token=zaisY5a6zNwjOwNyCkaSkFiI3HzfcjzVqzTbYZa6FvE&at_preview_index=1_2&at_
preview_listed_activities_only=true&at_preview_evaluate_as_true_audience_
ids=1557050&adobeTargetTrace=[authorization_token]***

Browsing in trace mode

When we browse in trace mode, we can check the trace call in the network tab. Enter the complete URL in your browser with the trace parameter as mentioned earlier. Press enter to navigate to the URL, then Ctrl + Shift + i to open the developer tools.

Depending on your version of at.js and your Adobe Target setup, the trace information will be available either in the Network tab or in the console itself.

In the case of MiaProva's website, it is available in the Network tab. Let's open it and filter the results with *trace*.

Let's use a different website than MiaProva's to see what things look like when the information is displayed in the console instead. If we open the Console tab, there are two lines, *a_b_trace* and *a_b_response_tokens*.

The first one, *a_b_trace*, contains a list of all the requests made by the page to the Adobe Target server, one per mbox. By clicking the arrow before Array, you can open and display these.

That's an intimidating amount of information, but never fear! Here are the main things to look at:

1. Click the arrow next to **request**. Under *request > mbox*, we can see the name of the mbox for which the request is emitted. If the mbox for the activity that you're debugging is not present anywhere, it means that it didn't send a request to the server. In my experience, this usually means there is an issue with the corresponding piece of code and you should talk to your software engineer.

```
a_b_trace                                                                              ?adobeTargetTrace=c1..d-c82fbc5cc38c:3903
▼ (2) [{…}, {…}] ⟨
  ▼ 0:
      clientCode:
    ▶ geo: {city: 'ashburn', connectionSpeed: 'broadband', country: 'united states', domainName: 'amazonaws.com', ip:         , …}
    ▶ profile: {afterExecutionProfileSnapshot: {…}, beforeExecutionProfileSnapshot: {…}, visitorId: {…}}
    ▶ qaModeTrace: {bypassEntryAudience: false, listedActivitiesOnly: false, tokenIsEmpty: false, tokenIsInvalid: false}
    ▶ request: {host:         , ipAddress:         , mbox: {…}, pageId: 'df9d874a-5c9f-4865-bdd9-edfe8e7cf13a', pageURL:       
      serverNode:
    ▶ [[Prototype]]: Object
  ▶ 1: {clientCode:         , geo: {…}, profile: {…}, qaModeTrace: {…}, request: {…}, …}
    length: 2
  ▶ [[Prototype]]: Array(0)
```

2. Click the arrow next to **profile**. Under *profile > afterExecutionProfileSnapshot > profileAttributes*, you can see the values returned by the profile scripts that were executed. We'll discuss profile scripts in the next chapter; just make a mental note that this is where you can see whether one was executed and if so, what it returned.

```
▼ profile:
  ▼ afterExecutionProfileSnapshot:
      modifiedAt: "2024-03-23T09:46:37.021-04:00"
    ▼ profileAttributes:
      ▶ firstSessionStart: {modifiedAt: '2024-03-23T09:46:37.018-04:00', value: '1711201597018'}
      ▶ previousSessionStart: {modifiedAt: '2024-03-23T09:46:37.018-04:00', value: '1711201597018'}
      ▶ sessionCount: {modifiedAt: '2024-03-23T09:46:37.018-04:00', value: '1'}
      ▶ user.FirstEntryChannel: {modifiedAt: '2024-03-23T09:46:37.018-04:00', value: 'organic'}
      ▶ user.fourGroups: {modifiedAt: '2024-03-23T09:46:37.021-04:00', value: 'GroupD'}
      ▶ user.landingURL: {modifiedAt: '2024-03-23T09:46:37.021-04:00', value:                             }
      ▶ user.newUserInclusionAB25v5: {modifiedAt: '2024-03-23T09:46:37.021-04:00', value: 'false'}
      ▶ user.newUserInclusionAB40v2: {modifiedAt: '2024-03-23T09:46:37.021-04:00', value: 'false'}
      ▶ user.newUserInclusionAB41: {modifiedAt: '2024-03-23T09:46:37.021-04:00', value: 'false'}
      ▶ user.newUserInclusionAB42v3: {modifiedAt: '2024-03-23T09:46:37.021-04:00', value: 'false'}
      ▶ user.newUserInclusionAB43v2: {modifiedAt: '2024-03-23T09:46:37.021-04:00', value: 'false'}
      ▶ user.newUserInclusionAB44v2: {modifiedAt: '2024-03-23T09:46:37.021-04:00', value: 'false'}
      ▶ user.newUserInclusionAB47: {modifiedAt: '2024-03-23T09:46:37.021-04:00', value: 'false'}
      ▶ user.newUserInclusionAB49: {modifiedAt: '2024-03-23T09:46:37.021-04:00', value: 'false'}
      ▶ user.referrerURL: {modifiedAt: '2024-03-23T09:46:37.021-04:00'}
      ▶ [[Prototype]]: Object
    ▶ [[Prototype]]: Object
```

The second line, *a_b_response_tokens*, contains all the responses that the Adobe Target server sent back. Again, let's click the arrow before *Array*.

```
a_b_response_tokens                                                                    ec59d4cd-cd1e-4ac9-b..-a004b6c6d5d2/:5213
▼ [{…}] ⟨
  ▼ 0:
      activity.id: "224927"
      activity.name:
      experience.id: "1"
      experience.name: "Experience B"
      profile.FirstEntryChannel: "organic"
      profile.activeActivities: "224927"
      profile.fourGroups: "GroupC"
      profile.isFirstSession: "true"
      profile.isNewSession: "false"
      profile.landingURL:
      profile.referrerURL:
    ▶ [[Prototype]]: Object
    length: 1
  ▶ [[Prototype]]: Array(0)
```

We'll cover response tokens in chapter 3.1, but for the purpose of QA and debugging, the first elements in the list are the most important:

- **activity.id** and **activity.name** tell us which Adobe Target activity we're looking at.
- **experience.id** and **experience.name** allow us to confirm which experience of the activity we've been assigned to (either through the QA parameters or through random assignment).

Using these first few elements of *a_b_trace* and *a_b_response_tokens*, I'm usually able to address most of the questions and issues that arise on an average day. (For example, "I'm not seeing the treatment experience when using the QA parameters; can you please confirm that the activity is working correctly?")

Chapter 1.3: Scheduling and Progressive Rollout

In the first chapter, we showed the existing experience (the current state of the website) to visitors. In the second chapter, we saw how you and other internal users can access a different experience to validate and debug it. In this chapter, we'll finally start showing a new experience to external visitors through a progressive rollout.

In a progressive rollout, a certain fraction of new visitors get exposed to the new experience while the others remain in the old experience. We then progressively increase the fraction exposed to the new experience over the course of several days or weeks, until all new visitors see the new experience. This allows us to ensure that the new experience works as expected in the face of increasing traffic. For instance, if you're rolling out a new algorithm or adding some animations or videos to your site, you might be worried about server load. A progressive rollout will allow you to only increase the traffic in incremental steps.

Progressive rollouts are not technically considered part of experimentation, and software engineers have been using them even without experimentation tools like Adobe Target. But these tools make it much easier to manage a progressive rollout.

This will also be our opportunity to learn about audiences and profile scripts, which are important concepts in Adobe Target. By creating the appropriate script and audience, we'll be able to assign only new visitors to an activity while keeping returning visitors in the same experience as in their last visit.

Activity setup

We'll start by duplicating the activity from the previous chapter.

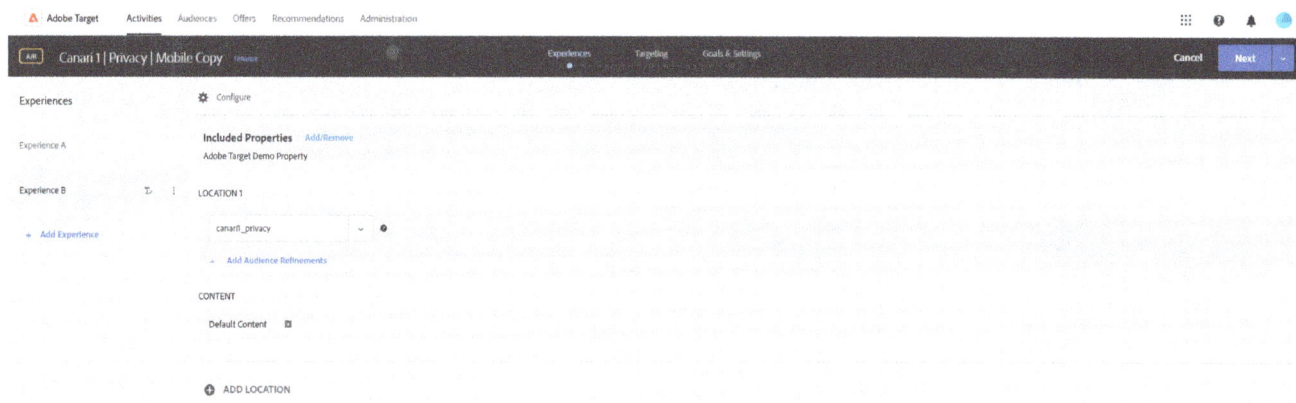

In this first screen, we'll update the name of the activity and its location in keeping with our established naming protocol.

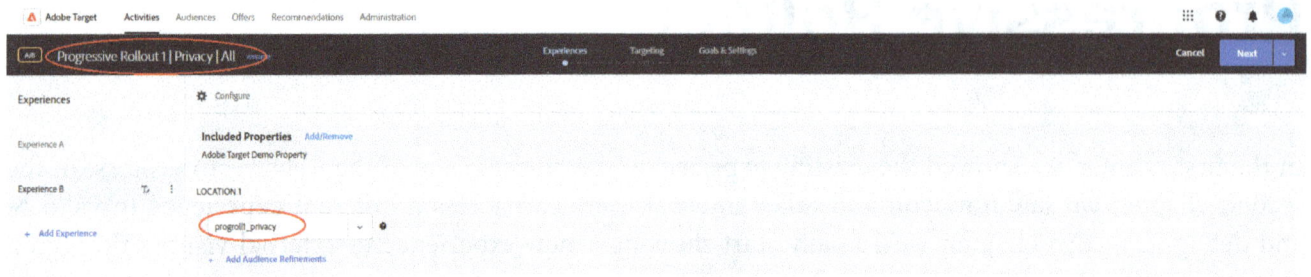

Clicking *Next* takes us to the Targeting screen, which we'll leave unchanged for the time being. We'll come back to it after we've taken some other preliminary steps, but for now, we'll go directly to Goals & Settings.

Scheduling start/end of activity

In the final screen, we'll set up the activity to start at a scheduled time. Click on the drop-down menu after Start and switch to *Specified Date & Time*.

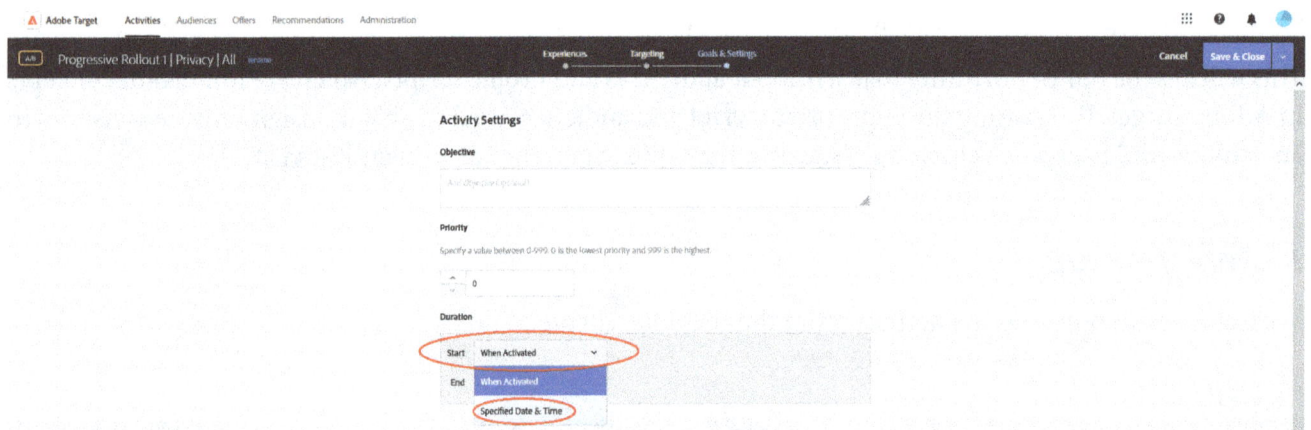

We can then select the date and time at which the test should start.

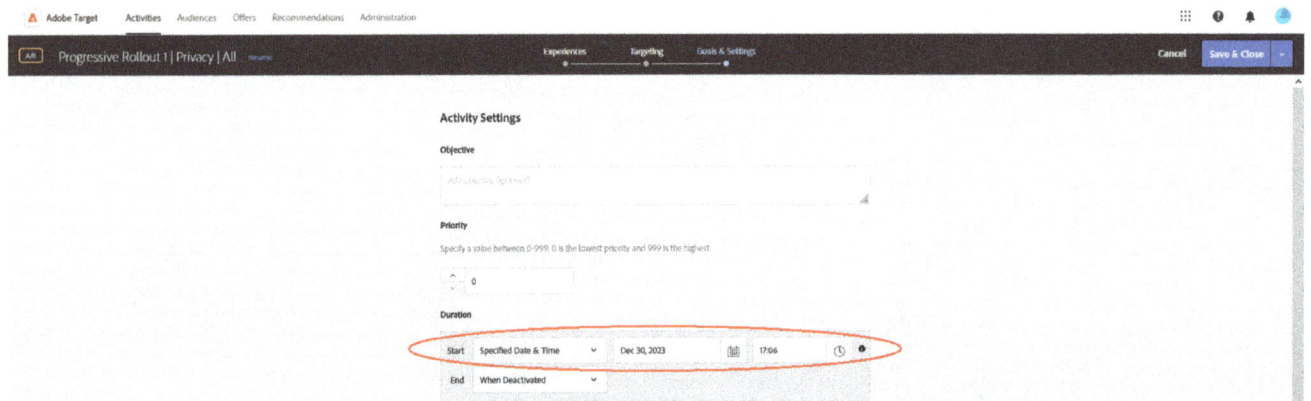

The process is similar for defining the date and time at which the test should end. As the information icon to the right of the date and time selectors reminds you, you'll still need to activate the activity beforehand for it to start at the scheduled time.

When you click on *Activate*, the activity status updates to Scheduled.

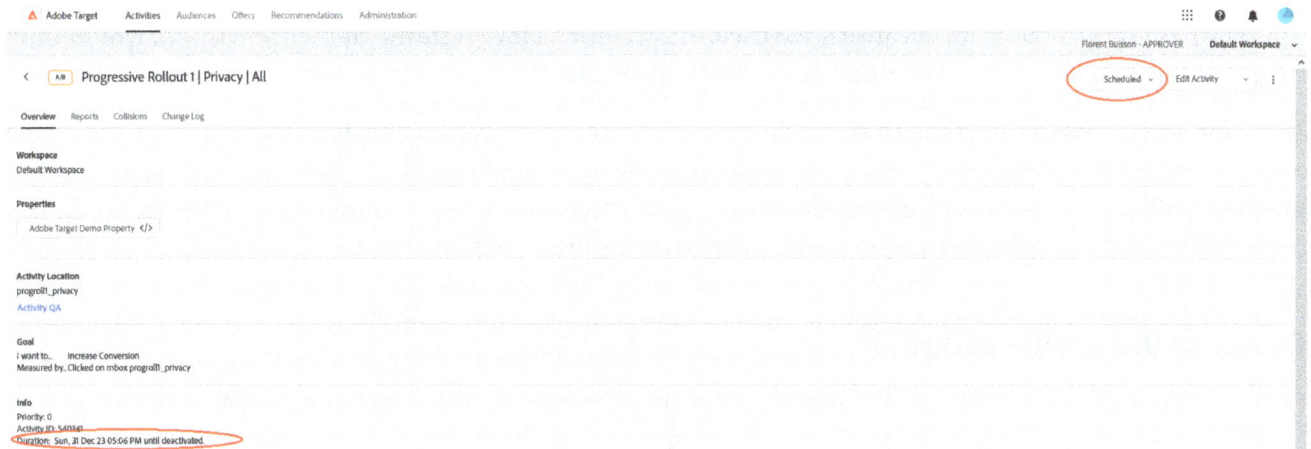

When to use scheduling?

I personally have never used scheduling to start an activity, but there are a couple of situations where it might be beneficial or even necessary. First, it ensures a neat and predetermined start time (such as noon or right after midnight) for limited-duration activities such as promotional events. In addition, if your company is rather bureaucratic, you may have to schedule a start time so that other teams and departments can be informed in advance and plan for it. However, it can be risky to start an activity when you're not around to monitor it.

On the other hand, I *have* used scheduling to end an activity. If the necessary duration for an A/B test based on sample size calculation concludes during a weekend or when you're out, scheduling an end time makes sense. You can also use it to ensure that you get a full day's worth of data without having to stay up until midnight to deactivate an activity.

Overall, my advice would be to not overthink scheduling: if you don't see a need for it, don't use it. But if you have a use case that requires it, now you'll know how to do it, and you'll be able to handle it without sweating it.

Profile script for new visitors only

Now that we're on the Summary screen, we can start working on the script for the activity. Prebuilt audiences, like the one for mobile browsers we used in the last chapter, are very powerful but somewhat static. They don't cover more dynamic situations, such as wanting to display a banner only on a visitor's returning visits. In these situations we instead want to use scripts, which can accommodate parameters (such as the visit number) that might change over time.

In the present case, our goal with using a script is to provide visitors with a consistent experience across visits as much as possible during the progressive rollout. We don't want a visitor who saw the default experience in their first visit, before the start of the rollout, to then be assigned to the treatment group and have a different experience in later visits. By default, Adobe Target does not discriminate between new and returning visitors: after an activity starts, every visitor who visits is eligible to be entered in the activity. This makes sense when new or anonymous visitors represent a small fraction of total traffic. If you're Amazon or Netflix, for example, testing only on fresh new users would dramatically reduce the available traffic and thus would be impractical. On the other hand, when non-logged-in or first-visit visitors represent the bulk of the traffic, and traffic volume is high enough to allow it, I prefer to include visitors in an activity from their first visit forward.

This is where scripts come in, because if we used the prebuilt "New Visitors" audience, visitors would only see the activity on their first visit, and not on following visits.

At a high level, what we're going to do is create an audience that says, "if this is a new visitor or they have a script that returns 'true', then they're eligible to be served the activity." The script that we'll create for that purpose will say "return 'false', unless the visitor ever enters the activity, then return 'true' forever". The combination of the audience and the script will generate the desired behavior.

Creating the profile script

Let's first write down the Activity ID number from the summary screen—in this case, 540361.

We then go to the Audiences tab and select *Profile Scripts* on the left-side menu.

When we click the *Create Script* button on the right, a new window pops up.

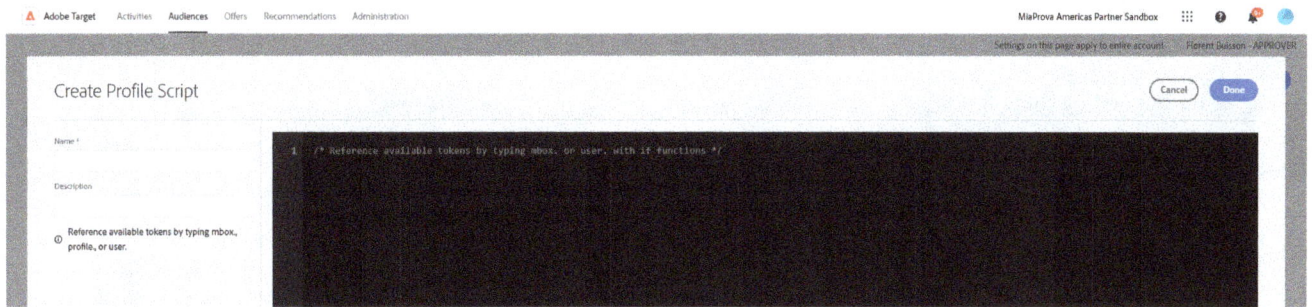

Beside the self-explanatory Name and Description fields, the window contains a code editor in which we can write a short JavaScript (JS) snippet that will run whenever an mbox makes a call to the Adobe Target server.

Here's the code for our script:

```
if(!user.get('progressiveRolloutPrivacy')){
    if (String(user.activeActivities).includes("540361") == true) {
        return true;
} else {
        return false;
}
}
```

Don't worry if you don't know JavaScript; we'll walk through the code piece by piece from the inside out, and we'll revisit profile scripts further in the second part of the book.

To start with, Target provides us with the `user.activeActivities` variable, a list of all the activities that a user has ever entered. We'll convert that variable into a string and use the JS function `includes()` to determine whether our activity is in the list of active activities for the current user:

```
if(String(user.activeActivities).includes("540361") == true){ … }
```

Adobe Target automatically persists `user.activeActivities` and adds new activities to it as a visitor enters them. So this condition will evaluate to false as long as our visitor hasn't visited the Privacy page. If and when they visit it, they may or may not be entered in the activity depending on the audience rules we set. For instance, if we configure the activity so that only 10% of visitors are included in it and our current visitor didn't make the cut, the script shouldn't fire. Assuming the visitor gets entered in the activity, the condition will now evaluate to true indefinitely.

A couple of notes about JS syntax:

- In JS an equality condition is expressed with two equal signs; this is to distinguish it from an assignment, which uses a single equal sign (e.g., x = 10). By contrast, in SQL an equality condition is expressed with a single equal sign (e.g., CASE WHEN price = 10 THEN …).
- In JS the condition is within parentheses, but the "then" part—the list of instructions to execute if the condition is true—is between brackets. If we want an "else" part, we just add the keyword after closing the previous bracket and follow it with another block of code within brackets. Compare this to the much more compact SQL code `IF(condition, do something, do something else)`.

Let's enter our script in the code area. We'll name it "progressiveRolloutPrivacy" and add the description "keeps returning visitors in the same experience". Finally, we save the script by clicking the *Done* button in the upper right corner.

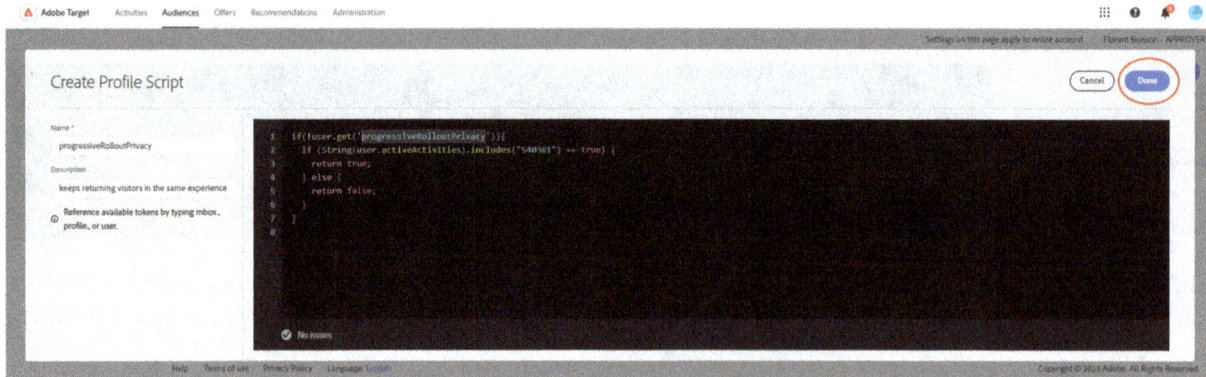

This way, we'll have solved our challenge of excluding from the activity visitors who didn't encounter it on their first visit. As a side note, maintaining the inclusion or exclusion from an activity across a visitor's visits is a fundamental feature in experimentation and optimization. Adobe Target, like many other tools, handles it for you by default through cookies. Thus, even if you don't use a script, you can expect a visitor to stay in the right experiences of the right activities as long as they don't clear their cookies, change browsers, etc. (nobody said that digital optimization was easy!). But the ability to only enter visitors in an activity on their first visit and then persist their experience for the following visits is where Adobe Target and its scripts shine compared to many other tools.

Script activation

We then need to activate our script by selecting it in the list, clicking the three-dot icon to the right of it, and selecting *Activate*.

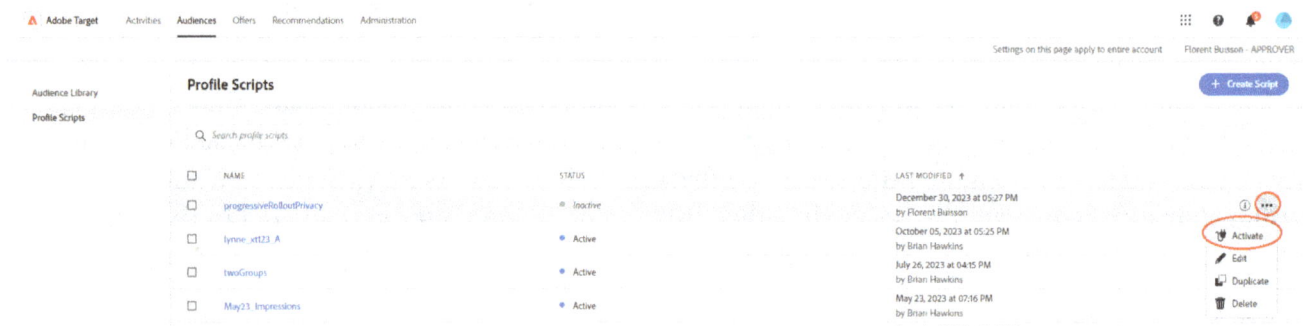

Using the profile script in an audience

Once you are satisfied that a profile script does what it's supposed to, it's time to use it for an activity's audience.

From where we are, let's create a new audience by clicking on *Audience Library* in the left-side navigation menu and then *Create audience*, as we did in the last chapter.

In the pop-up screen that opens, let's scroll down the list of Attributes on the left and select *Visitor Profile*.

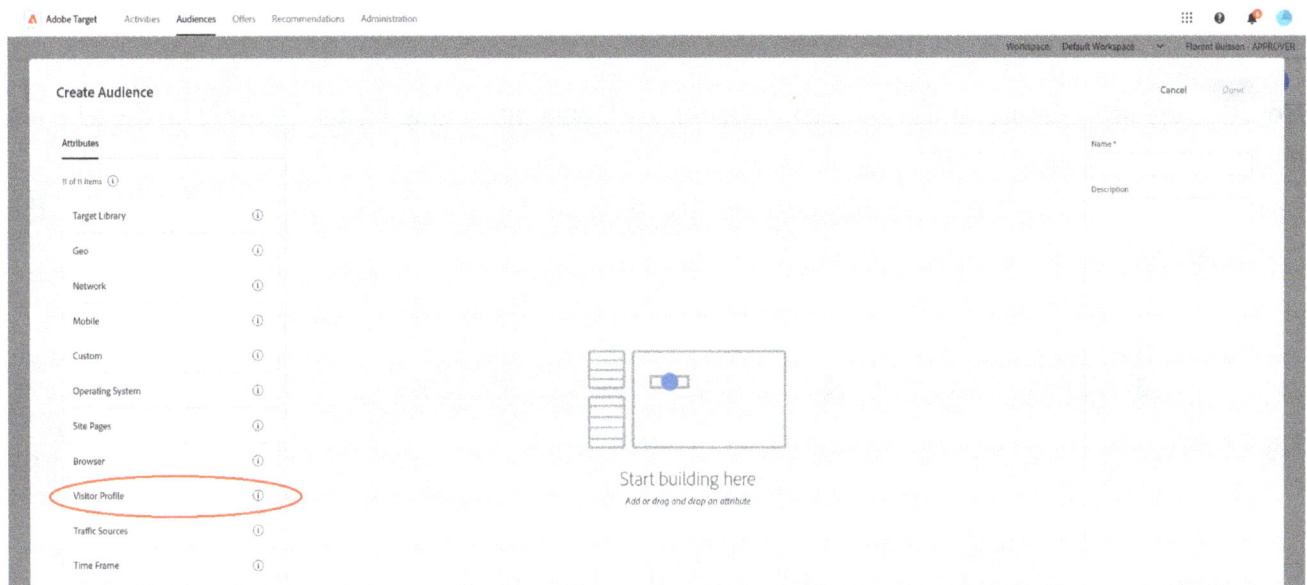

We need to drag and drop *Visitor Profile* into the central area, and then more options become available. We want to define our audience as including two categories of visitors:

- New visitors
- Returning visitors who were previously entered into the activity

This will implicitly exclude all returning visitors who were not entered into the activity during their first visit.

Let's click on *Select attribute* and select *New Visitor*.

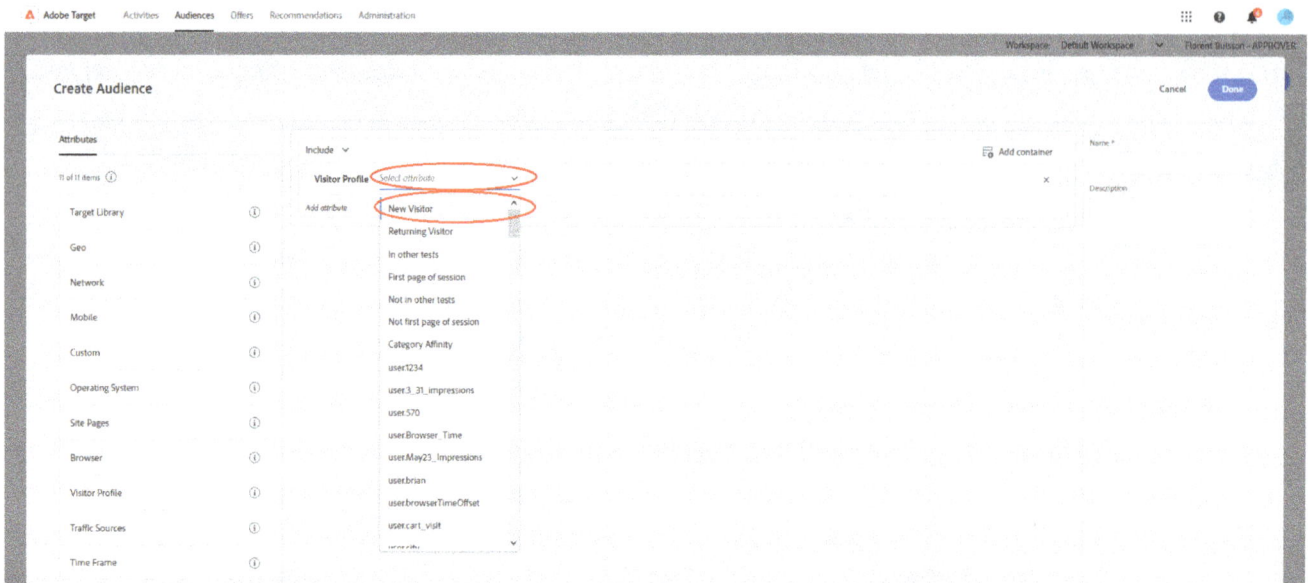

Note the *Add attribute* area under our first criterion. We'll once again drag *Visitor Profile* from the left-side menu, dropping it into this area.

By default, Adobe Target automatically assumes that we want the new criterion to be a restriction on the previous one, so it adds an *And* connector.

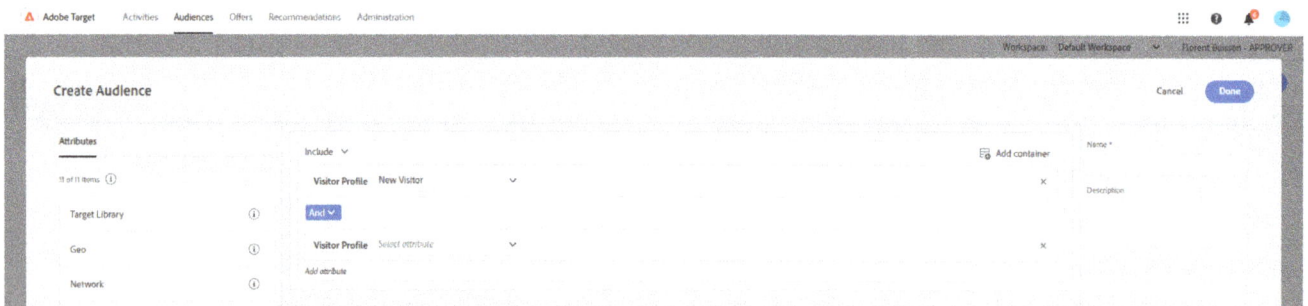

But what we want is an *Or* connector. We want visitors who are new **OR** who are returning and have previously been entered in the activity. Let's switch the connector.

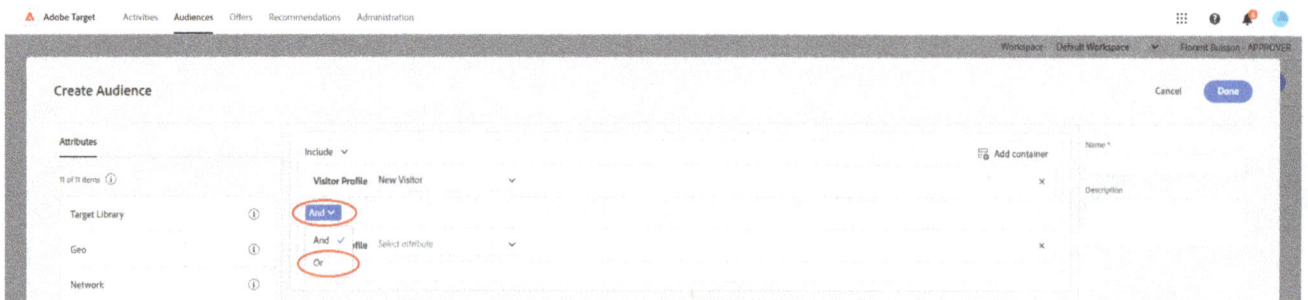

We then find our script by clicking on the *Select attribute* box and typing "user." followed by the name of our script. As we begin to type the script name, Adobe Target will automatically suggest it.

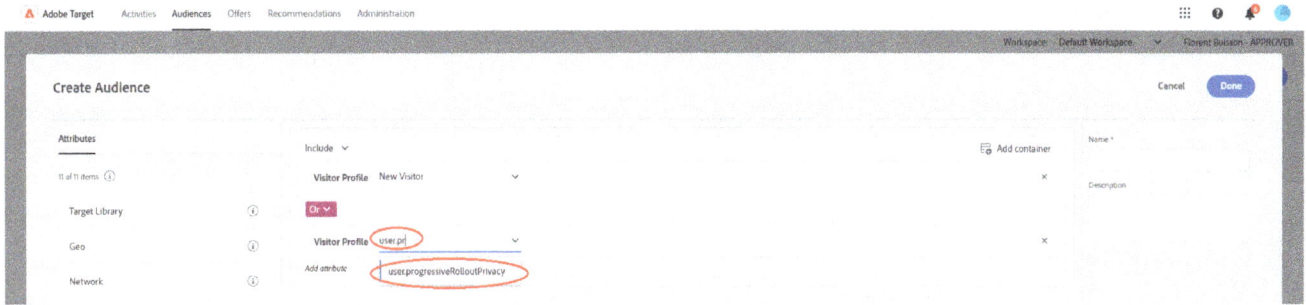

After we select our script name as suggested by Target, a *Choose evaluator* selector appears. We'll select *Equals (case insensitive)*.

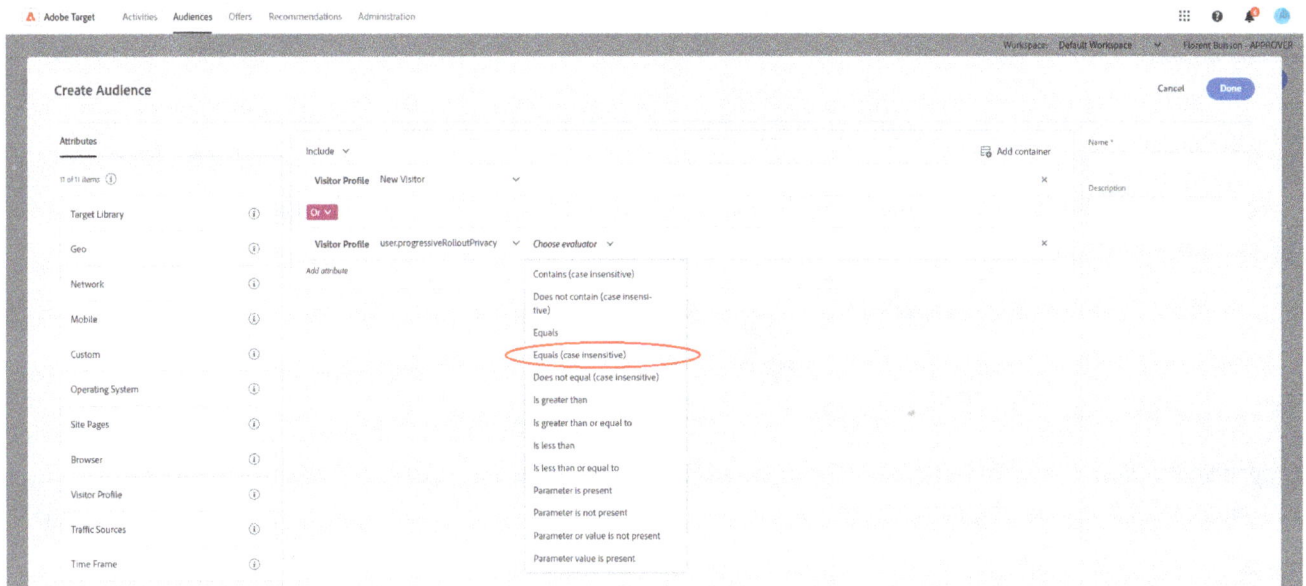

The next selector, *Choose Comparison Type*, appears, and we select *static value*.

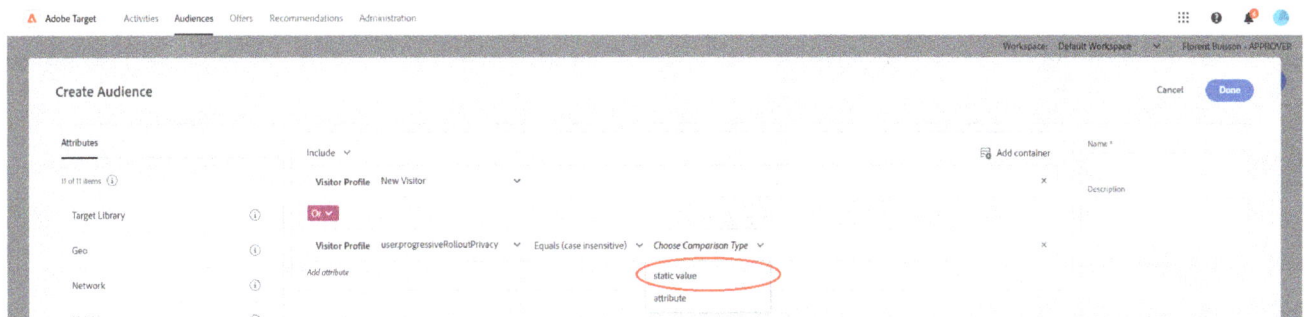

In the open text box that appears, we enter "true".

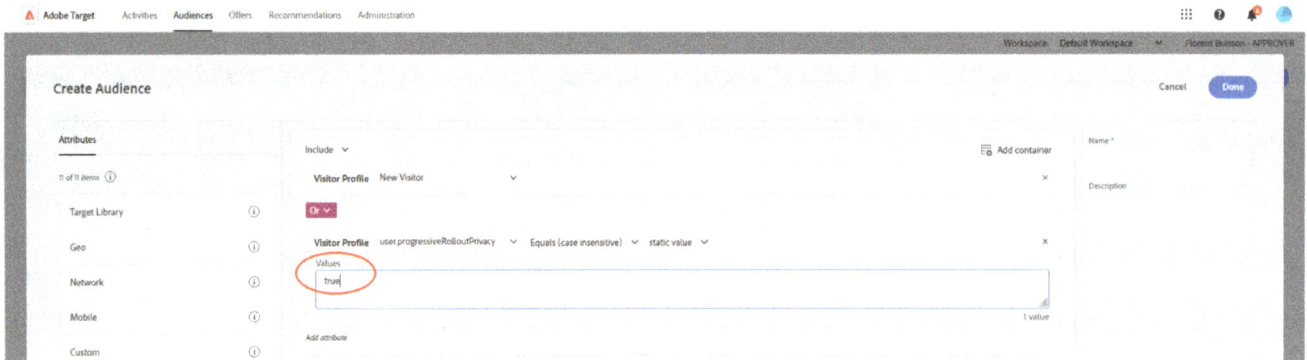

Finally, we need to name and describe our new audience.

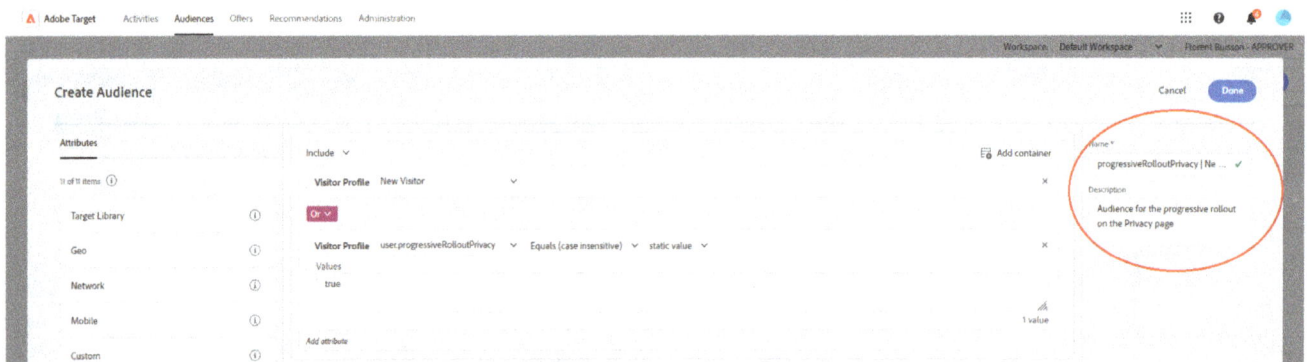

You'll often need to find, remember, or refer to an audience name, so it's best to follow a consistent template and make it as informative as possible. This audience includes visitors for which *New Visitor* is true or *progressiveRolloutPrivacy* is true, so let's put these in the audience name. Of the two, *New Visitor* is common to many audiences, so let's put the unique part first to make auto-complete easier and faster in the future. Our new audience name is thus "progressiveRolloutPrivacy | New Visitor". (If we had two criteria and we wanted both of them to be true for a visitor to be assigned to an activity, we would use "&" instead of "|".)

We can then click *Done* and return to the Activities tab to select and edit our activity.

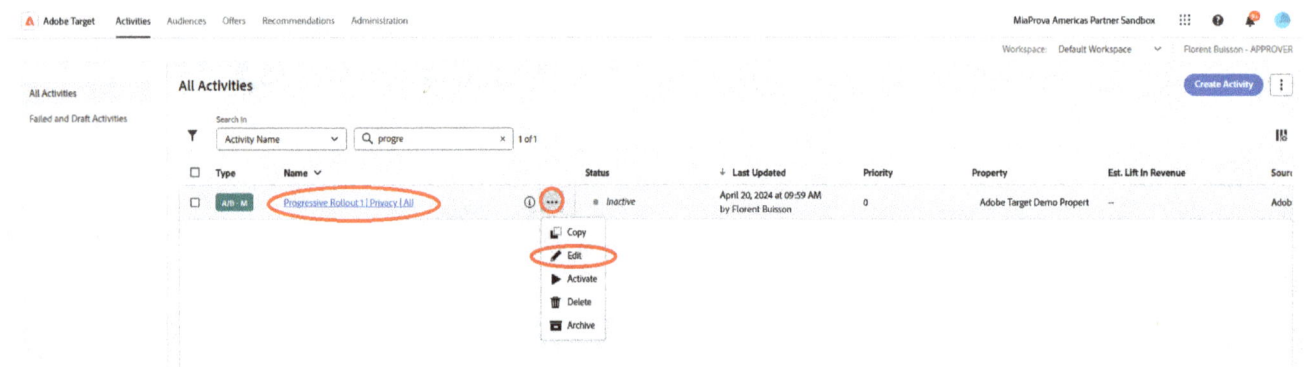

Then we'll go to the Targeting screen to replace the audience.

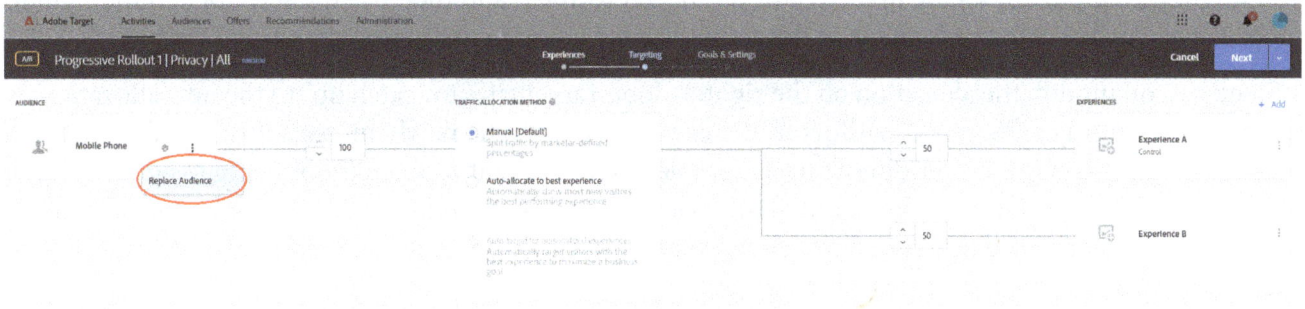

Let's assign the newly created audience to our activity.

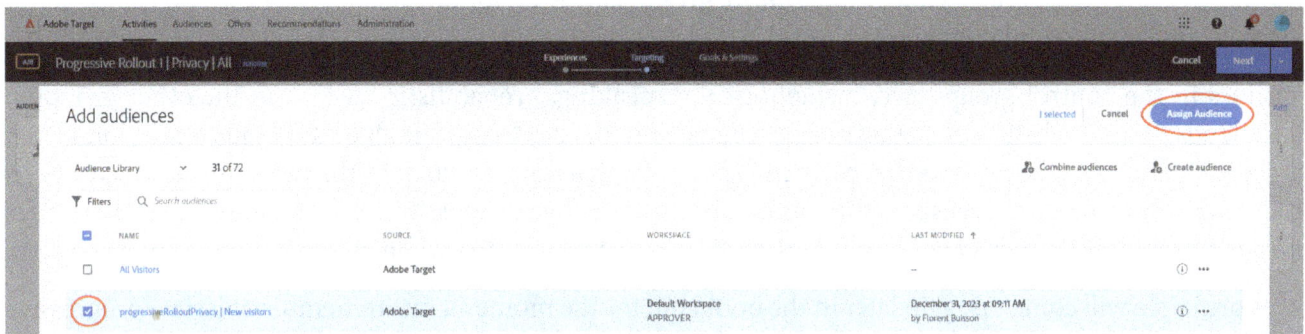

Traffic allocation for progressive rollout

We have now scheduled our activity start and set it up to apply only to new visitors; it will then keep them in the activity during any subsequent visit. Now that we're ready to launch the activity, it's time to talk about how we're going to implement the progressive rollout.

Let's recall our goal: we want to roll out the new feature to an increasing share of new visitors to make sure that it doesn't negatively impact our site performance and business metrics. We'll start at 1% of traffic.

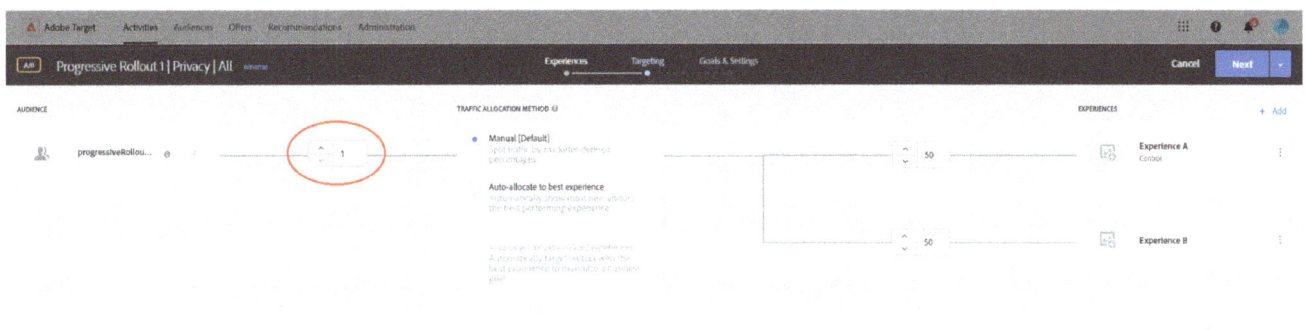

We can then wait for our activity to begin on its scheduled start date. If nothing has gone wrong after a period of time—between one business day if you're comfortable with how things are going and one week if you want to be thorough—we'll go back to the screen above and edit the activity to increase the percentage of traffic it affects.

Changing traffic allocation over time

You might be tempted to set the first selector on the left to 100% and then use the selectors on the right to progressively increase the percentage of the activity traffic going to the new experience. *Don't do it.*

Whenever you modify the allocation on the right, Adobe Target tries to "catch up" to the new allocation by temporarily sending an excess of visitors to the experience with the newly increased share of traffic. This means that an incoming visitor doesn't have a stable and consistent probability of being assigned to each of the activity groups. On the other hand, when you use the selector on the left to increase the percentage of visitors that get entered into the activity, a new visitor still has the same probability of being allocated to each of the two experiences. This is what we want.

There is a deeper underlying principle at play here that is worth elaborating on. In almost all cases, visitors *outside* of an activity will get the same experience on your website as the visitors in one of the groups of the activity, sometimes referred to as the *control* group. However, for our purposes, these two categories of visitors are fundamentally different.

Visitors in the control group have, metaphorically speaking, probabilistic "twins" in the other group(s). Alex lands on the website at 9:00:00 and gets allocated to the control group; Barbara lands one second later, at 9:00:01, and gets allocated to the treatment group. With a different luck of the draw, it would have been the other way around. This ensures the comparability of the two groups. Visitors outside of an activity have no such probabilistic twins and therefore should never be considered when analyzing the results of a test.

This principle will come up again later in the book, but for the moment, just remember this: in a progressive rollout, we should increase the share of visitors that go to the new experience through the left selector, the one determining the share of total traffic going to the activity—not the right selectors, which determine the share of the activity traffic going to each experience.

Chapter 1.4: Experimentation and A/B Testing

We're now getting to the *pièce de resistance*, running A/B tests for the purpose of determining whether a new experience outperforms the current one on your website. This will be the opportunity for us to discover the Visual Experience Composer (VEC), a cornerstone of Adobe Target's offering. The VEC allows analysts and business users such as marketers to test small changes to a site's layout and content without the need for developers to modify the site's code.

Using the Visual Experience Composer

To start the VEC, let's go into the Activities tab, click *Create Activity*, and select *A/B test*. In the following pop-up, the Visual experience composer is selected by default, so we don't need to change that. We'll only need to enter the URL of the page where we want to place the test.

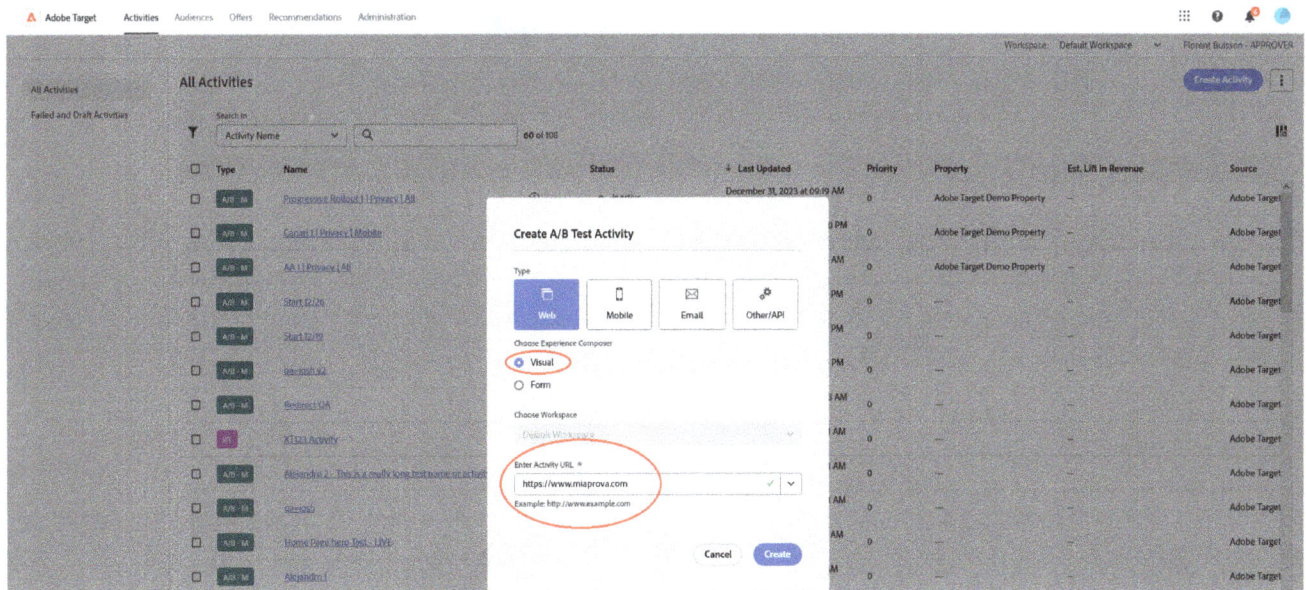

Once we click *Create*, the VEC window opens, displaying the page of the URL we entered.

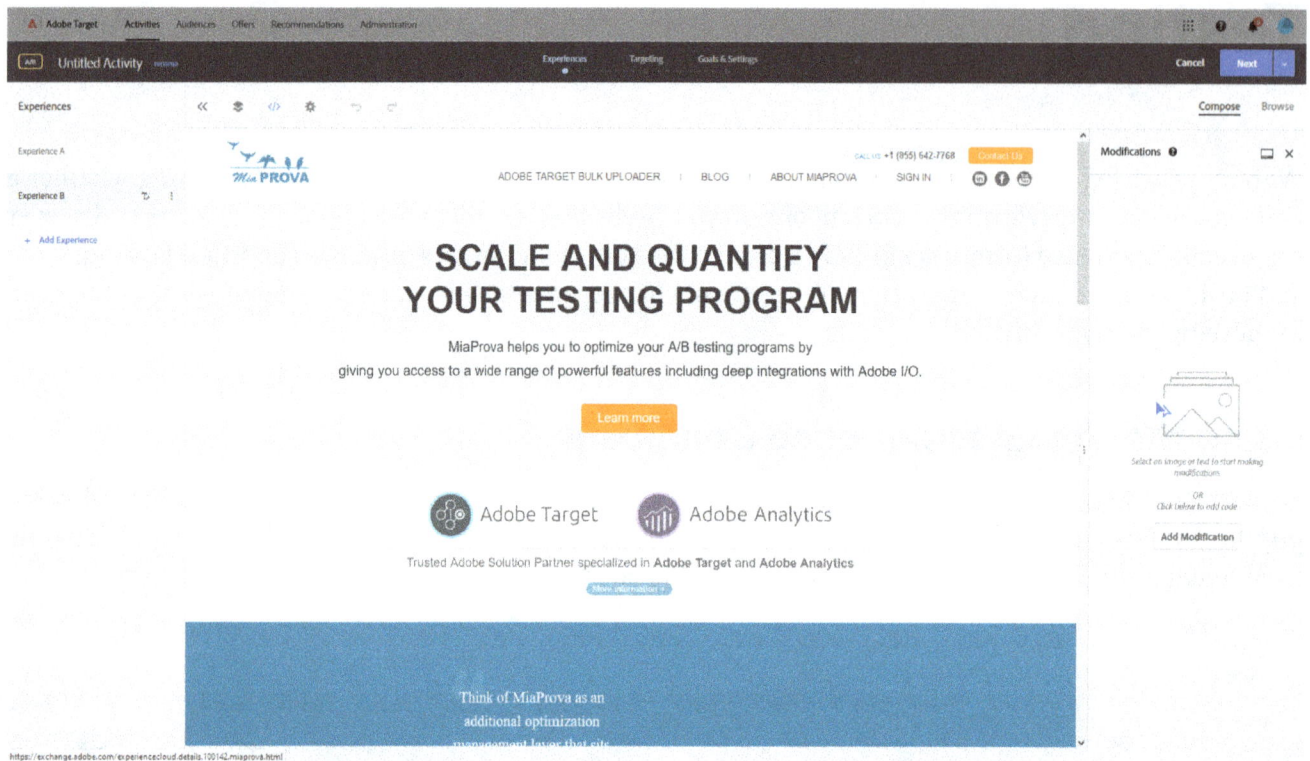

The window has three main components:

- A list of experiences (left), where we can select the one we want to modify, rename it, or add a new one
- A rendering of the page whose URL we selected (center), where we'll make modifications on the fly
- A list of modifications we made to the currently selected experience compared to the default experience (right), which is empty at this point

If needed, you can choose to hide or show these components using the first three of the six buttons above the central pane.

These buttons do the following actions:

1. Toggles the left-side *Experiences* menu between visible and hidden
2. Toggles the central page rendering between visible and hidden
3. Toggles the right-side *Modifications* menu between visible and hidden
4. Opens a configuration menu
5. Undoes the last modification when relevant
6. Restores the last modification

Modifying a component on the page

When you hover your cursor over any component in the page, it is surrounded by a blue rectangle to indicate its content and limits, with a label indicating the component's type.

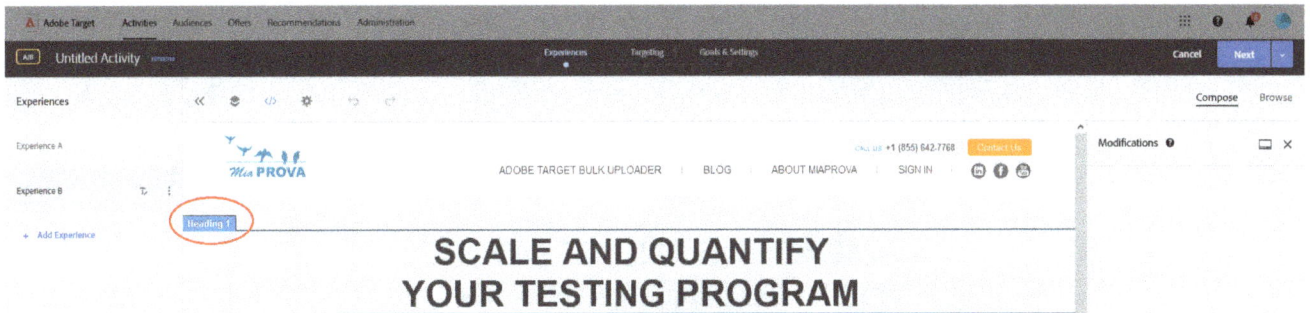

If you click on the component, the rectangle turns orange and a contextual menu pops up.

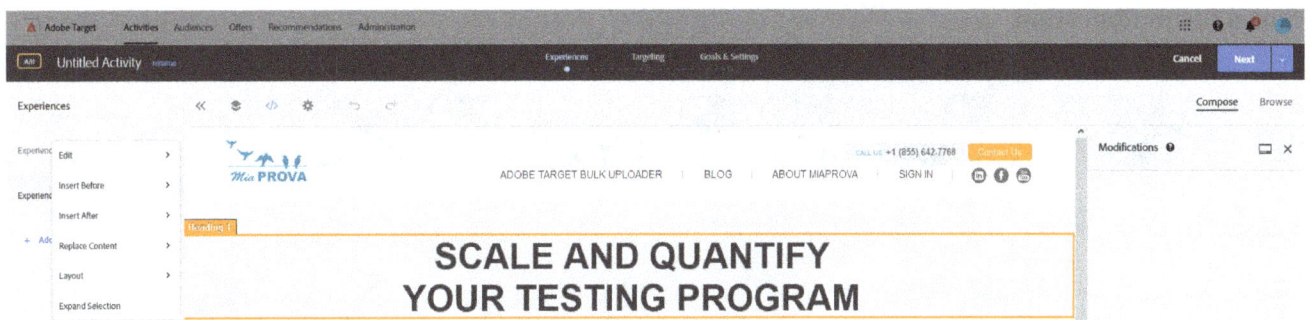

For instance, let's select *Edit*, then *Text/HTML* in the corresponding contextual menu. An editor pops up.

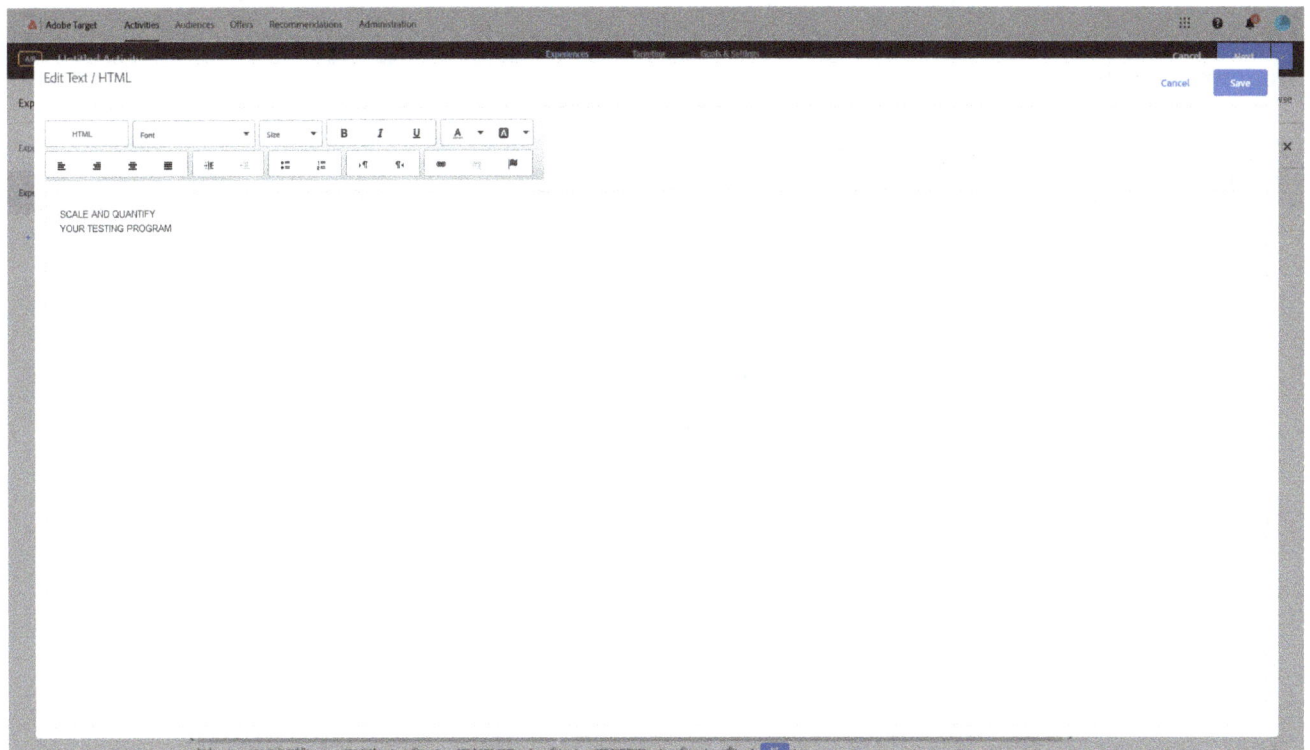

Let's replace the text "Scale and Quantify" with "Measure and Grow" (I know, I know, I missed my calling as a star copywriter) and click *Save*. When we get back to the main window, we can see that the change has been implemented in the page display and now appears in the right-side list of modifications.

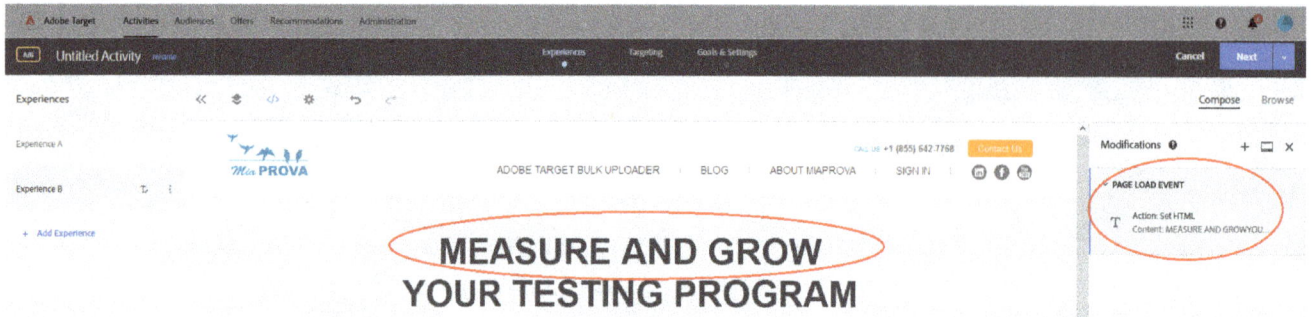

If we hover over a modification on the right, contextual icons appear that allow us to visualize, edit, or cancel the modification.

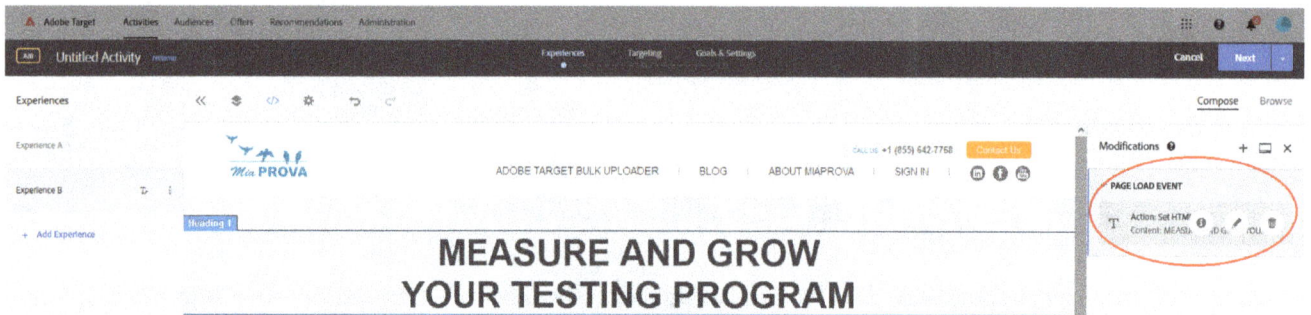

As a side note, advanced users can also click the "+" button above the list of modifications to enter changes programmatically.

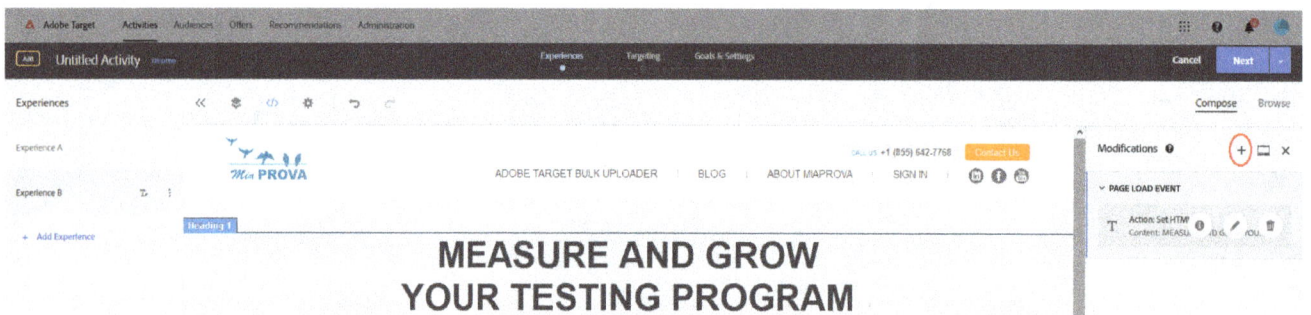

This opens a form in the right-side menu.

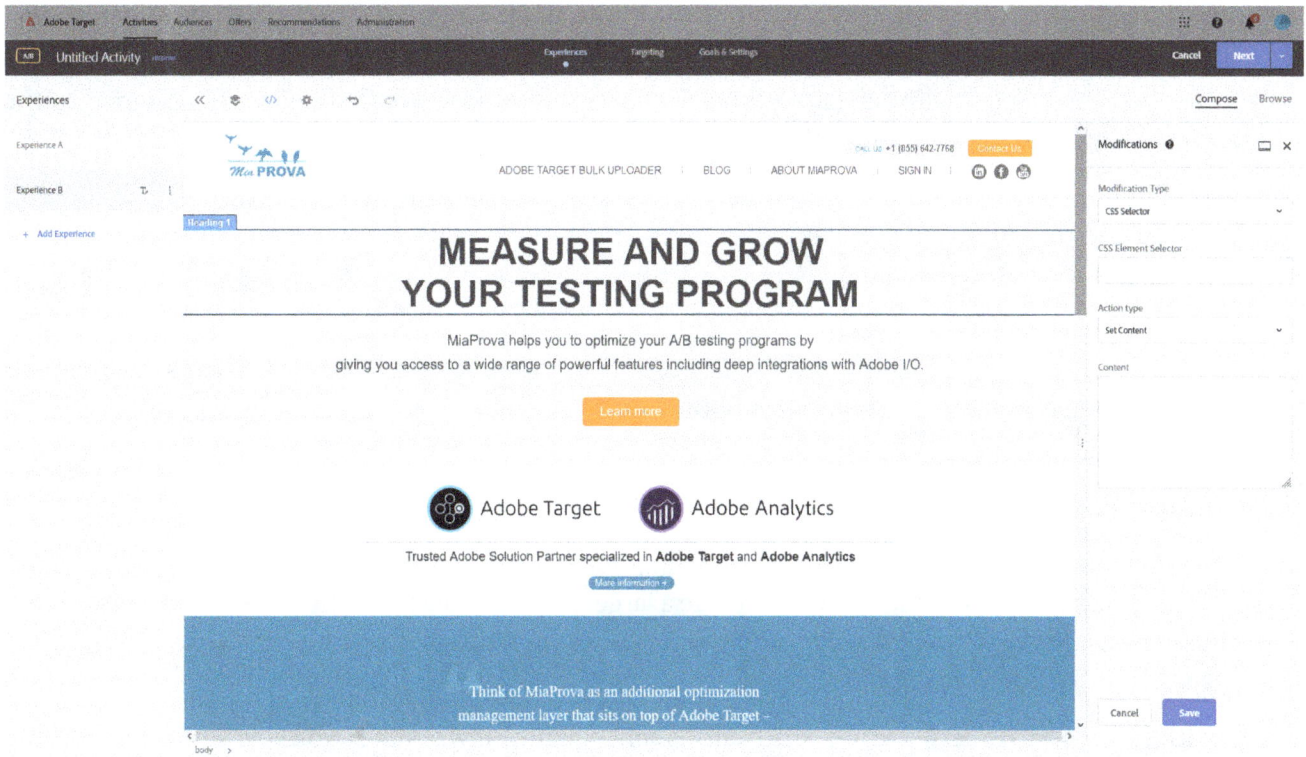

This form can be used to add JavaScript code to the page—but that's outside of the scope of this book.

Once we have made all the changes we want to the treatment experience, we can click *Next*, which brings us to the Targeting screen.

Targeting

Targeting for A/B testing

The Targeting screen looks the same as before, except that when you use the Visual Experience Composer, small screenshots of the experiences are added in the corresponding section.

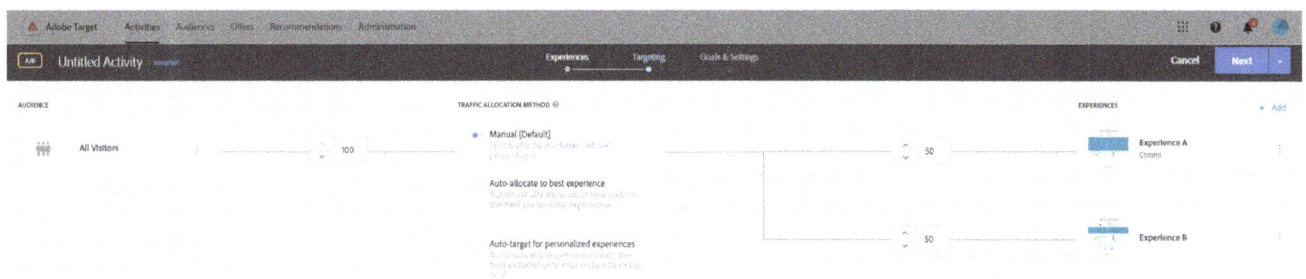

For an A/B test, the traffic assigned to the test should be split between the different experiences with fixed percentages that remain the same for the whole duration of the test. If you're using a progressive ramp-up by running the test on a small fraction of traffic first before reaching the desired share of traffic, it is best to exclude that early data from the final analysis.

Typically, we'll split the traffic we're sending to the test equally between the different experiences. In the present case, that amounts to a 50%-50% allocation. If you're concerned with sending 50% of a page's visitors to a new and potentially flawed experience, you would reduce the share of traffic assigned to the test as a whole by using the selector on the left side.

The fixed-duration, fixed-allocation configuration is the standard one, for two good reasons: A/B tests are easy to set up and interpret, and they minimize the duration required to achieve a predetermined level of statistical significance. You should definitely stick with this approach unless you have a strong rationale to pick an alternative.

One such alternative that is available in Adobe Target is the Auto-allocate model. We'll discuss in a moment some of the reasons you may want to use this option, but for now, let's take a look at how it works.

Auto-allocate to best experience

The Auto-allocate mode is Adobe Target's implementation of a statistical method known as a "multi-armed bandit." The general idea is to progressively allocate a larger share of the test traffic to the experience(s) that appear to perform the best, while still allocating some visitors at random across all experiences to continue learning about their true performance.

For activities with only two experiences, the traffic is split equally between the two experiences until Adobe Target is 75% confident that one activity is performing better than the other. At that point, the traffic gets split 2/3 to the better-performing experience and 1/3 to the other. Once Adobe Target reaches 95% confidence that one experience outperforms the other, it will switch to a 90%-10% split, heavily favoring the outperforming experience without completely shutting down the other one.

For activities with more than two experiences, the traffic is split equally at first until each experience has received a minimum of 1,000 visitors and 50 conversions. Then the traffic split gets updated at least once per hour, with 20% of traffic always being split at random across all experiences and 80% of traffic being allocated to the two experiences with the best performance so far.

To set up Auto-allocate, we simply select *Auto-allocate to best experience* in the Targeting screen.

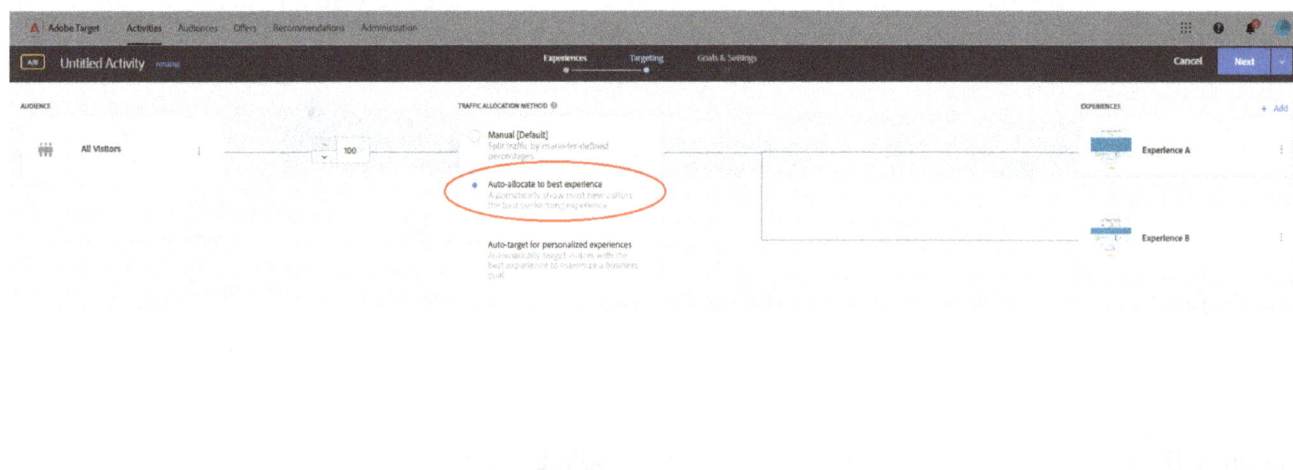

Goals and settings

Choosing a success metric for Auto-allocate

When creating an A/B test activity with a fixed allocation such as 50-50, the goals and settings you choose in the last screen are only for information purposes, as they don't have any material impact on how the test is run. When using Auto-allocate on the other hand, the success metric you select will drive the allocation during the test.

For instance, let's say that the new experience (or *treatment*) reduces the number of pages viewed but increases conversion because visitors find what they need faster. If you select conversion as the success metric, Auto-allocate will progressively drive more traffic toward the treatment experience, whereas if you select the number of pages viewed as the success metric, Auto-allocate will progressively drive more traffic towards the control experience.

Remember that the whole point of choosing Auto-allocate instead of a traditional A/B test is to minimize traffic going to the worse-performing experience during the test. Therefore, choosing the wrong metric can defeat that purpose. When in doubt, use a fixed-allocation A/B test.

Defining a success metric from the VEC

If you've used the VEC to implement the changes you want to test, you have the option of defining the goal (success metric) within the VEC, which can be simpler than trying to identify the relevant action in your analytics tool.

In Reporting Settings > Optimization Goal > My Primary Goal, let's select *Conversion*, and then in the dropdown menu *Clicked an element*. We then click on *Select elements*.

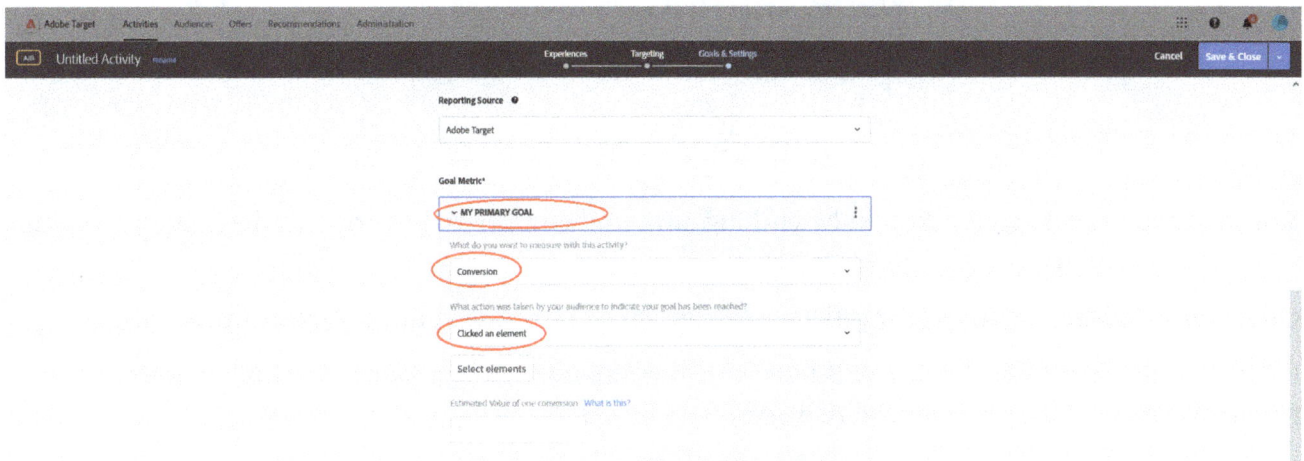

This opens a slightly modified version of the VEC entitled *Select elements to click track*. Note that the right-side menu reads Selected Elements instead of Modifications.

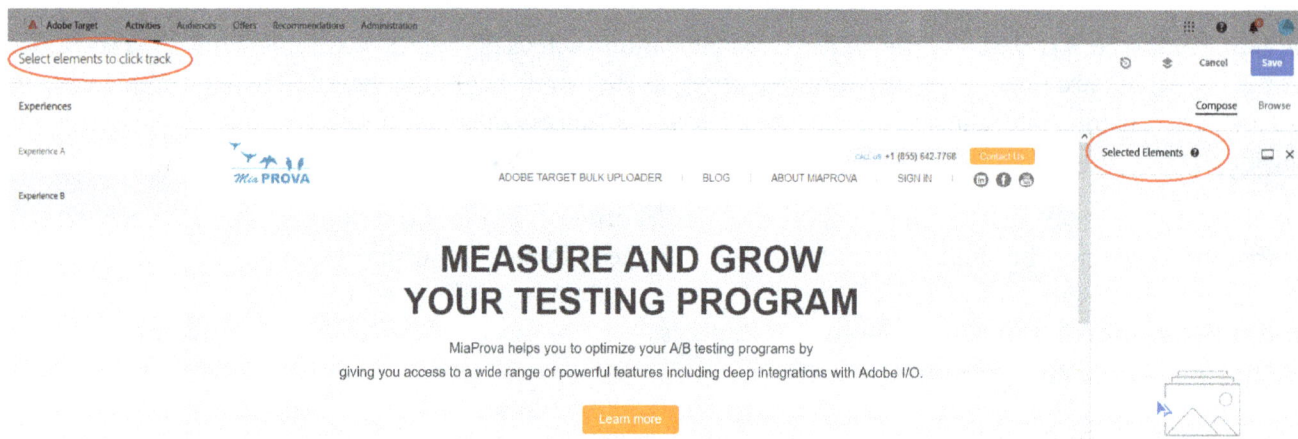

If you click on an element in the page—typically the one that is modified in the new experience you're testing—it is highlighted with a blue box labeled *selected*. The name of the element you selected also appears in the Selected Elements menu on the right side of the screen.

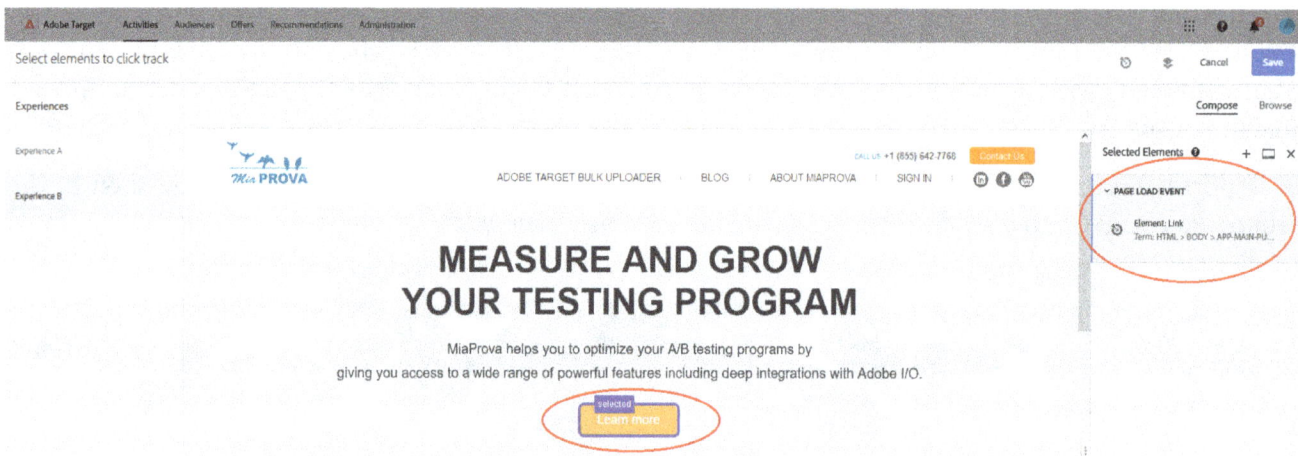

You can then validate your selection by clicking *Save* in the upper-right corner of the VEC screen. This takes you back to the Goals & Settings screen

Once you've finished creating your activity, you can activate it or schedule its start, as we saw before.

Final note: in the list of activities, A/B tests with Auto-allocate are marked A/B - AA, whereas A/B tests with a manual allocation are marked A/B - M.

When to use Auto-allocate

There are two main reasons to use Auto-allocate. The most common one is when we have multiple new experiences we'd like to test and we're only concerned with choosing the best one (e.g., we have several variants of the same idea). Auto-allocate will shift traffic from the bottom performers to the top performers, allowing us to learn sooner which of the top performers is the very best one. This comes at a cost, however: we will never know the precise ranking of the bottom performers.

The second reason is somewhat murkier. Think of it as choosing between two different safety systems for your water meter: would you rather be protected against your dishwasher overflowing and causing $5,000 of damage to your carpets in one day, or against a pipe slowly leaking inside a wall and reducing the value of your house by $10,000 over several years?

Auto-allocate protects us against the dishwasher overflowing but leaves us exposed to pipe leaks inside the wall. If a new experience badly underperforms the control experience in a test, Auto-allocate will quickly decrease the percentage of daily traffic exposed to the new experience, but it does so at the cost of running the experiment for a longer period of time. This reduces the maximum loss we might incur within a single day but increases the potential for loss overall.

On the other hand, traditional A/B tests protect us against leaks in the pipes but leave us exposed to the dishwasher overflowing. As we saw earlier, A/B testing minimizes the total sample size required to reach statistical significance, therefore decreasing the total loss incurred in the long run from tests with negative impacts.

In other words, with Auto-allocate, more people in total will be exposed to underperforming experiences, but they'll be spread out over time. With A/B testing, fewer people in total will be exposed to underperforming experiences, but we might have some really bad days along the way.

This is a complex trade-off and a difficult one to get right. That is why I suggest you stick with A/B tests and don't even consider Auto-allocate until your testing program is consistently running at a moderate velocity (around one new test per week) and you have a few dozen tests under your belt.

Chapter 1.5: Multivariate Testing (MVT)

In an A/B test, we only compare two different versions of the website, usually the current version and a new version that we're considering implementing instead. However, this can limit your velocity if you need to wait until an experiment on a page has completed prior to running the next one. In addition, you might be missing out on interaction effects.

For instance, let's imagine that you want to highlight top products and you're considering adding one of two possibilities to the product details page: user reviews or a "great deal" badge. The current conversion rate is 10%. For this hypothetical example, let's say that the true effects are as follows:

- Adding only user reviews would increase CR to 13%.
- Adding only the badge would increase CR to 12%.
- Adding both would increase CR to 11% because the two partially cancel each other out.

Clearly in this situation, adding user reviews only is the best course of action overall. But we wouldn't know that if we evaluated the two options with two successive A/B tests starting with the badge:

- The first A/B test, of the badge against the status quo of no highlight, would lead us to implement the badge.
- Then in the second A/B test, we would evaluate having both the badge and the user reviews against the new status quo of only the badge. Because having both options results in a lower CR than having the badge only, we would conclude that user reviews "don't work", and we would stick with the badge only.

The solution to this problem is obvious in theory: we should test each of the two features alone *AND* test them together against the current status quo of no highlight. Doing so can become complicated and cumbersome in practice, especially when you have more than two features under consideration. This is where multivariate testing (MVT) comes in, letting Adobe Target handle the complicated parts for you under the hood.

Please note that creating an MVT requires using the Visual Experience Composer, so the VEC must be available on your account.

Implementation

To create an MVT activity, we start as usual by going into the Activities tab and clicking on *Create Activity*. We then select *Multivariate Test* in the dropdown menu.

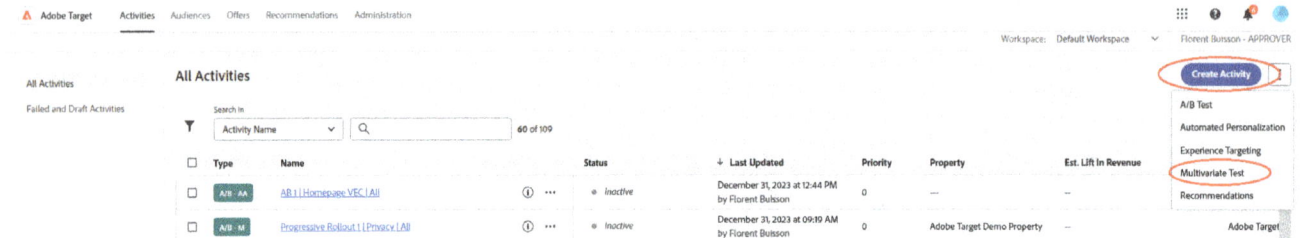

This opens the pop-up to enter the URL of the page where we want to make changes. We'll click *Create*.

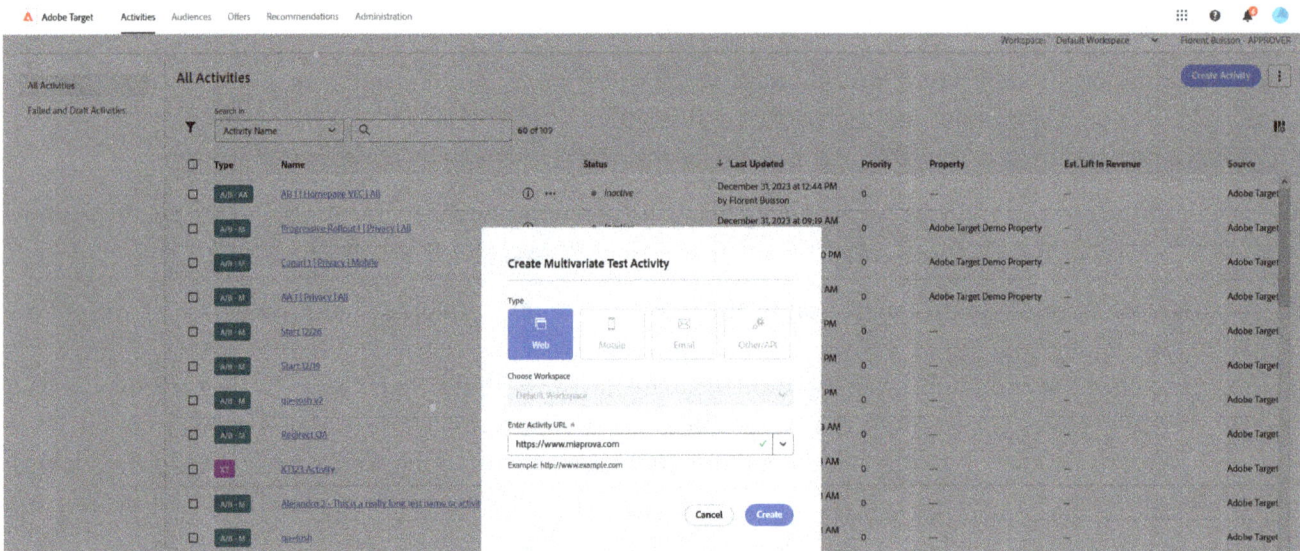

First step: create

Once the VEC has opened, we can make changes as we did in the previous chapter on A/B tests. First, we'll add "About" as an alternative to "About MiaProva." The modified element is then surrounded by a blue box, and highlighted by blue diagonal stripes.

SCALE AND QUANTIFY
YOUR TESTING PROGRAM

Note that each change we make is called an **offer**. The relationship between offers and experiences is important to understand when building an MVT activity. Offers are individual building blocks, while experiences are combinations of offers across multiple places on the website. As such, an MVT activity requires us to create variations in more than one place. In addition, MVT activities allow us to economically combine and test variations, so this is the opportunity to try out multiple variations in a single location.

In the editor that pops up, let's add "Learn More" and "Get Started" as alternatives to "Contact Us," then hit *Next* to get back to the VEC.

As you can see in the screenshot on the next page, the second element for which we created variations is also highlighted by blue diagonal stripes. Its label now includes the number of variations we have created (three, including the default one), and if we click on it, a contextual menu offers several options:

- **Rename Location**. In Adobe Target lingo, the element of a web page for which variations are created is called a **location**. It's often simply an HTML "div" element (you can see the element's name and position in the page structure at the bottom of the VEC), so renaming it helps keep track of the changes we've made to a page.
- **Delete Location.** We can delete all the variations made in one place by deleting the corresponding location. This reverts the web page element to its original version only.
- **Remove "[current variation name]".** This instruction allows us to directly delete the variation that is currently displayed without having to go back into the corresponding editor. For reference, all the variations we created are listed at the bottom of the contextual menu, with a check mark before the one currently displayed.
- **Edit Content….** This option opens the editor we used to create the variations.

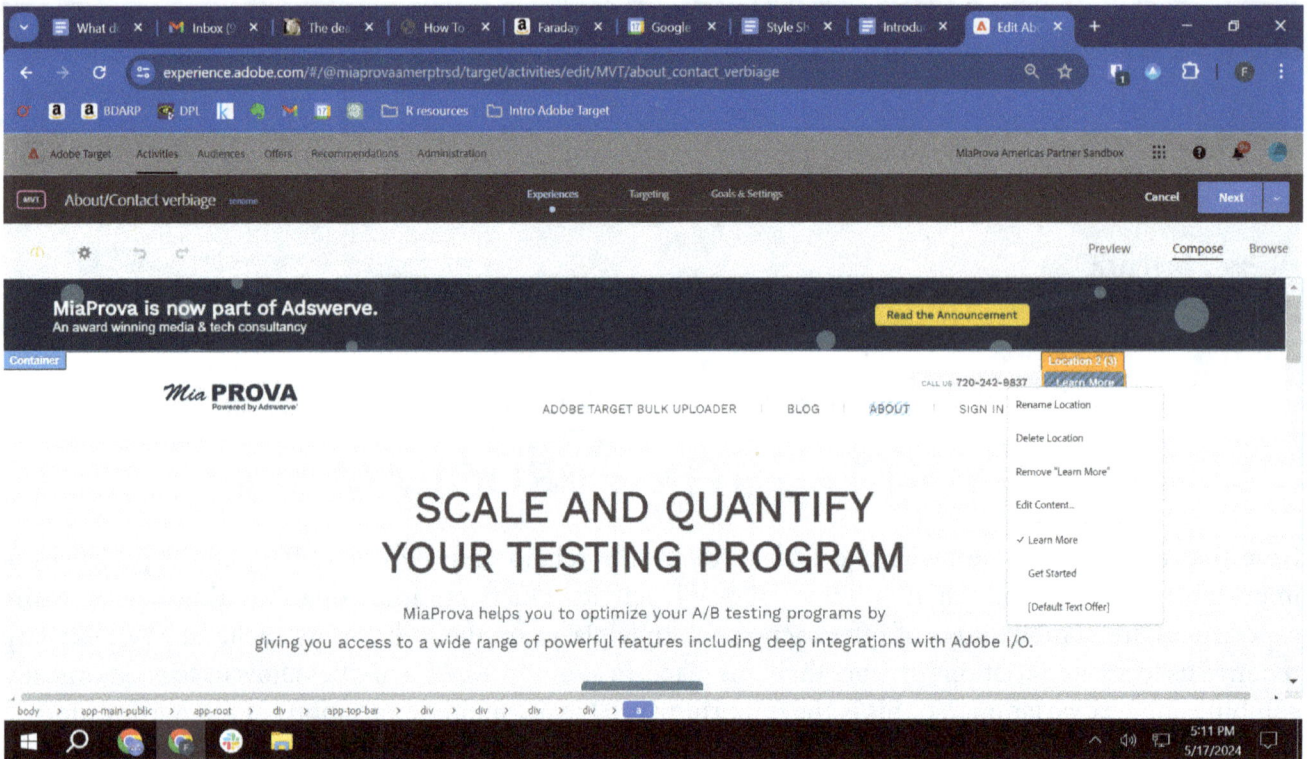

Once we have added new variations in at least two locations, we can preview the corresponding experiences by clicking on *Preview* in the upper right corner of the screen.

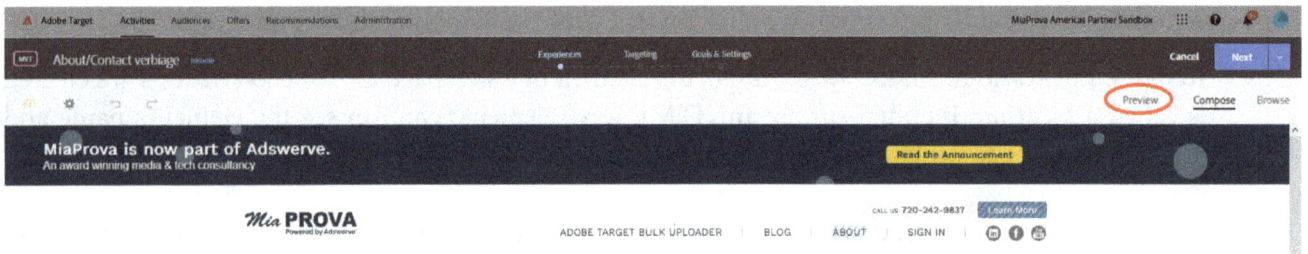

In the Preview mode, we can validate all the combinations of the variations in the different locations. We have two variants in one location and three in another. Multiplying them together gives us six different combinations, which are listed in the left-side menu.

We can see that by default, all the combinations are included. We can change the status of an experience by selecting the checkbox to the left of its name and then clicking on *Include* or *Exclude*. This is where the value of an MVT activity resides: we can effortlessly test a myriad of different experiences and decide which interactions to include or exclude. We could achieve the same result through a more traditional A/B test, but it would require creating each experience manually, a time-intensive and error-prone process.

A final word of caution: it's easy to go overboard with the number of variations in an MVT. But statistics still apply, and the amount of traffic you'll need to reach a decision at a satisfactory level of uncertainty can quickly become unmanageable. To help you avoid this fate, Adobe Target provides a traffic estimator when you click on the yellow fuel gauge above the list of experiences.

By entering the typical (e.g., recent past average) conversion rate and visitors per day, you can get the estimated test duration. If it's too long, you can adjust your plans—for instance, by excluding some combinations from the activity.

Second step: target

When we click *Next*, we get to the Targeting screen. There, as usual, we can determine whether to apply the MVT to all visitors who enter the page or restrict it to a predetermined audience. We can also determine what percentage of the traffic for that audience will be entered into the activity.

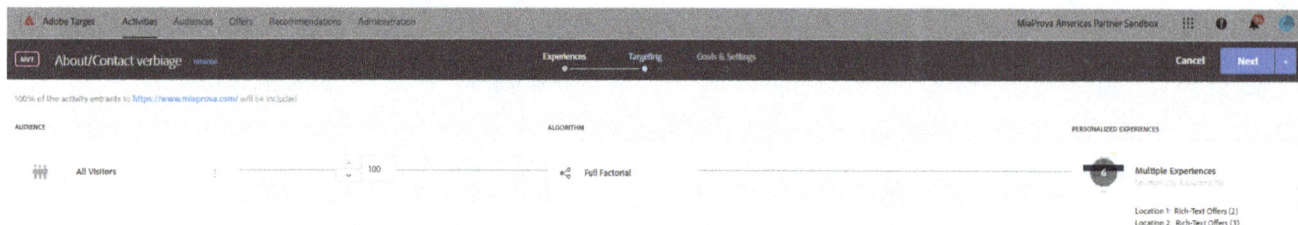

As I mentioned at the beginning of this chapter, an MVT activity is a form of multi-armed bandit whereby Adobe Target will manage and optimize over time the traffic allocation between experiences, so there is no Allocation box: it's replaced by a ***full factorial algorithm*** that you can't modify (meaning that all the combinations you included will be tested).

Third step: goals and settings

The Goals & Settings screen is identical to what we've seen before.

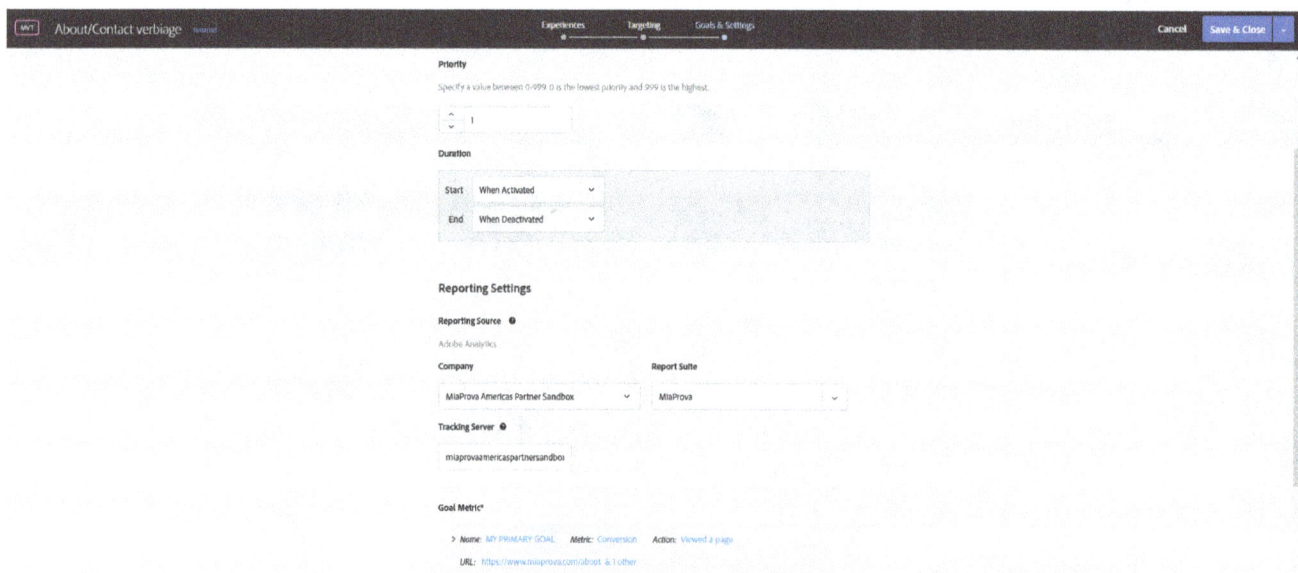

Just remember that whenever the traffic split between experiences is handled automatically by Adobe Target, it's very important to have the correct Goal Metric set up in this screen. I have set the goal to be conversion, i.e., the visitor seeing one of the two pages behind the links that I modified.

Reporting and validation

After saving and closing, we'll wait for the activity to be live for a little while—long enough to get at least a few hundred visitors—prior to moving on.

At that point, we'll take a look at the Reports tab.

In addition to the usual Table View and Graph View subtabs, this tab also has a Location Contribution subtab, which is specific to MVT activities and is selected by default.

First, though, let's look at Graph View, which allows us to visualize how the conversion rates for the different experiences have been trending over time.

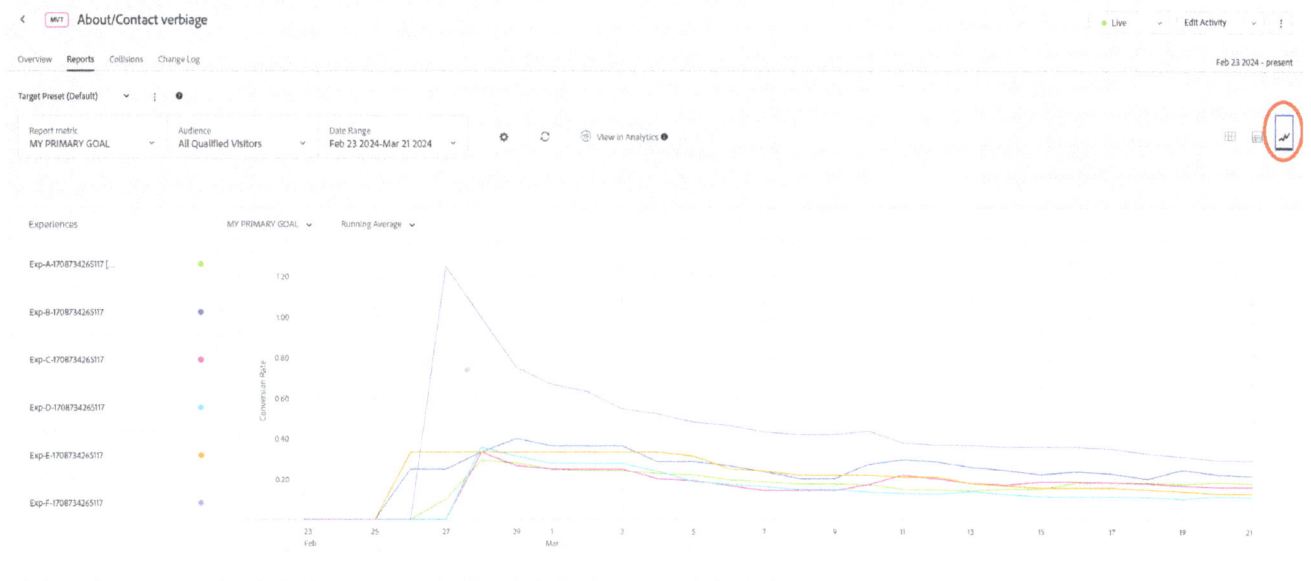

Remember that each experience corresponds to a combination of the offers in the two locations where we've made changes. As we can see, Experience F has been outperforming the others.

Table View provides summary statistics for each of the experiences. The current winner has a star before its name, but the confidence level is still too low to call it.

The Graph and Table Views allow us to determine which specific experience is the best overall, but it can be difficult to understand at a glance which parts of the experience are driving the results—especially when you have a high number of locations and offers.

This is where Location Contribution comes in with additional information that is unique to MVT activities.

There's a lot of information on this screen, so let's review it from the bottom up. At the very bottom, we can see the average Conversion Rate for each Offer in each of the locations.

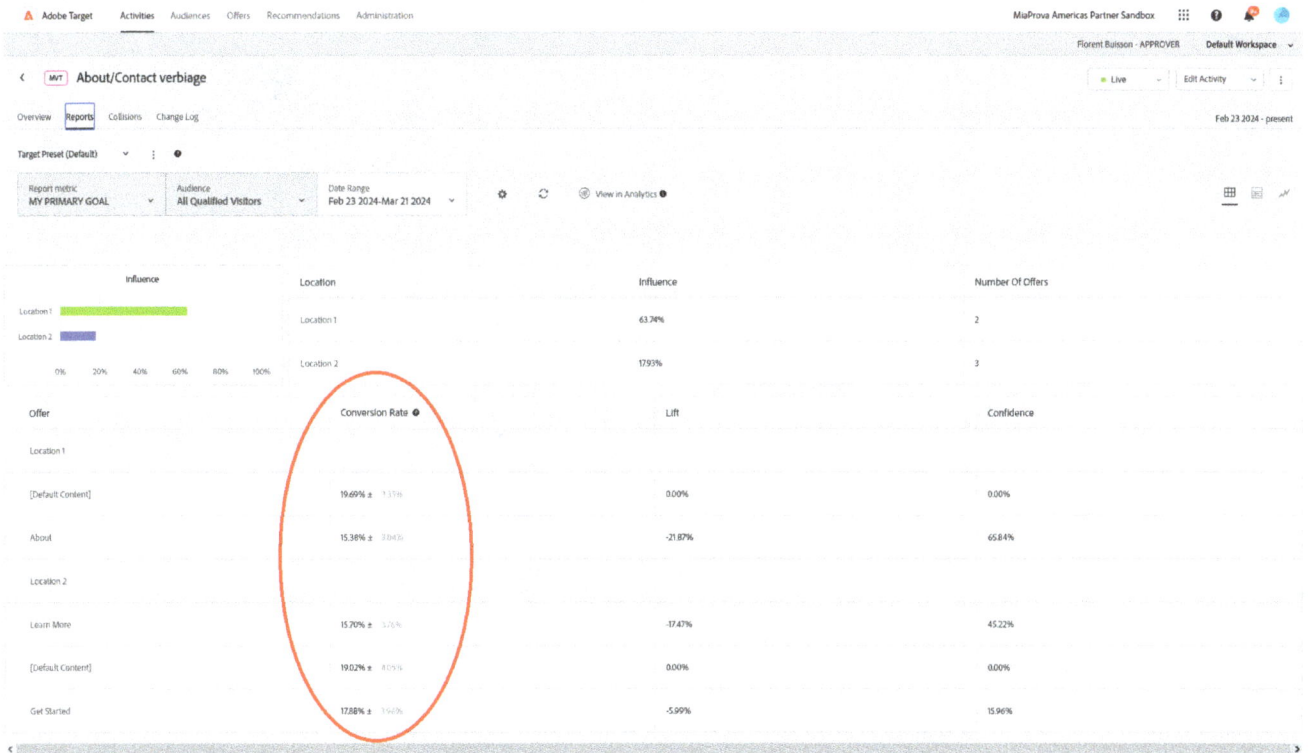

In our example, the conversion rate for Learn More in Location 2 is 15.70%. This is the average taken across all the combinations with the other location(s)—in this case [About MiaProva, Learn More] and [About, Learn More]. Conversely, the conversion rate displayed for About in Location 1 would be the average between [About, Learn More], [About, Contact Us] and [About, Get Started].

To the right of the Conversion Rate, we see the average Lift compared to the default in each location, as well as the degree of Confidence. Both lift and confidence are always zero for the default offer in each location (it can't outperform itself). Here, none of the new offers outperformed the control on average. But remember that Experience F was the winner! This is where MVT activities shine: if we had tried making changes in only one location at a time, we would never have found the unique combination of changes with a positive lift.

Finally, the Influence section above the table gives us some additional insights for future experiments.

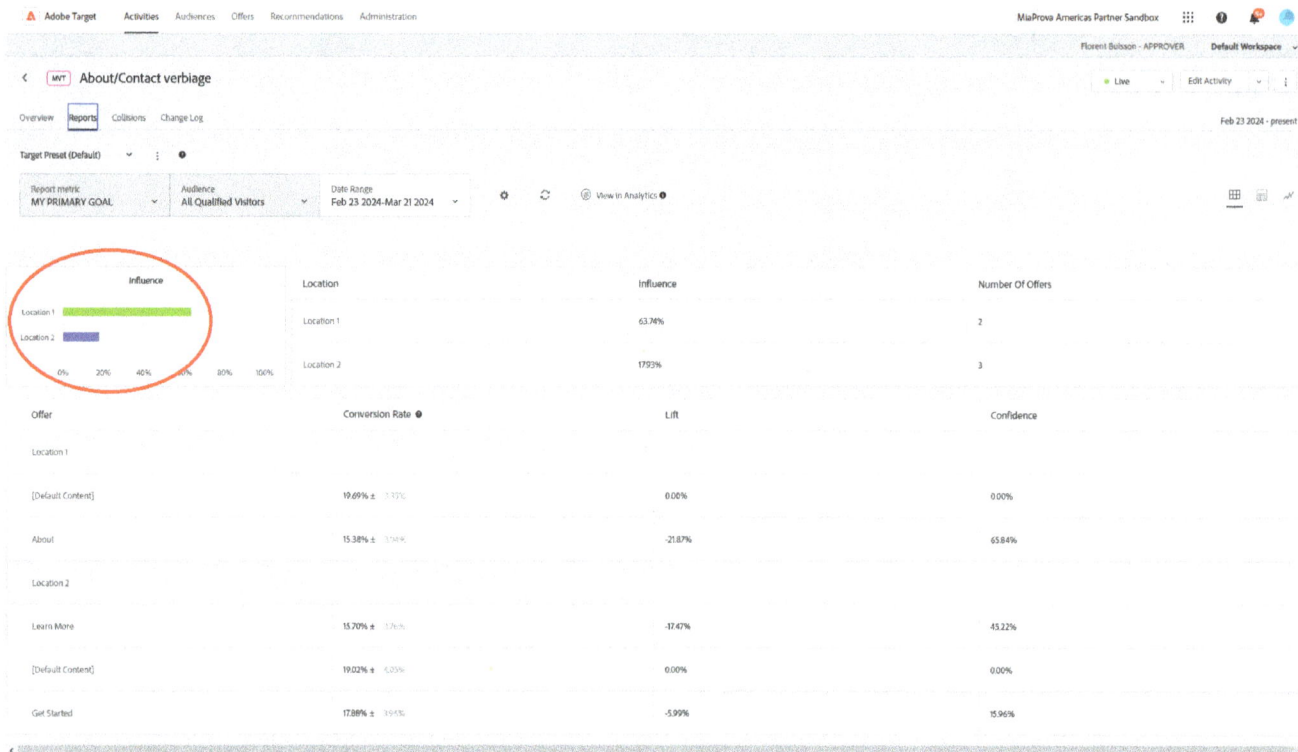

The bar plot on the left and the table to the right of it show the same information—namely, which of the locations we've been experimenting on has the most impact on conversion rate. Here the data suggests we should prioritize the first location (the About MiaProva link) for future testing.

To conclude and recap, MVT activities allow us to test multiple offers in multiple locations—and all their combinations—in a very economical manner.

Chapter 1.6: Experience Targeting (XT)

All the activities we have seen so far are designed to be temporary: whether it's a progressive rollout or an A/B test, the idea is that once you have learned what you wanted to learn, you should deactivate the activity and get back to a single version of the website until your next rollout or test. We're now getting into the world of ongoing personalization, where different visitors will be served different experiences on a permanent basis.

Personalization is often looked upon as a holy Grail, a very advanced and slightly scary approach that is only for the experts but promises untold riches to those who master it. In my opinion, both the fears and the expectations are somewhat misplaced. Personalization is easier from a technical perspective than most people think, but it also introduces a permanent layer of complexity that people don't expect—think of it as "technical debt" on which you'll pay interest forever while never being able to pay off the capital.

Implementation

In chapter 1.4, while discussing A/B testing, we tested the phrase "Measure and grow your testing program" against the current default of "Scale and quantify your testing program." Let's say that ex-post analyses showed that the new verbiage performed better for mobile phone users and for authenticated users, whereas the old one performed better for computer and tablet users and for anonymous prospects. Instead of using the verbiage that performed best on average across the board, this gives us an opportunity to extract additional lift by personalizing tour content depending on the audience. In Adobe Target, Experience Targeting (XT) allows us to do just that through a rule-based approach.

As usual, our journey begins by clicking on *Create Activity* in the Activities tab and selecting the type of activity we want to create.

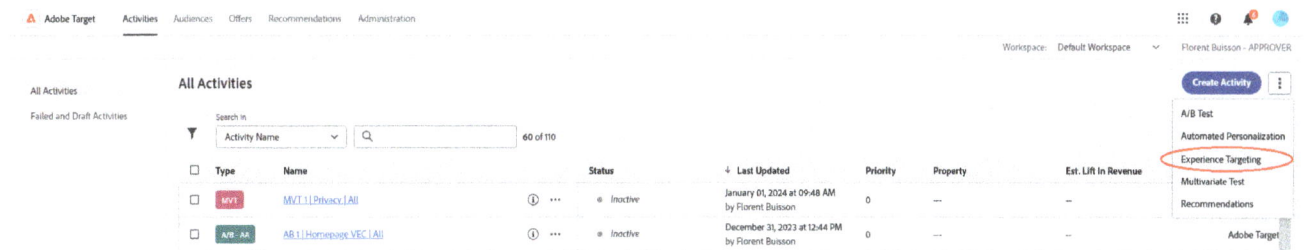

In the next screen, as before, we can choose between *Form* and *Visual* Experience Composer; we'll use the *Form* Composer for the sake of brevity. Let's assume that the engineering team has created the appropriate call in the code for the *xt1_homepage* mbox, with two experiences labeled "Scale" and "Measure" corresponding to the respective verbiage.

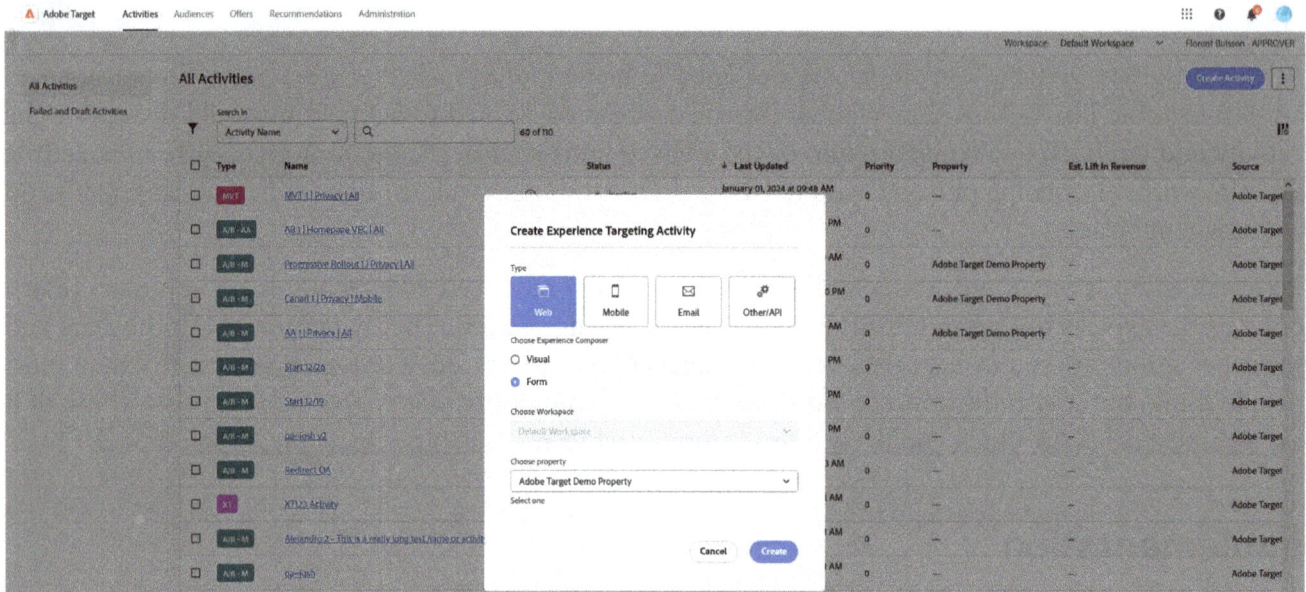

In the next screen, we'll first name our new activity "XT 1 | Home Page" and indicate the corresponding mbox.

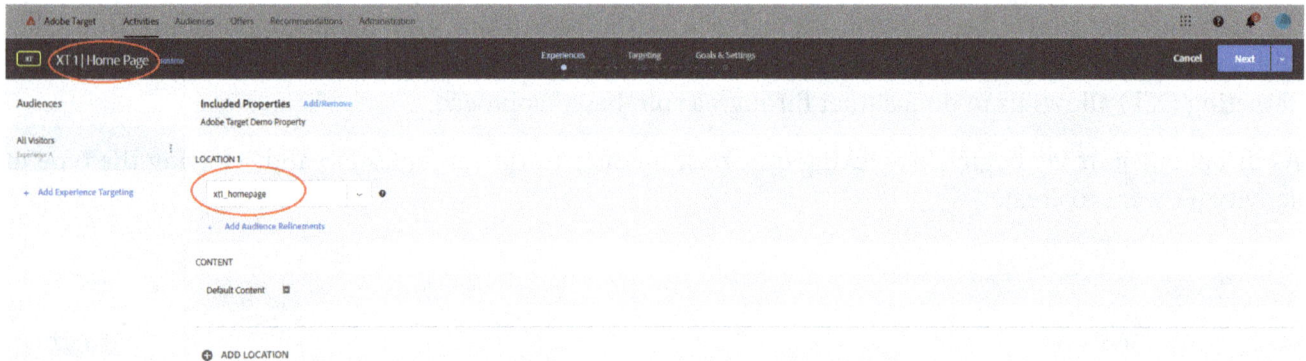

When using the Form Composer, we have to use and work around the experience names that have been defined and implemented by the engineering team. Therefore we'll start by renaming our default experience under All Visitors; it is now titled "Scale."

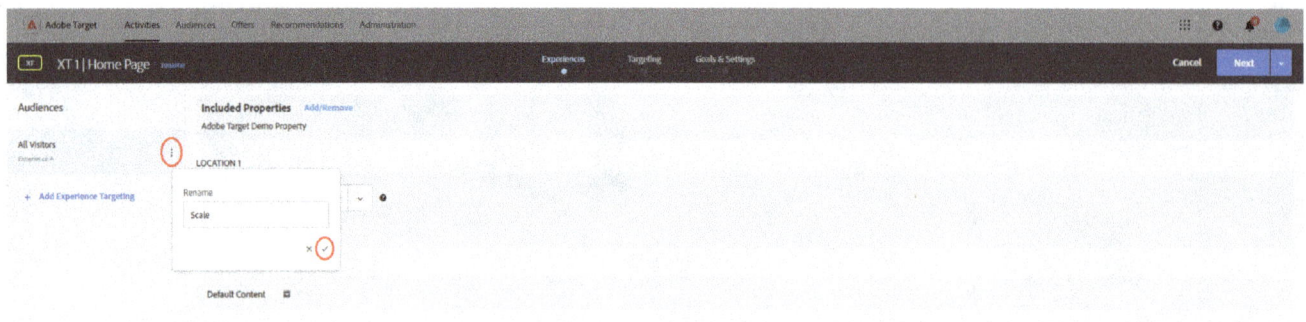

We'll then click on *Add Experience Targeting* to define the audience that will be served the Measure experience. This opens the *Add audiences* screen.

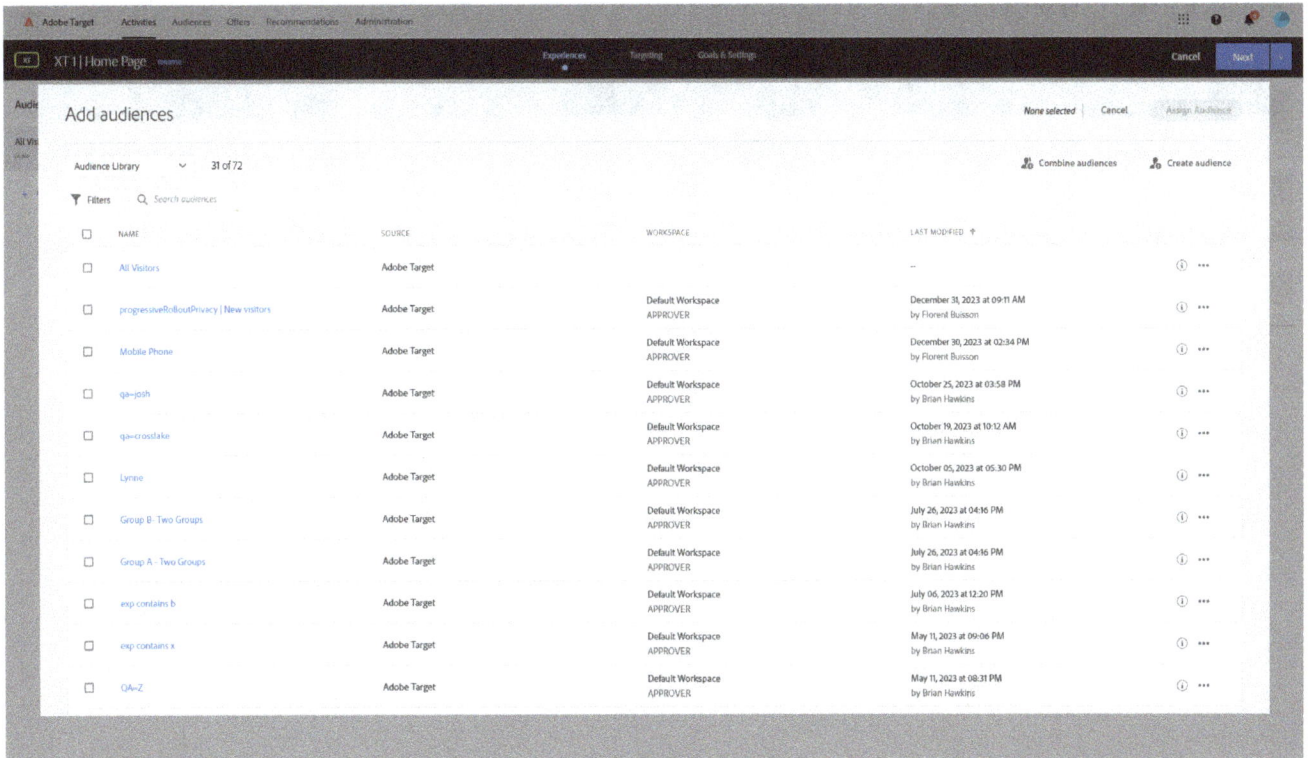

We'll need to combine the two criteria we have identified (i.e., mobile phone users and authenticated users). We have already created an audience for mobile phone users but we'll need to create a new one for authenticated users. Let's do this first.

In our implementation, authenticated users are defined as those with a non-null value for *mbox3rdPartyId*. We'll drag *Visitor Profile* to the central section of the screen and select *mbox3rdPartyId* and *Parameter value is present* before naming our newly created audience. We also need to make sure that we save this audience to the Audience Library (the default) so that it's available for our combined audience.

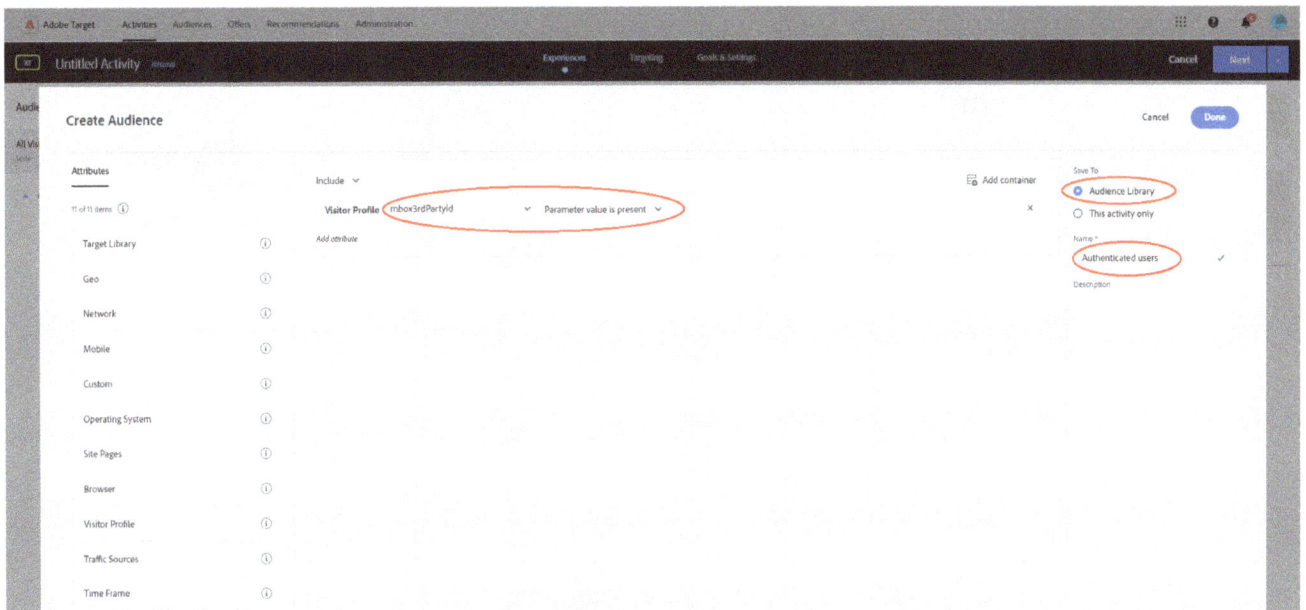

Clicking *Done* takes us back to the previous screen. This time we click *Combine audiences*, which opens a similar editor with Audiences instead of Attributes in the left-side menu. Here you can save combined audiences, which are specific to a single activity (as you can see on the right side of the screen).

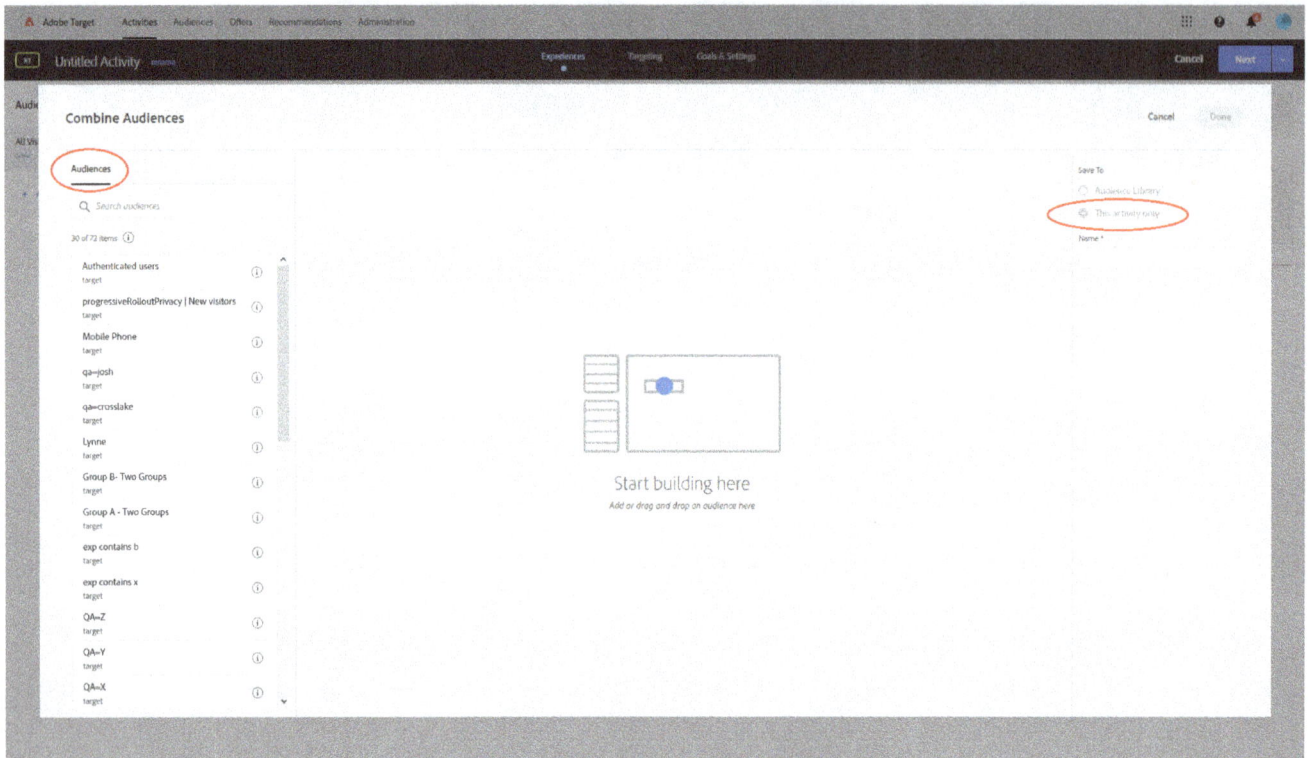

We'll drag and drop *Authenticated users* and *Mobile Phone* from the left-side menu and switch the joining operator from *and* to *or*. We'll name our audience "Authenticated users || Mobile Phone" to make crystal-clear the underlying logic.

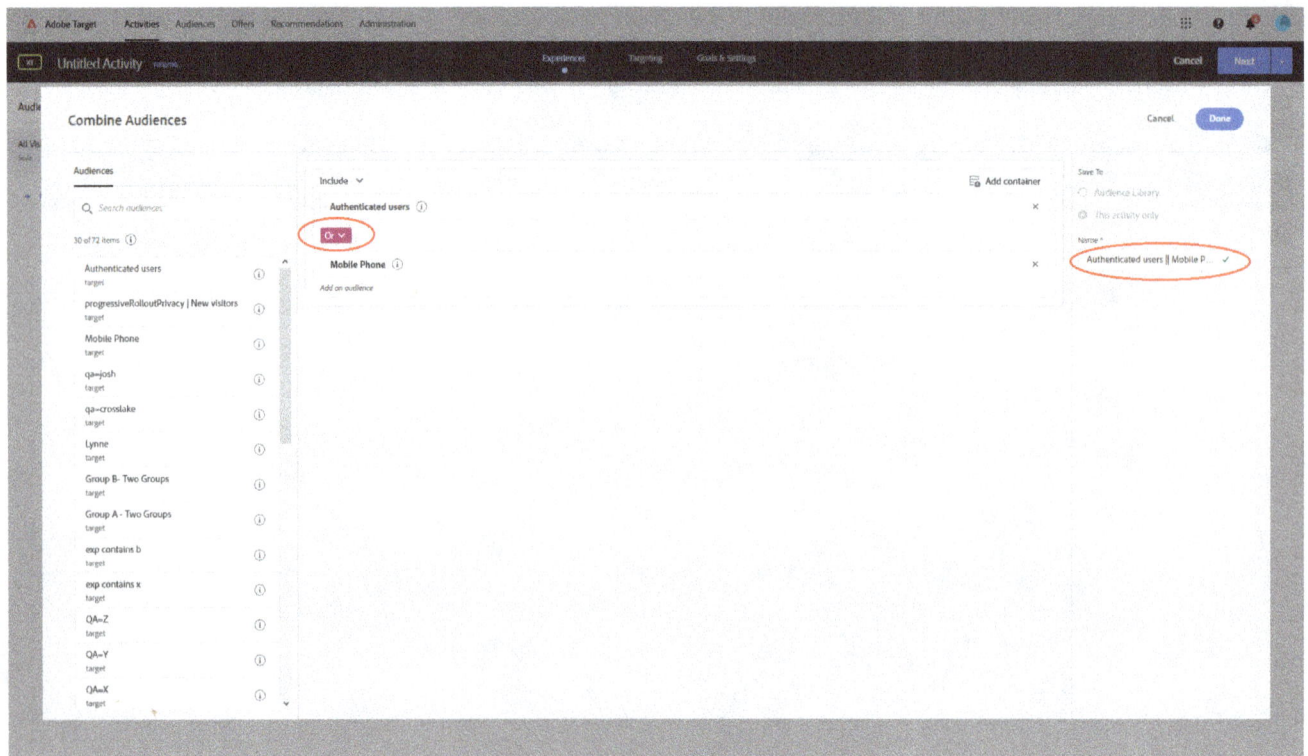

After assigning our newly created combined audience to the second experience, we'll click *Next* to move to the Targeting step.

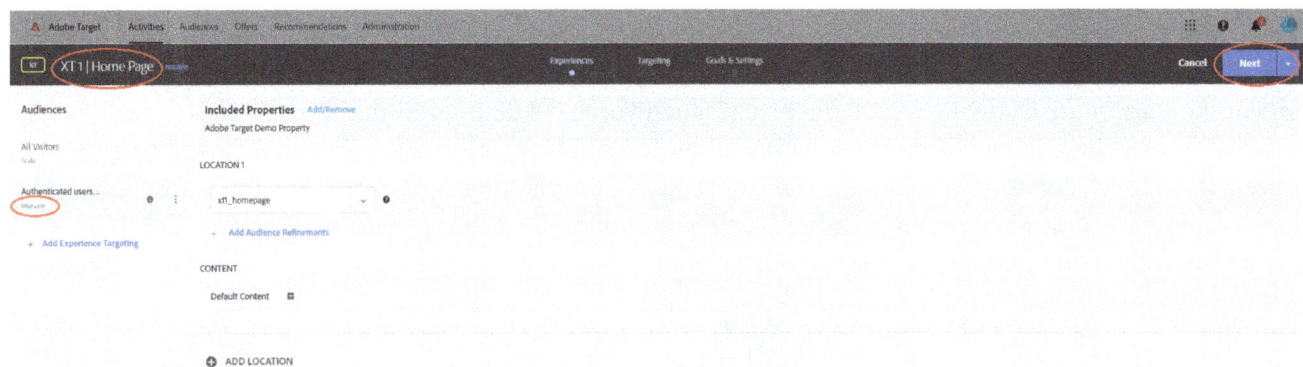

The Targeting screen for XT activities displays the audiences and the experiences that are served to them, listed in the order that they are evaluated.

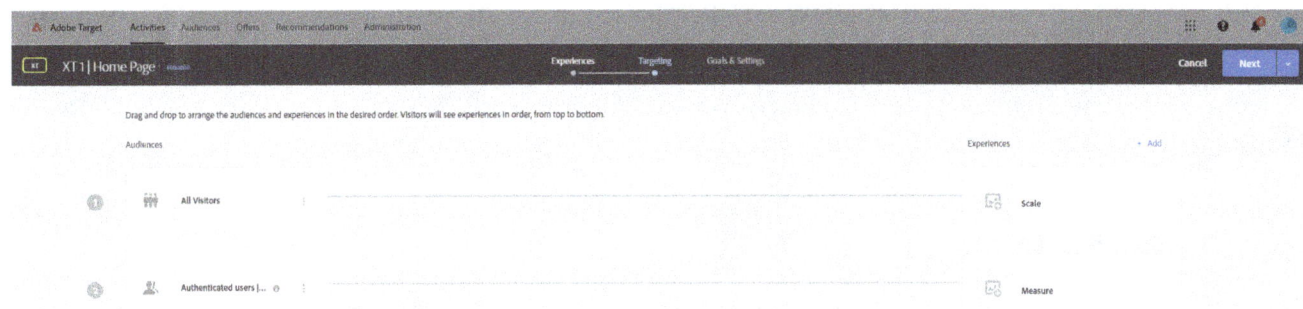

If the audiences that we have defined are strictly mutually exclusive, their order in this screen doesn't matter. For instance, instead of having a catch-all All Visitors audience, we could have defined that audience as the opposite of the other, i.e., "nonauthenticated AND nonmobile". But I prefer to have a fallback All Visitors audience because you never know what may go wrong or when you may make a typo. Since our audiences are therefore not mutually exclusive, we want the narrower audience(s) on top and the broader one(s) at the bottom. If necessary, we can reorder them by dragging and dropping.

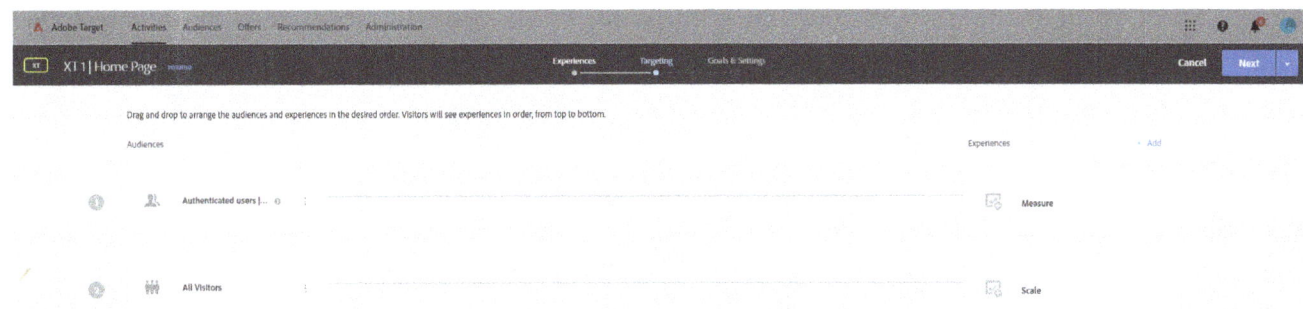

One thing to keep in mind is that behavior- and preference-based audiences can change over time. For instance, a visitor who is not authenticated at the beginning of a visit may sign in in the middle of the visit. Similarly, if an audience is based on the number of products viewed, a visitor will never be labeled as such when they first enter the website but may acquire the label after some time browsing. Even geo-targeted audiences can become applicable or inapplicable if a visitor from one geographic location travels to another and then returns to your site.

Thus, audience assignment for experience targeting is not permanent but gets updated based on changes to a visitor's profile. A visitor will "trade up" if they become eligible for a higher-priority experience, *but only at the start of the following visit*. Conversely, when you have defined multiple audiences in the activity, if a visitor stops qualifying for a given audience but qualifies for a lower-priority audience, they will be served the experience for the latter on their next visit. If a visitor stops qualifying for an audience and doesn't qualify for another existing audience, they will default to the generic experience of visitors who don't qualify for any audience.

As a side note, this means that technically we could have built our XT activity with only the Authenticated Users || Mobile Phone audience being defined and served the Measure experience. This would rely on the Scale experience being served by default to everybody else. Unfortunately, what happens when you have defined only one audience and a visitor stops qualifying for it is a bit counterintuitive: they keep seeing the corresponding experience nonetheless. My guess is that in this case, Adobe Target prioritizes providing a consistent experience to a given visitor, whereas when you define multiple audiences, you implicitly agree to visitors potentially encountering different experiences. This is another reason why I prefer to have a fallback All Visitors audience at the bottom of the targeting hierarchy.

When we're done with that step, we can click *Next* and get to the Goals & Settings step. This will be the same process we've used for our previous activities, so I won't elaborate again here.

Reporting and validation

Reporting in Adobe Target for XT activities is similar to what we've seen so far (this screenshot is from a prior activity in order to have a large enough number of unique visitors to report on).

However, the interpretation of the results needs to be slightly different. In an XT activity, we have different audiences seeing different experiences. Even though Adobe Target will highlight a "winner" with the usual green star, we can't know that this experience would perform best for the other groups as well. Therefore, it is best to dismiss the idea of a winning experience and focus instead on how to improve the conversion rate for the underperforming groups.

In the previous screenshot, we can see that the experience for Group B is not performing very well, so that's where we'll want to focus—for example, by running an A/B test specifically focused on that audience or by investigating its characteristics through UX research.

PART II:
PREMIUM ACTIVITIES

Chapter 2.1: Personalization

We saw in the last chapter that Experience Targeting allows us to serve a specific experience to a specific visitor segment. This is a powerful first step into personalization, but it requires us to know in advance which experience will perform best for that segment. Figuring that out by looking at the results of A/B tests and slicing them by segments can be a very manual and time-intensive process. To truly unleash the power of personalization, we'll have to move from manual to algorithmic (or automated) personalization, which is available for premium licenses only.

Adobe Target Premium offers two types of activities for personalization. Automated Personalization (AP) was developed first and is still available. Auto-Target (AT), on the other hand, is the new kid on the block. It is based on the same algorithm under the hood as Automated Personalization, but it has a more streamlined process and a greater number of features. Therefore, in this chapter we'll start with AT, and then we'll see what remaining use cases are still best served by AP.

Auto-Target

Auto-Target (AT) brings together elements of A/B testing and Experience Targeting: you define competing experiences and then let AT figure out which experience is the best one for a visitor based on their profile characteristics. As with Auto-Allocate, AT will strike a trade-off between exploration and optimization; it does this by serving experiences at random to a subset of visitors (for exploration) and serving its best guess to the rest of the visitors (for optimization).

This is one area where there is a significant difference between Auto-Target and Automated Personalization: in AP, you have to set up the percentage of traffic that should be allocated to a random experience—typically 10% or 15%—and that percentage remains constant over time. Conversely, AT optimizes that percentage by setting it at a higher level at first to accelerate early learnings, then decreasing it progressively down to 10% to take advantage of the learnings accumulated so far.

Testing the waters with a time-bound activity

As a first step to familiarize ourselves with personalization, we'll run a temporary activity as a follow-up to an A/B test. A good candidate would be an A/B test in which one experience performs well with a certain segment of visitors but the other experience performs better for another segment. This suggests that there might be benefits to keeping both experiences live on your website and directing visitors to one or the other based on their profile. However, this means having to maintain and continually update a larger code base, which entails a cost; therefore, we'll want to get a clear measure of these benefits (the "lift") compared to only using the best-performing experience across the board.

As in the last chapter about Experience Targeting, let's build upon our two competing phrases, "Measure and grow your testing program" and the current default of "Scale and quantify your testing program." We'll start by copying our existing A/B test.

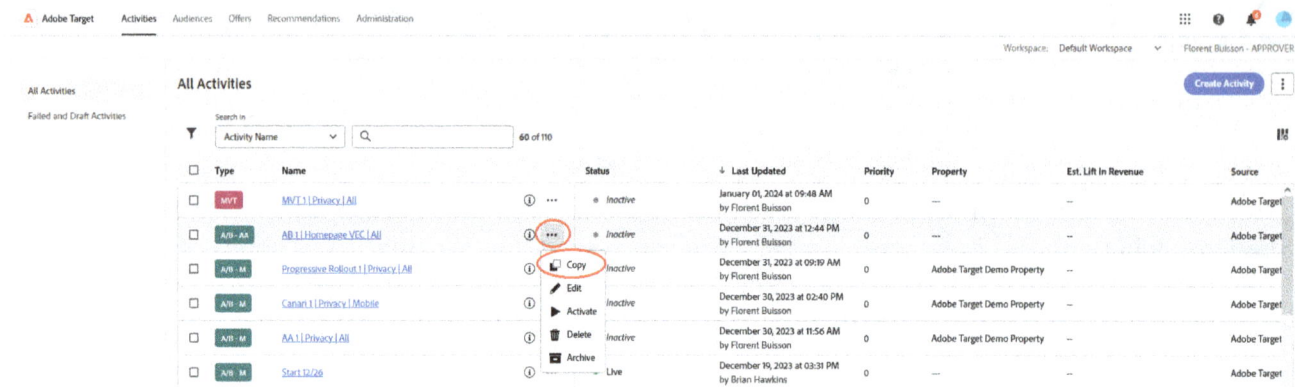

In the Experiences step, we need only to update the name of the activity.

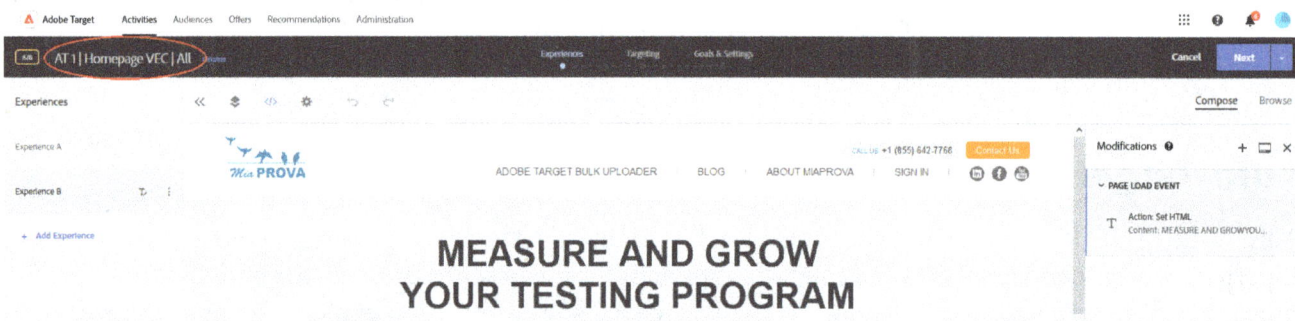

If we were creating an AT activity from scratch, this step would entail the same process as it would for an A/B test.

The Targeting step is where things become different. Under Traffic Allocation Method, we'll select *Auto-target* . This will immediately modify the right side of the screen, generating a 50/50 split between a Control branch and a Personalized Experiences branch.

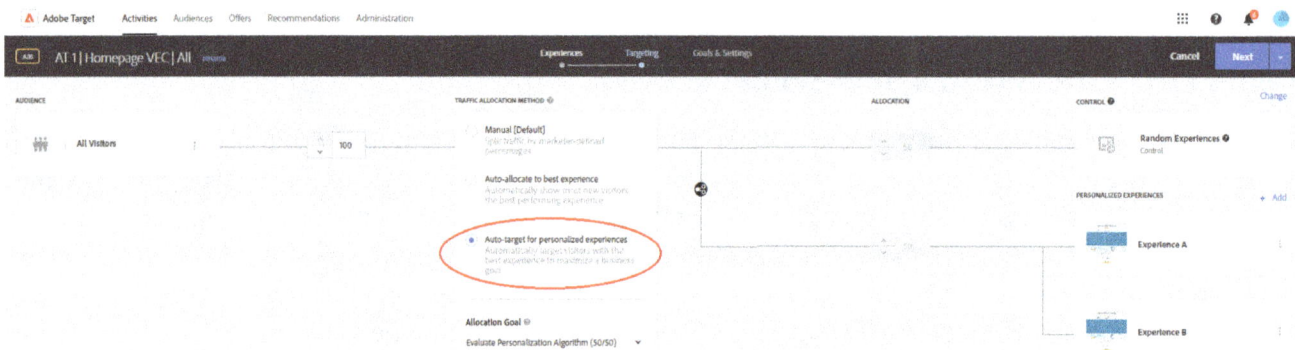

This modification occurs because the default setting for Auto-target, shown directly beneath it under Allocation Goal, is *Evaluate Personalization Algorithm (50/50)*. This is the setting we want, so no need to change it at the moment. Let's move on to the branches.

The default for the Control branch is *Random Experiences*, which means that when a visitor is allocated to that branch, they will be served at random one of the experiences we have defined. This is *not* what we want here, because it doesn't represent a viable option that could reasonably be implemented as a long-term solution. We want to determine the lift from personalization compared to the best performing experience overall—the one we would implement if we decided against personalization.

Let's change that setting and choose *Experience B* as our control instead.

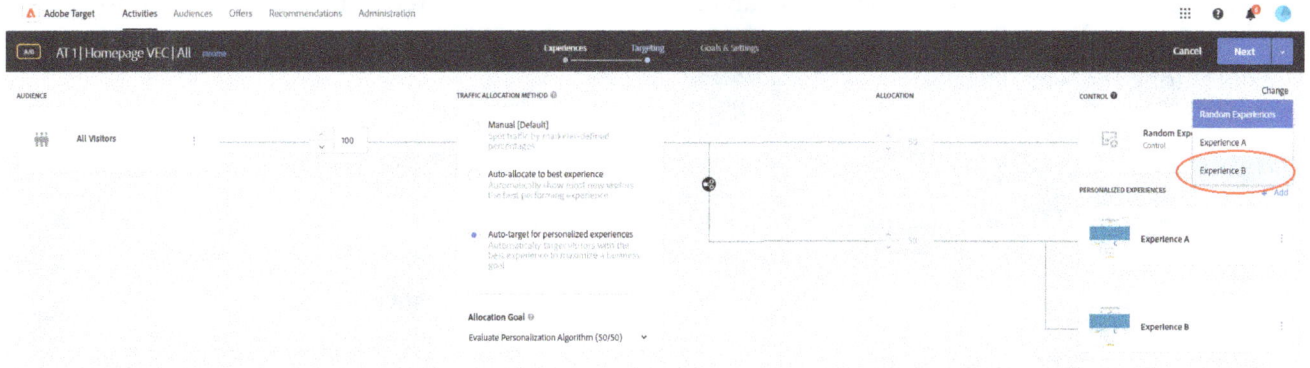

In the Personalized Experience branch, you can see all the experiences you have defined. Whenever a visitor starts a new visit, they'll be assigned to one of these experiences based on the information on their profile. Let's see how that works.

How the algorithm works

The algorithm used for Auto-target takes into account basically *all* the information that is available in a visitor's profile: not only basic data such as location, device type, current time and day of week, but also behavior such as the number of pages viewed. The overall algorithm is updated every 24 hours to integrate new information about how well its past assignments have worked.

One thing to keep in mind is that the experience is assigned at the visit level: at the beginning of a visit, a visitor is assigned to a certain experience and stays in it for the entire visit, but they might be assigned to a different experience for their next visit, based on the new information collected in the meantime (such as their behavior during their previous visit).

Analyzing the results of the activity

The Reports tab for Auto-Target activities is similar to what we've seen so far.

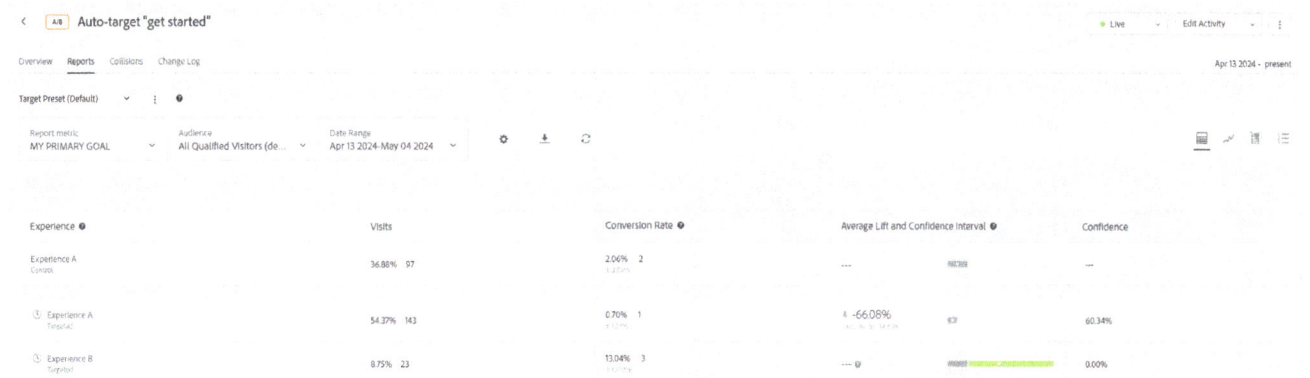

Always-on personalization

Once we are satisfied that personalization would be beneficial as an "always-on" activity, we can create the corresponding Auto-target activity. This time in the Targeting step, as our Allocation Goal we'll select *Maximize Personalization Traffic (90/10)*. With this setting, Adobe Target will drive 90% of traffic to the optimal experience based on the visitor's characteristics and send the remaining 10% to a Control. This is where it makes sense to use *Random Experiences*, so that the algorithm can keep learning as much as possible along the way.

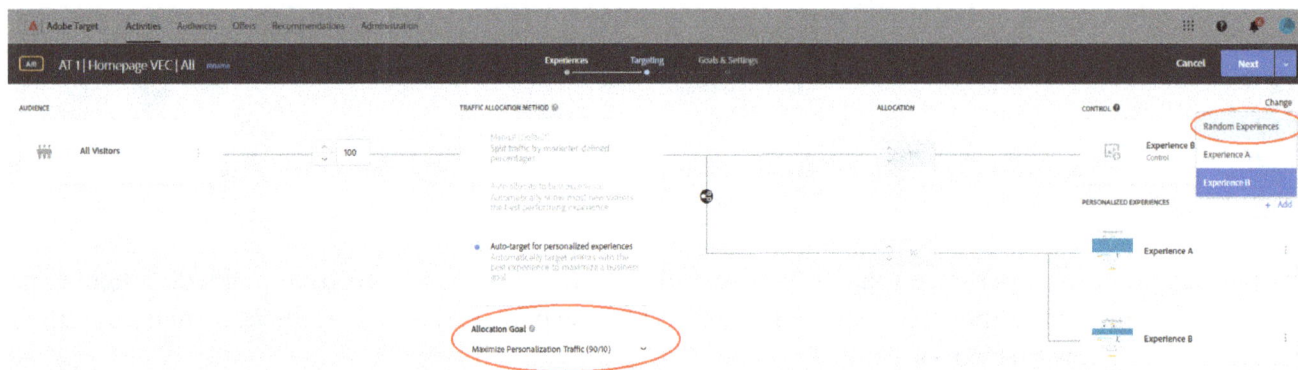

Automated Personalization

Given all the benefits of Auto-Target we've seen so far, why would you ever want to use Automated Personalization instead? There are two minor reasons that we'll review quickly and one major reason we'll discuss a bit more at length. The two minor reasons are:

- Automated Personalization offers you some additional flexibility in that you can choose which algorithm to use, whereas in Auto-Target you must rely on Adobe Target's modified version of the Random Forest algorithm.
- Similarly, you can choose the percentage of traffic to be used for learning rather than letting Adobe Target dynamically optimize it over time.

While Adobe calls out these two reasons, I don't find them compelling, and I would leave AP to its well-earned retirement were it not for the last reason:

In Auto-Target, you have to build the different experiences by hand, as in an A/B test. Automated Personalization, on the other hand, like multivariate testing, automatically generates all the possible combinations between the variants you have introduced in different locations. There are certain situations in which this automatic generation will be far more efficient. For instance, let's say you have three different possible headlines and three different possible pictures, all of which are compatible with each other. In this case, you'll want to optimize across the nine possible combinations based on a visitor's profile. This will be much faster and easier to handle with AP.

Implementation in Adobe Target

While Auto-Target activities are a special type of A/B testing activities, Automated Personalization activities are a top-level option under the *Create Activity* button.

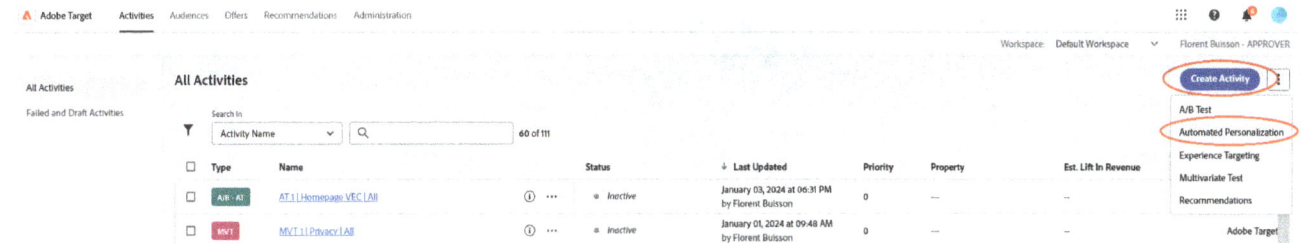

After selecting *Automated Personalization*, you can then choose between *Form* and *Visual Experience Composer*. Note that if you want to use the Visual Experience Composer, you'll have access to only a limited array of capabilities. Some options, such as injecting custom JavaScript code, will be unavailable, as these capabilities can be leveraged only in an Auto-Target activity.

The VEC is otherwise similar to what we're used to, with some minor differences that we'll detail below.

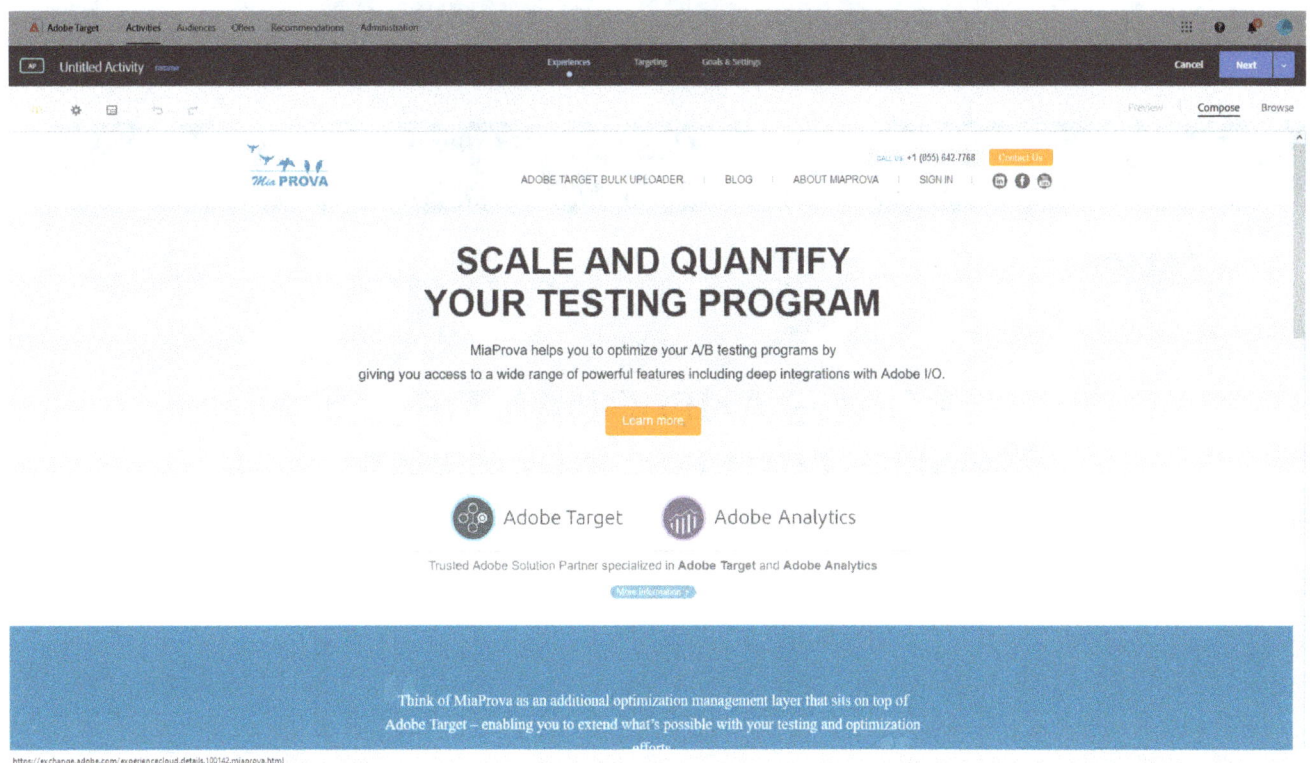

We can create new experiences by clicking on an element and introducing modifications such as differences in verbiage.

In the first location, we'll try "About" versus the current default, "About MiaProva."

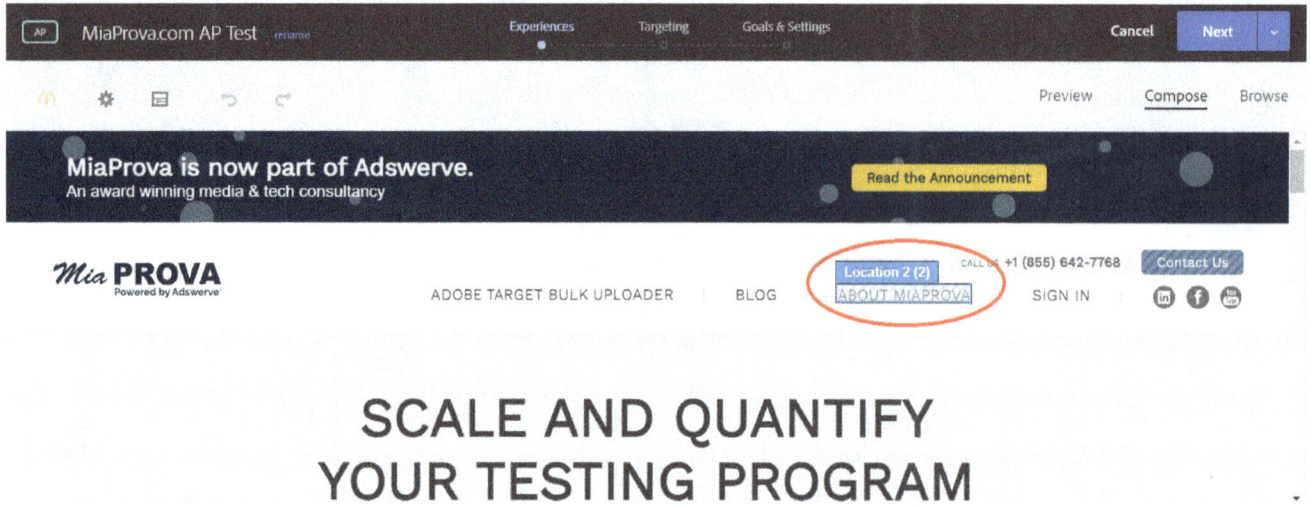

In the second location, we'll try "Get Started" and "Learn More" against the current default, "Contact Us."

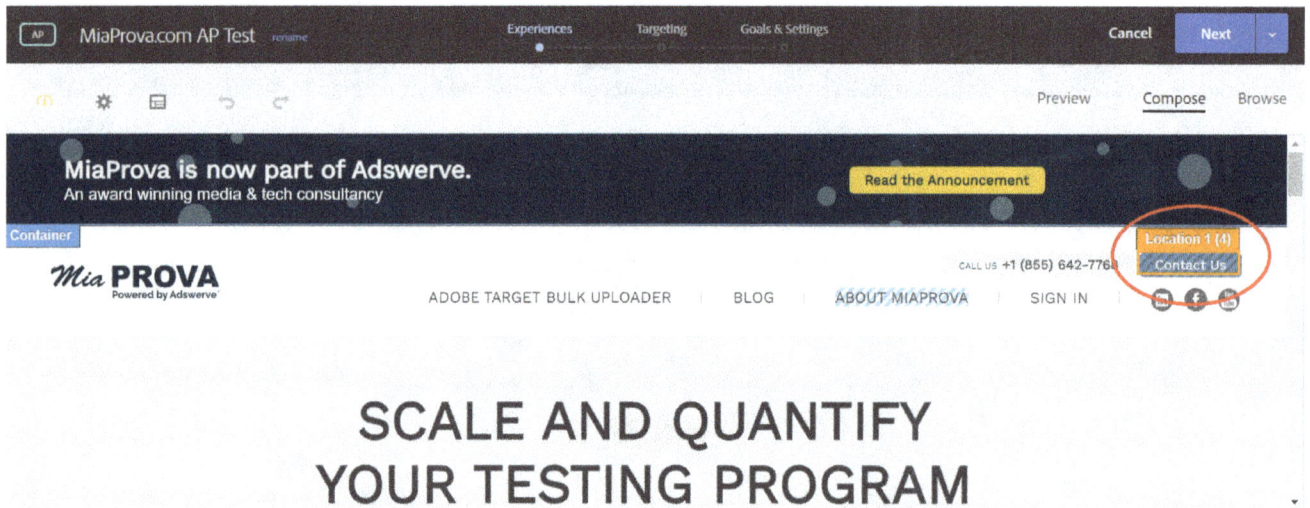

After having made these changes, we can check the duration required to reach robust results by clicking on the *Traffic* button, represented by a gauge, at the far left of the menu.

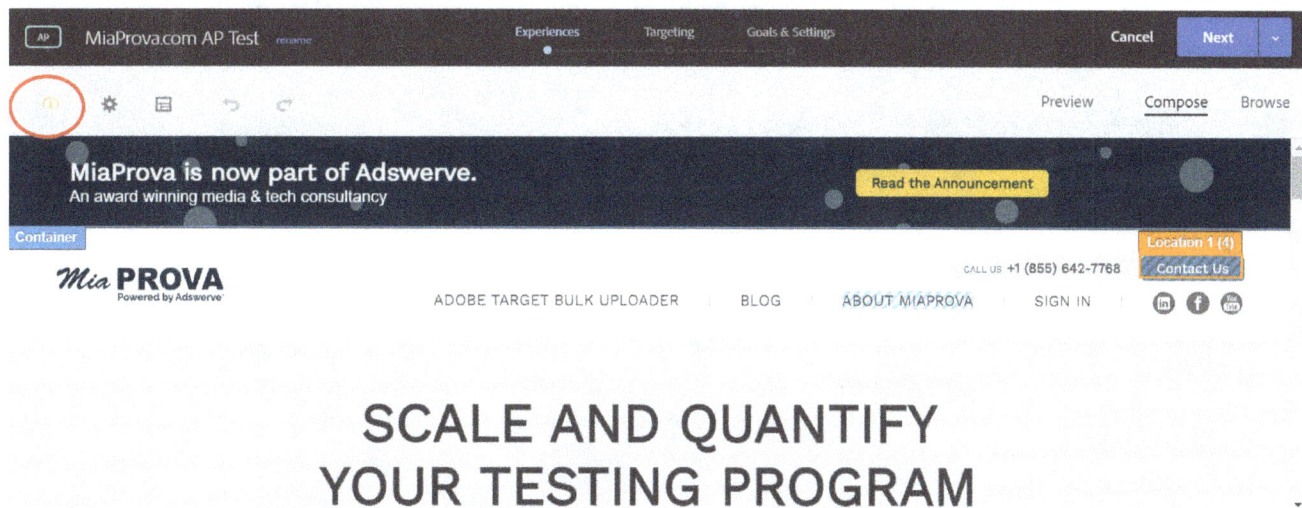

Next to the Traffic icon is the familiar Settings button, and the third icon is for managing content.

This button allows us to easily include or exclude specific combinations of changes, or in Adobe Target parlance, experiences that combine offers.

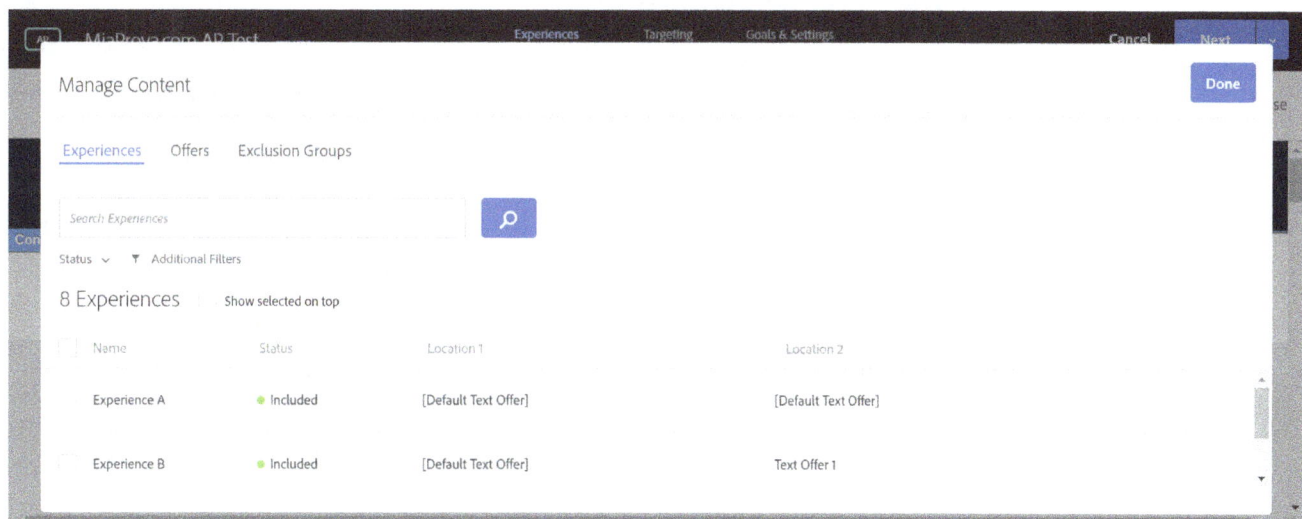

In the present example, we don't need to exclude any experience. But let's imagine, for instance, that we had one offer with a banner offering a time-limited 10% discount and another offer with a pop-up offering a time-limited 20% discount. We wouldn't want any visitor to be served both of these offers; therefore we would exclude the corresponding combinations in the Experiences tab. However, as the number of locations and offers increases, tracking all the experiences that combine two specific offers can become cumbersome and error-prone. For example, if you are testing ten different background colors in a third location, you would need to find and exclude all ten experiences that combine the two discounts.

Adobe Target gives us an easier solution to this problem: Exclusion Groups. By selecting the corresponding tab, we can select offers that should never be combined.

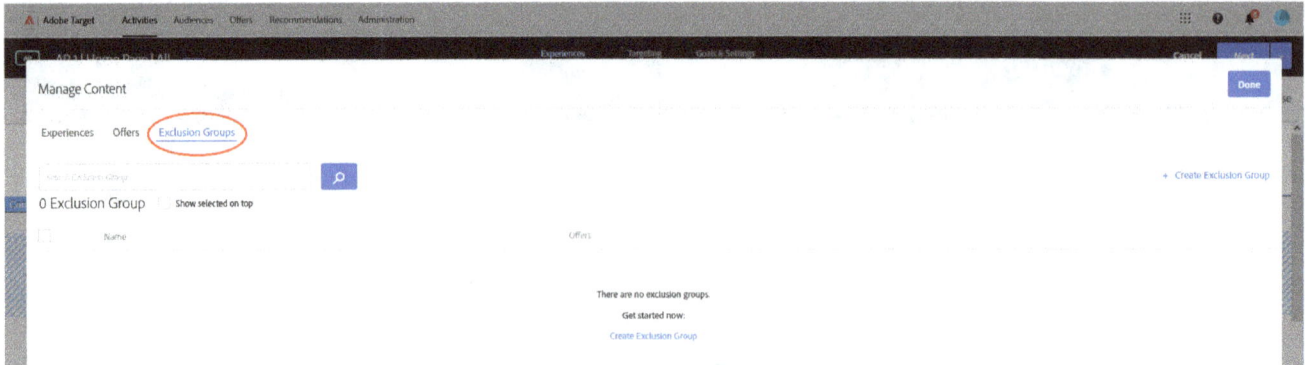

After the Experiences step, the Targeting step is very similar to what we've seen for Auto-Target, with a drop-down menu to select our allocation goal.

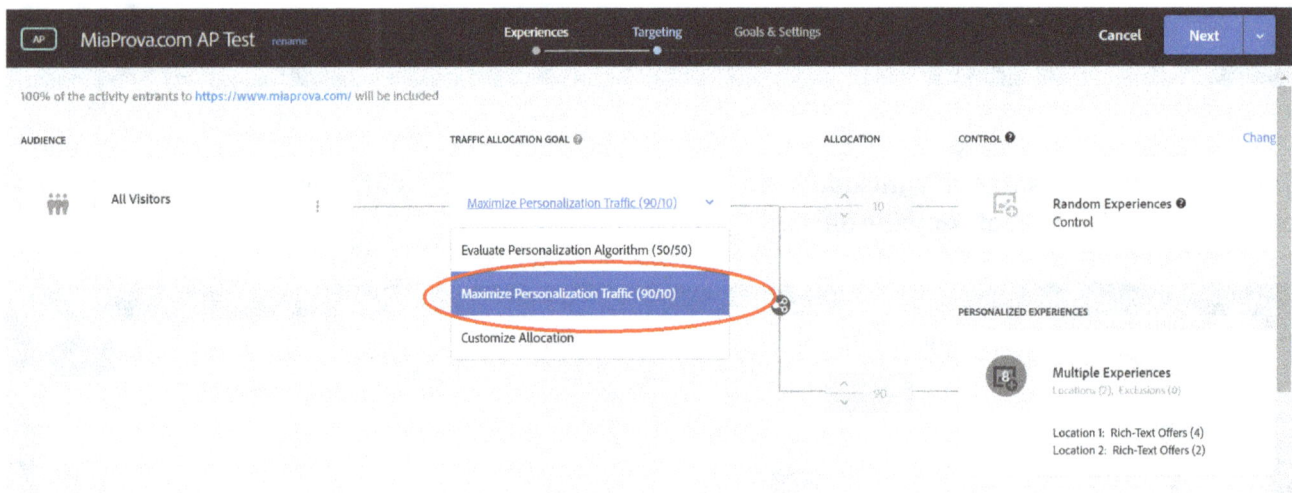

The Goals & Settings step is identical to what we did previously, so no need to go over it again.

Analyzing the results of the activity

Once the activity has been running for a little while, we can jump to the Reports section and set the desired metric, audience, and time frame.

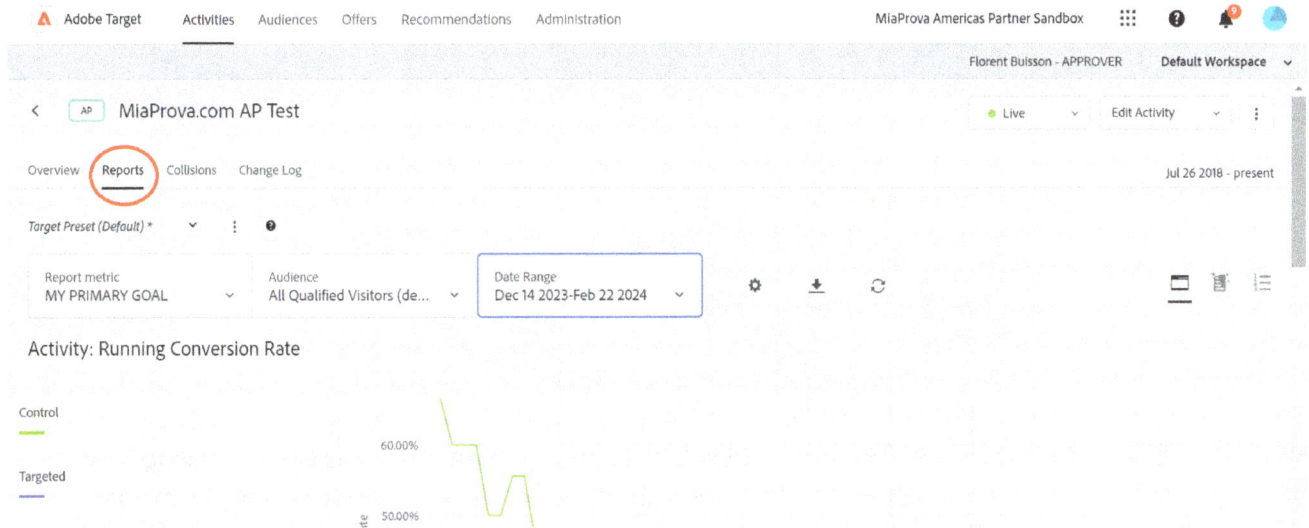

Lower in the screen, we can visualize the average conversion rate of the AP-targeted experience versus the control experience.

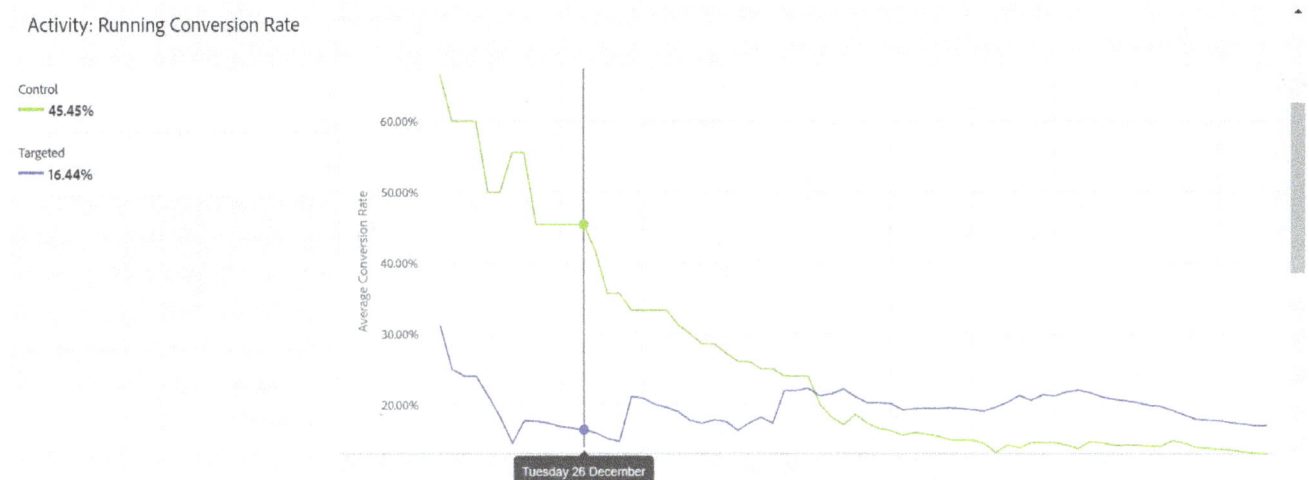

In the present case, the control experience started on top, but then, as its performance degraded over time, the targeted experience rose slightly above it. To be clear, in the long run, with a stable environment, the targeted conversion rate should always be at least equal to the control: if serving the control experience to everybody is the optimal solution, it can always do that. So seeing "some" lift above control is not impressive per se, the question is whether that lift is high enough to justify the added complexity.

To answer that question, let's scroll further down the page to where we can see the numbers and their confidence intervals.

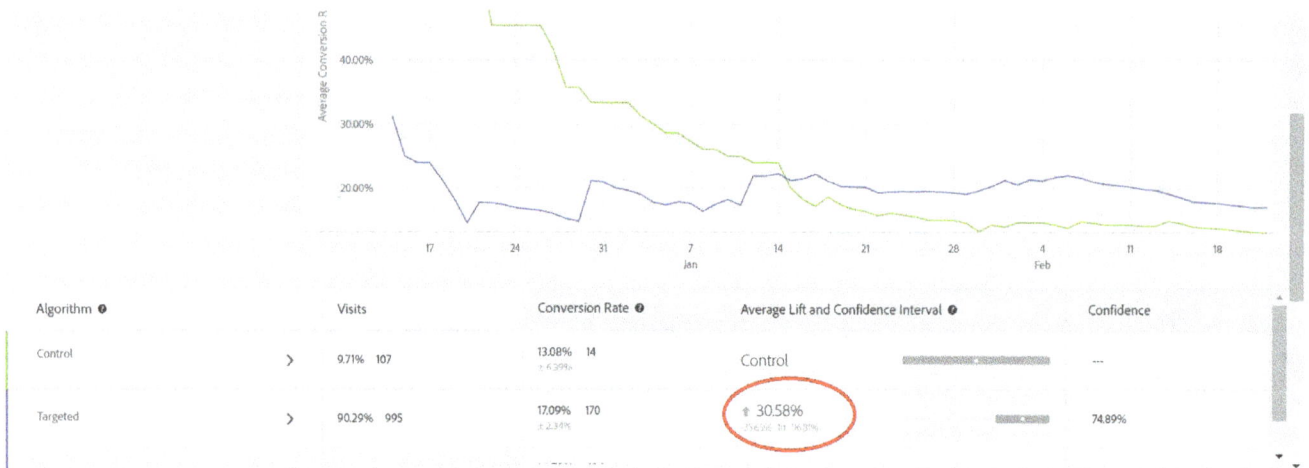

With a confidence interval of -35.65% to +96.81% for the difference between the two experiences, we can't be fully confident yet that the targeted experience indeed outperforms the control, but the average lift at the moment does look pretty good.

Chapter 2.2: Recommendations

In many ways, recommendations are a part of personalization: we have a collection of elements—be it movies for Netflix, consumer products for Amazon, etc.—and we want to serve a different sample of them to different visitors based on relevant context, filters, and business rules. But recommendations have evolved into a distinct subfield with dedicated processes and algorithms, which is probably part of the reason why they have their own tab in Adobe Target.

Recommendations configuration

Our first step is to create a catalog of elements that are eligible to be recommended, called *entities* in Adobe Target. A fixed catalog would very quickly become obsolete as new elements become available or unavailable over time, and having to update manually each time it happened would be unmanageable, especially if the catalog is large. Therefore, Adobe Target uses the concept of *feeds*, sources of data that are checked for updates at regular intervals.

Let's start by clicking on the dedicated tab in the top-level menu.

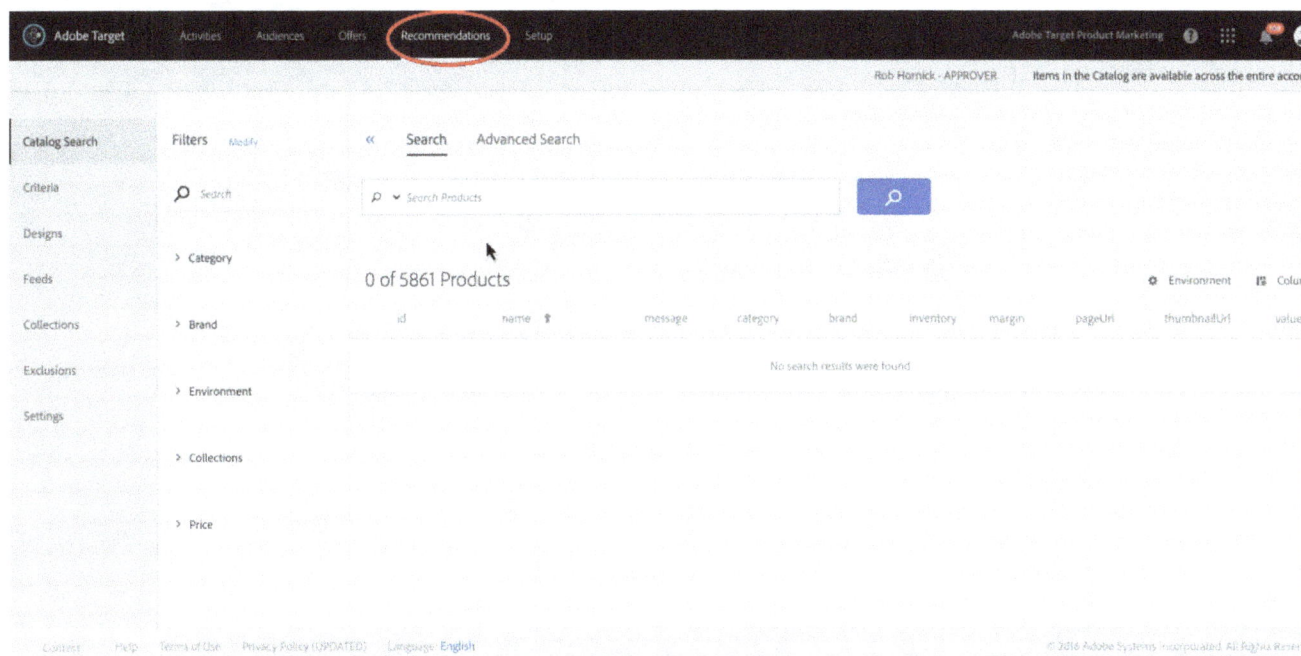

Catalog Search

The first option on the left-side navigation menu is *Catalog Search*, which allows us to visualize the current state of our catalog. In this example, it contains 5861 products at the moment. We can also select specific collections to visualize their content.

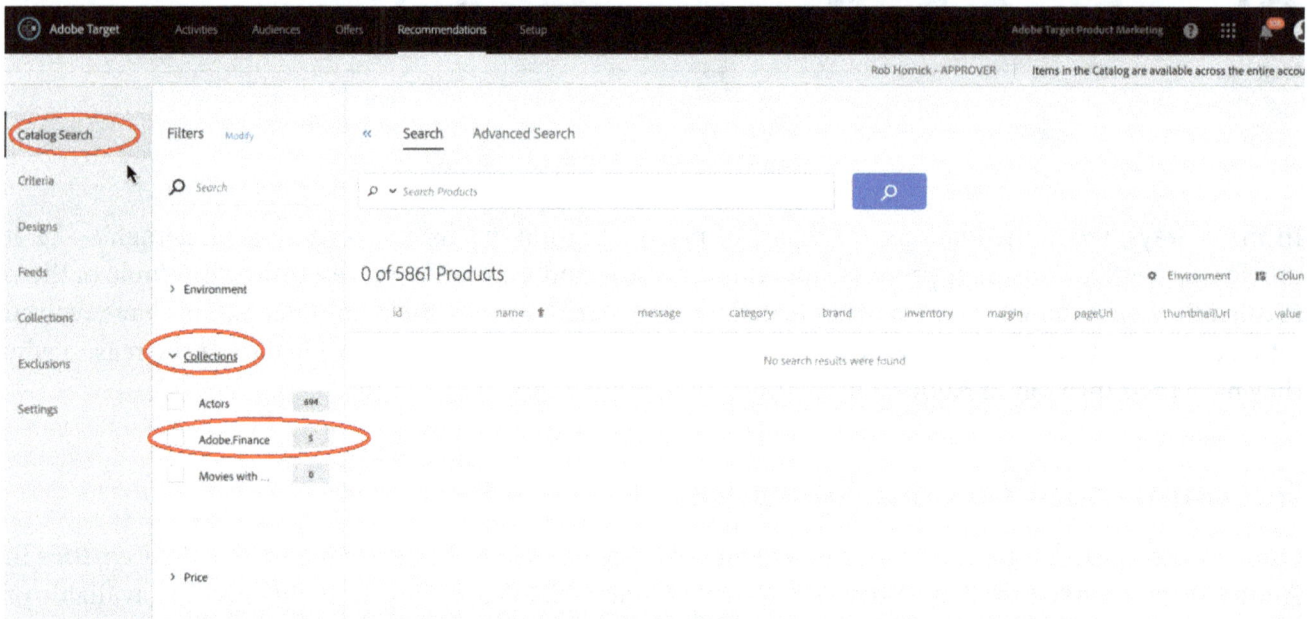

As soon as we select a collection, the corresponding items are displayed.

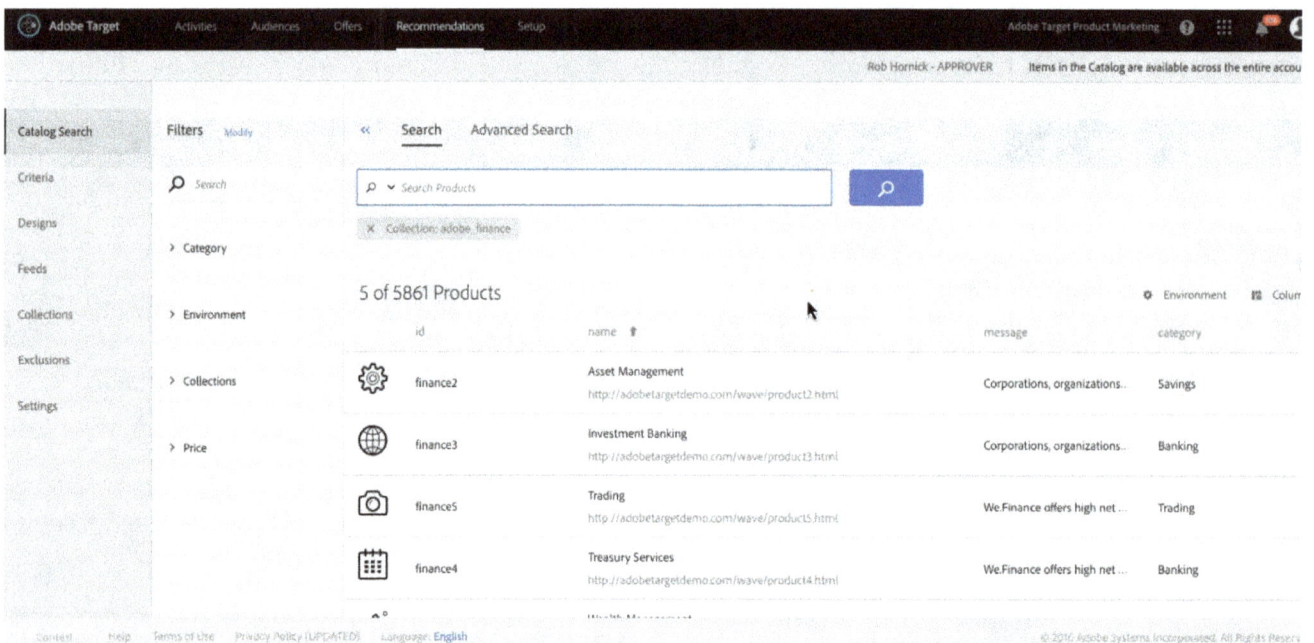

Criteria

The second option on the left-side navigation menu is *Criteria*, which offers a variety of recommendation algorithms you can choose from. When you have a criterion selected, you can choose to edit it. Let's choose *Most Viewed Products* as our criterion and hit the *Edit* button.

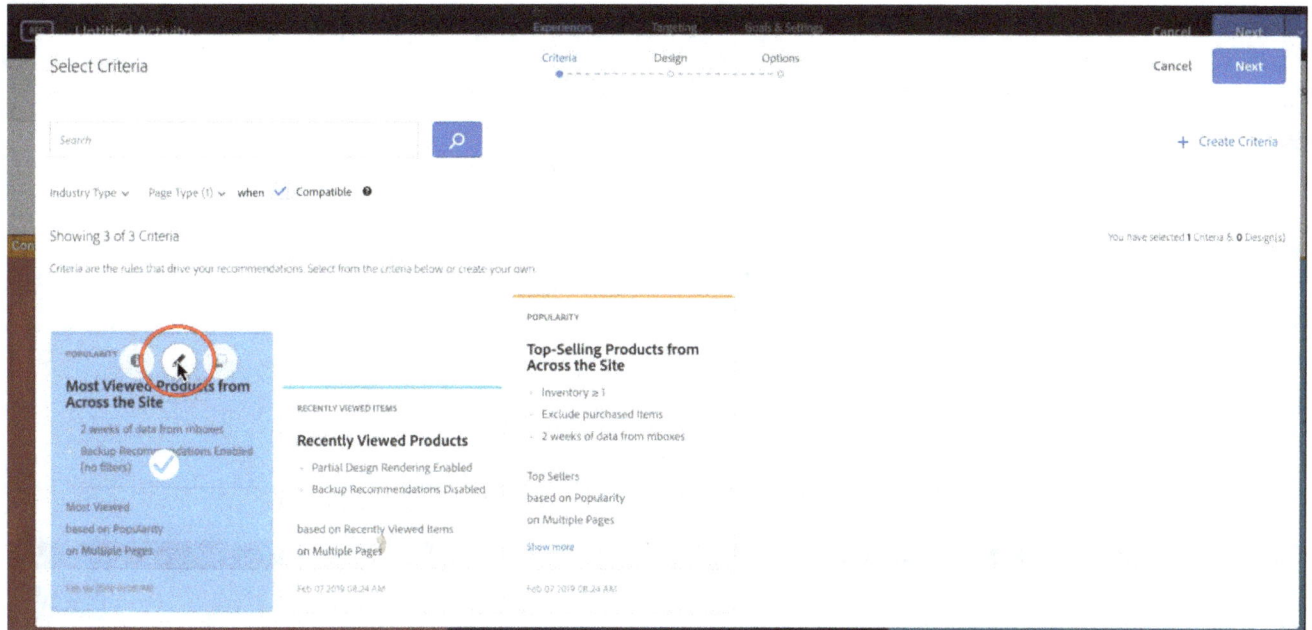

This pulls up the Update Criteria screen, where we can choose the variable to use for ranking recommendations along with the underlying logic. Here we'll select *Popularity* and *Most Viewed*. (Additional options may be cart-based, such as *People Who Viewed These, Viewed Those*, or user-based, such as *Recommended for You*.)

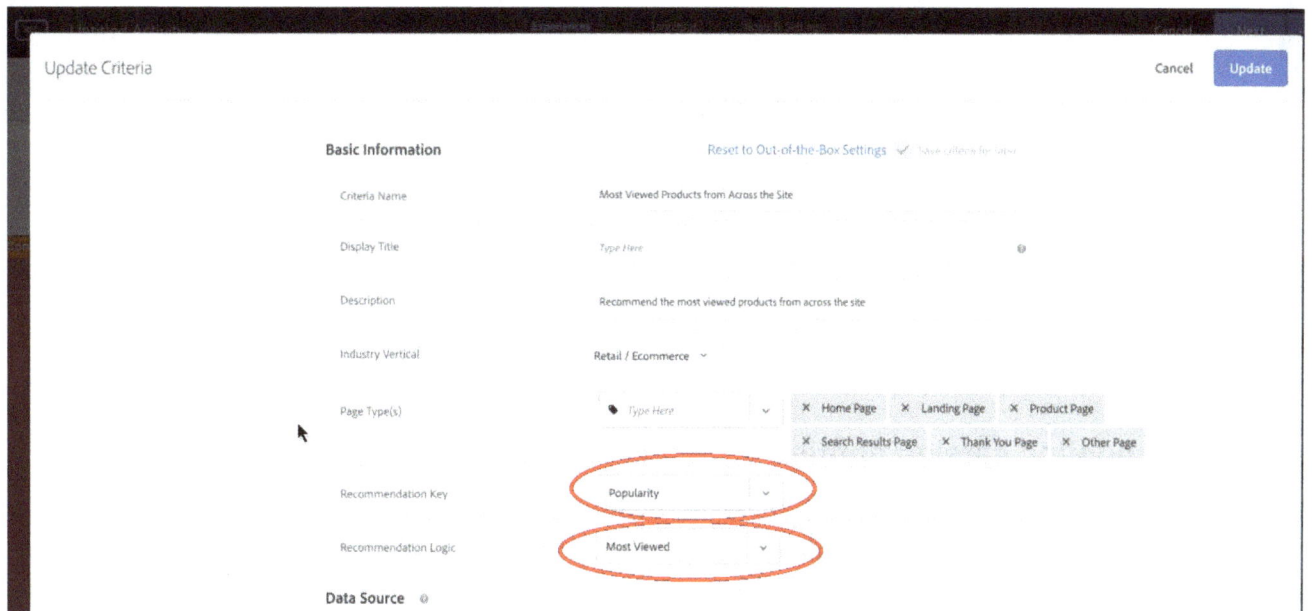

Scrolling further down on the page, we see options for Data Source and Content.

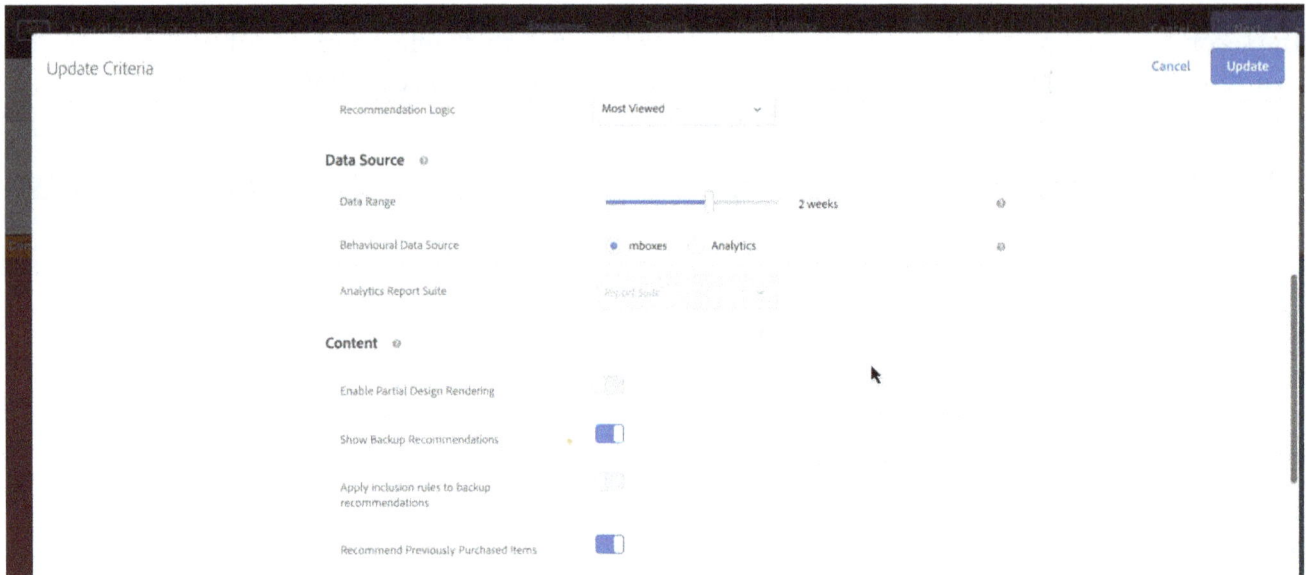

And then further down are options for Inclusion Rules and Attribute Weighting.

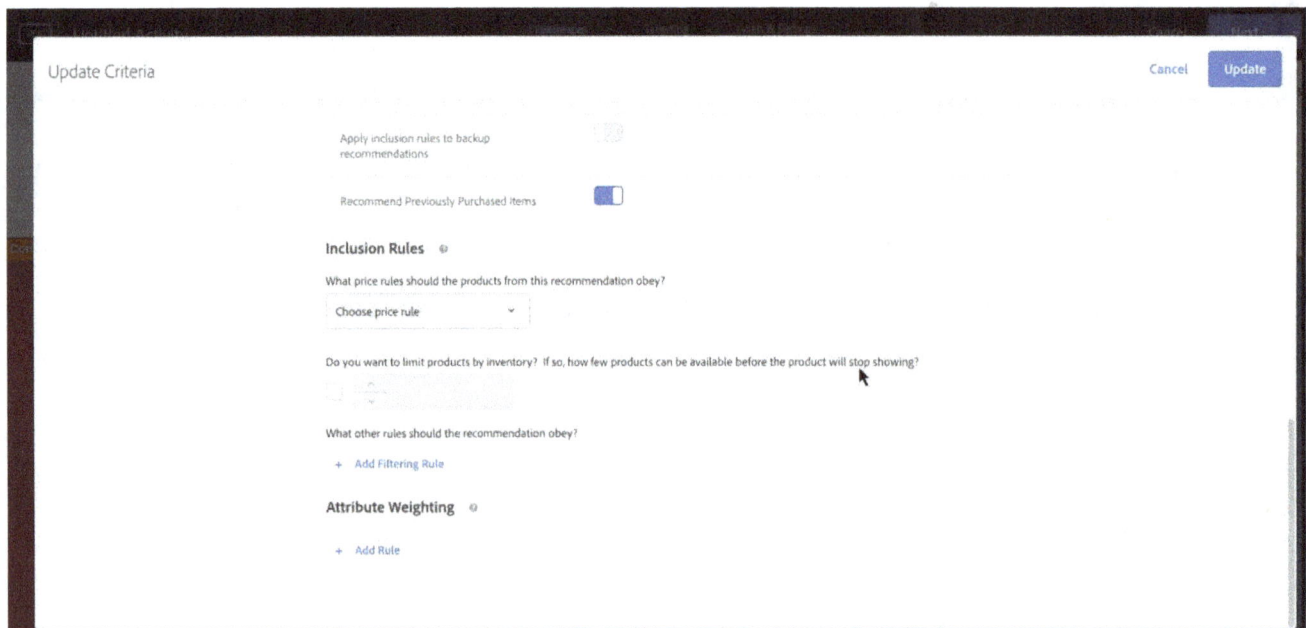

Creating/updating catalog entities through mboxes

For e-commerce companies and similar companies with a relatively stable pool of products, the most common approach to populate the catalog is to tag the relevant pages (such as Product Detail Pages, or PDPs) and pass the current information (such as price) to Adobe Target through page parameters. Your software engineering team will handle the details of the implementation, but it might help you to have a rough idea of what's going on. Typically, the `targetPageParams()` function will be used to capture page-specific information, as in the following template:

```
function targetPageParams() {
    return {
        "entity": {
            "id": "<i>1234</i>",
            "categoryId": "1",
            "inventory": 326
        }
    }
}
```

Feeds

Returning to the left-side menu on the Recommendations page, we'll skip the *Designs* option for the time being and move on to *Feeds*. Feeds allow us to add offline information to our entities, such as inventory or margin. The simplest approach is to use a CSV file provided through an HTTPS URL or an FTP server, although we can also use a Google Product Feed (if we're already indexing our products in Google) or an Analytics Product classification.

Once we've selected our source, we'll need to provide an update schedule to tell Adobe Target how often it should refresh the data by reloading it from the source.

If we don't want to set up an automated schedule, we can select *Never*. Note, however, that Adobe Target will remove an entity from the catalog once its data is more than 61 days old, so if we go with this option, we'll need to manually provide updated data at least that often in order to avoid issues.

Finally, we can provide a mapping between our file's headers and the categories in Adobe Target.

Collections and Exclusions

Once you have added entities to your catalog, you may want to group them, for example, by type (products in one group, blog articles in another) or by category (summer products versus winter products). Conversely, you might want to segment entities by use, separating products that might be recommended as alternatives and products that might be recommended as complementary to the product the visitor is currently seeing. The *Collections* option allows you to do just that.

Note that collections are refreshed only once a day and therefore are best used for entities with permanent, or at least stable, attributes. Criteria, on the other hand, are evaluated in real time, making them more appropriate for entities with dynamic attributes.

Exclusions work similarly to collections but allow you to identify entities that should *not* be included in recommendations, such as clearance items. Note that entities in exclusions will *never* be shown in any recommendation location on your site even if they otherwise fit the bill, so criteria are a better approach if you just want to exclude certain products from certain recommendations.

Creating the activity

With all that setup behind us, let's now create an actual, specific Recommendation activity, using the three-step process (Experiences, Targeting, Goals & Settings) as usual. In the Create Activity menu, we'll select *Recommendations*.

The next screen offers the usual choice of Experience Composers. We'll choose the *Visual Experience Composer*.

Experiences

Location

In the VEC, we'll select the container where we want to display our recommendations. Note: we typically want a Recommendations activity to display multiple entities. This may require the activity overwriting multiple elements on the page, as in the current example. When that's the case, we can tell the VEC to select not only the container we clicked on but also its siblings in the page structure, by clicking *Expand Selection*.

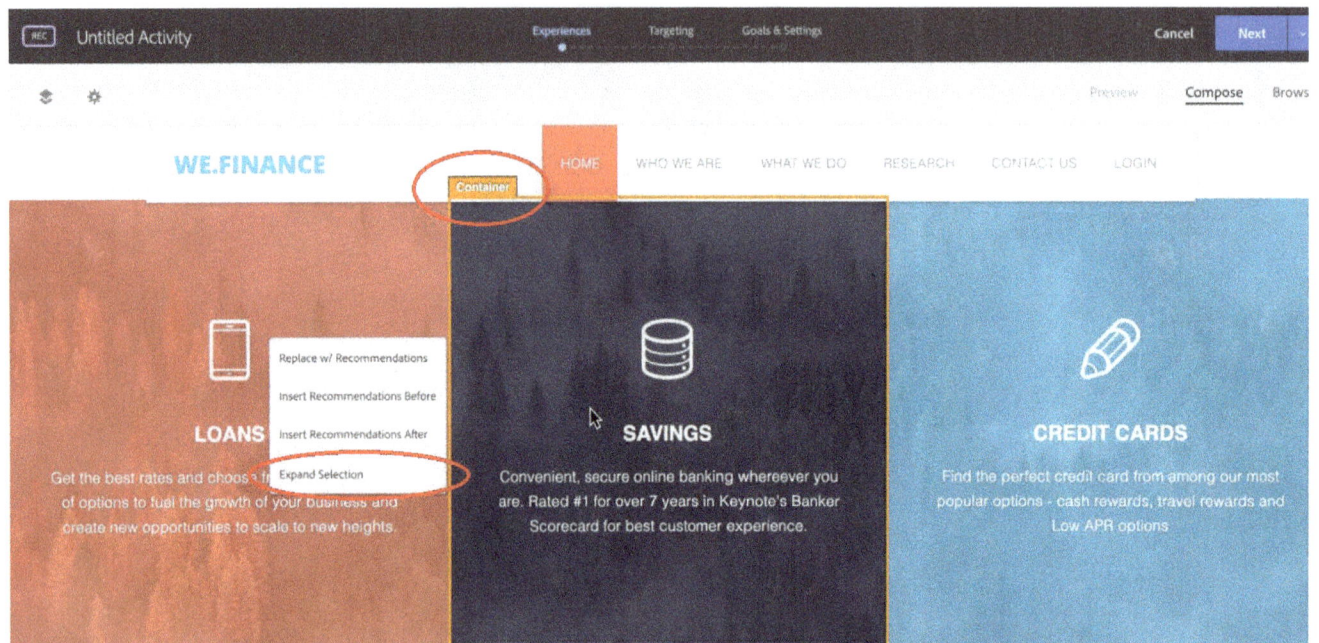

Once we have selected the desired container(s), we can click on *Replace w/ Recommendations*.

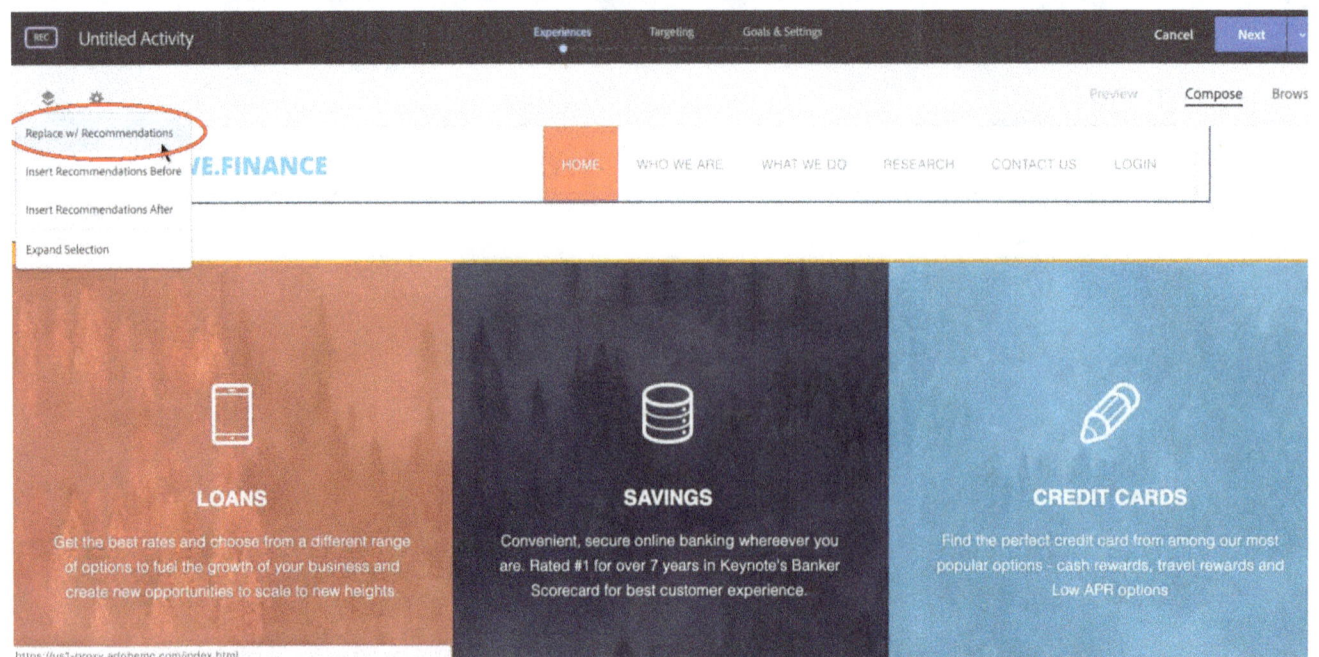

This opens a Select Page Type pop-up.

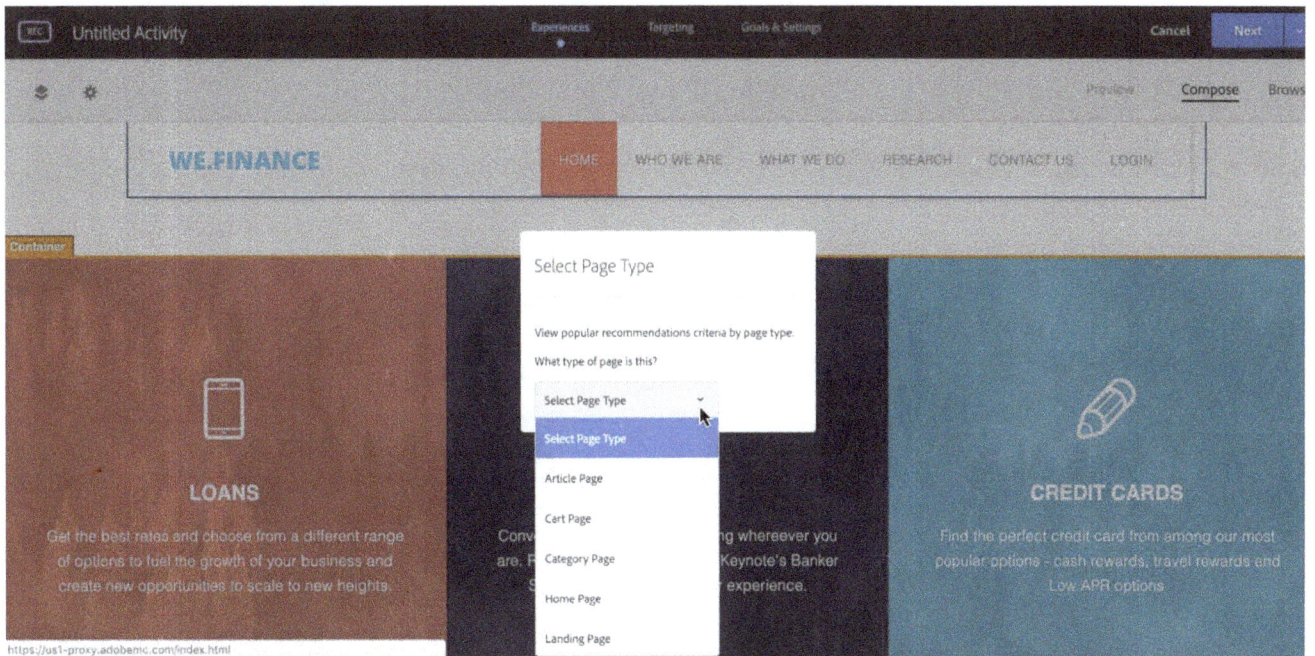

The set of criteria available in the next step may vary depending on the page type that we select. However, we'll also be able to change page type in that next step, so don't worry too much about it. Just select the page that makes the most sense to you and then click *Next*.

Criteria

The next step is to select Criteria.

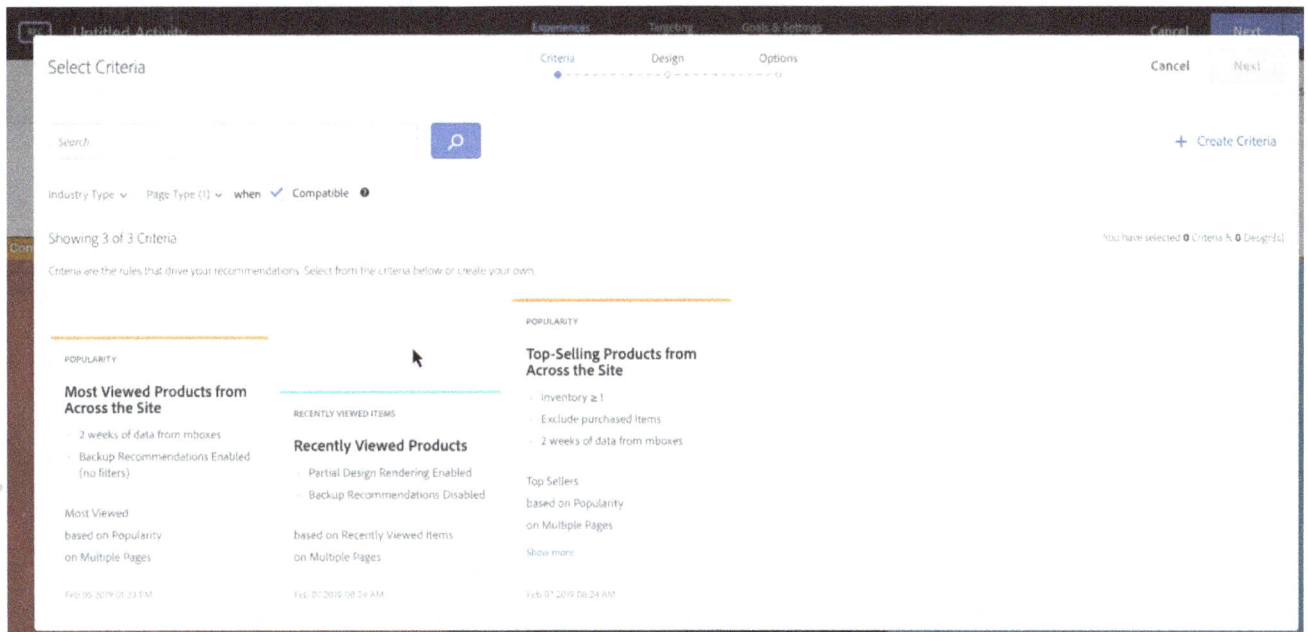

We can select one or several criteria here. We can also edit the criteria if we want to make tweaks on the fly.

Design

Clicking *Next* takes us to the Select Design step.

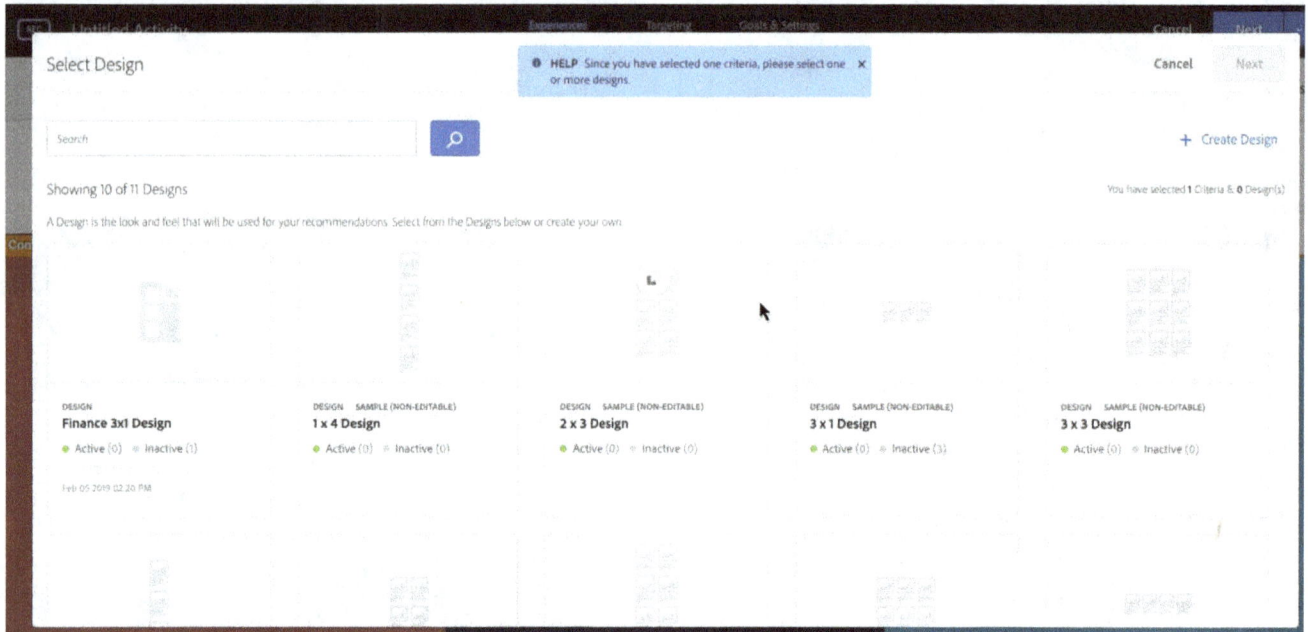

A design describes the arrangement of recommendations in the location—a single row, a single column, a 2x2 table, and so on.

Options

In the Options step, we can select a collection we've created. Finally, we'll click *Save*.

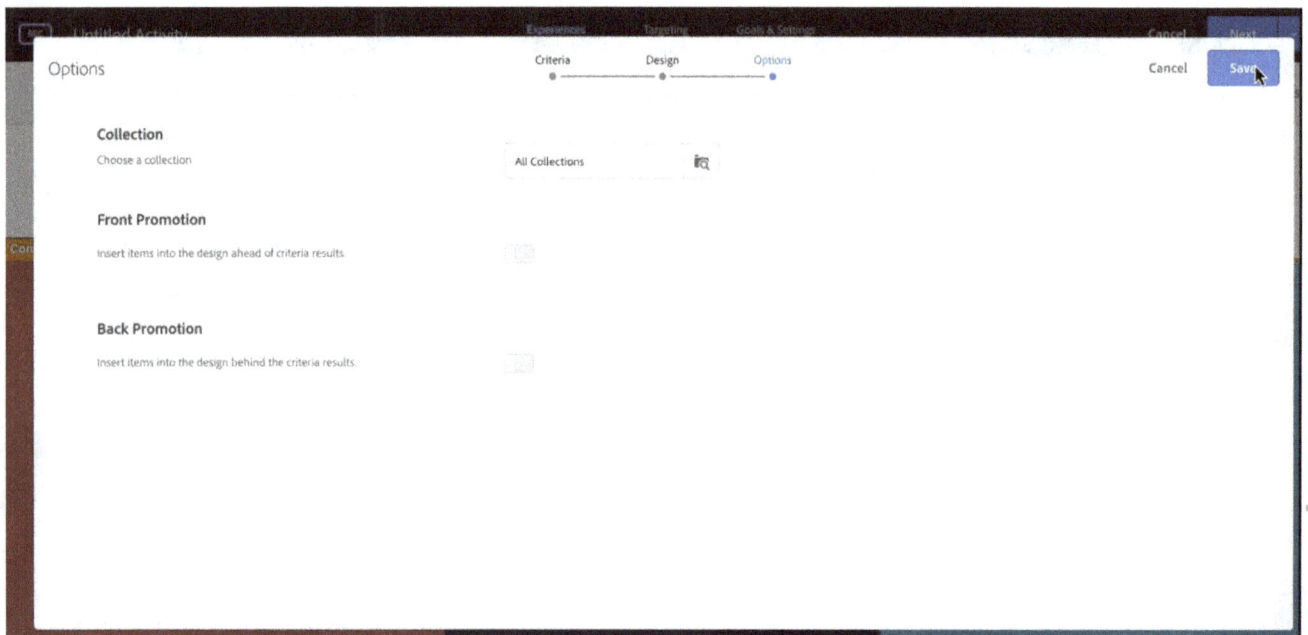

Targeting

The Targeting screen is similar to what we've seen for other activities, with some specific differences.

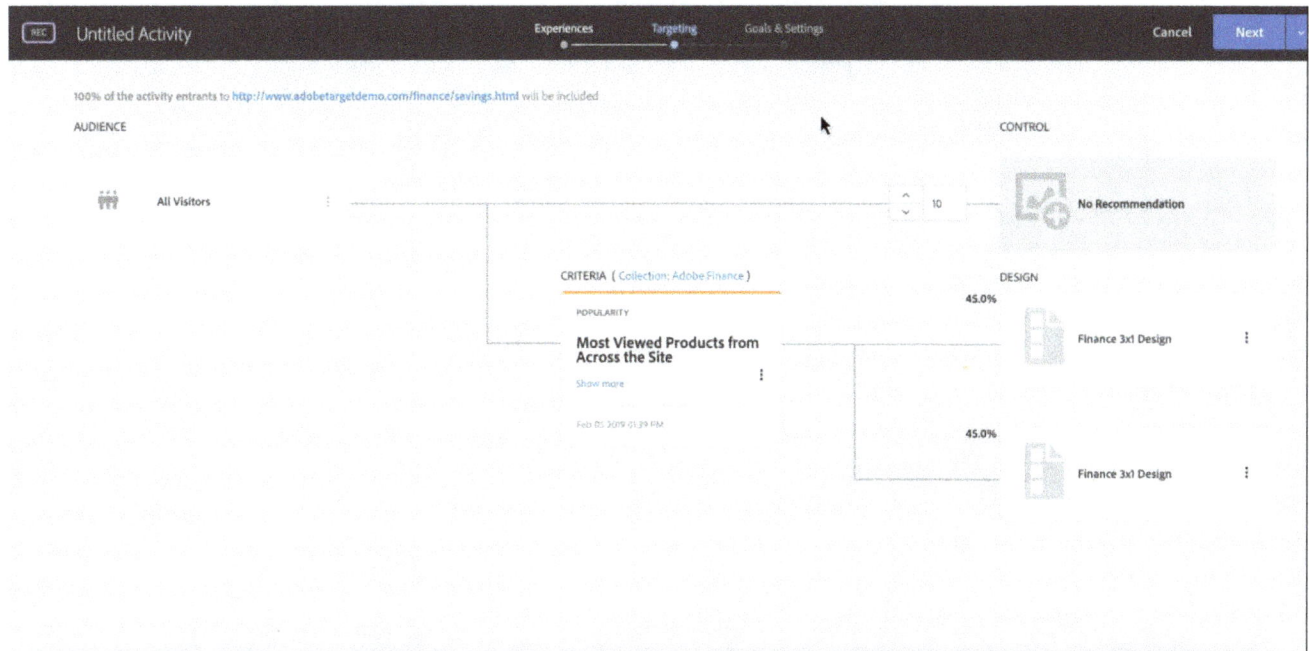

By default, the activity is set up with a control group that doesn't see any recommendations, along with a branch for each of the criteria and designs that we have selected, with audience percentage split equally between the latter. We can click on the three dots on the right side of an experience to modify or delete it, and we can change the percentage of total traffic for the relevant audience that goes to the control group, but we can't directly modify the percentage of traffic going to one recommendation experience versus another.

Goals & Settings

This step is the same as for other activities. The only change is that if we select Conversion as the primary goal of our activity, we can then select whether to have the visitor action "Clicked on recommendation" counted as a success.

Case studies

- Testing Shifts into High Gear for Intel

PART III:
TRANSVERSAL TOPICS

Chapter 3.1: Audiences and Visitor Profiles

The fundamental building block for experimentation is the ability to generate a random number when a visitor lands on your website and then serve different experiences depending on the random number. Building such a tool is not very hard from a software engineering perspective, and many companies have created their own version of it. Things start to get much more complex at the next level of capabilities, such as the ability to use visitors' characteristics to determine whether they should be included or excluded from a test or to determine when to trigger conditional behaviors. In Adobe Target, this is where audiences and visitor profiles come in.

In part I, we discussed how to create an audience based on the visitor's device, and how to exclude from an activity returning visitors who had not been assigned to it during their first visit with the help of a profile script. In this chapter, we'll do a deeper dive into the building blocks of audiences:

1. profile parameters,
2. profile scripts, and
3. response tokens.

Metaphorically speaking, audiences represent a declaration of intent ("when to do what to whom"), and those three building blocks work together to implement the corresponding nitty-gritty details, a.k.a. visitor profiles. I'll review them one by one and then show you how to use them to build audiences.

Profile parameters

The most basic bricks for building audiences and profiles are *profile parameters*, variables that are defined/captured by the Adobe Target servers when answering a request from your website. To visualize and browse through them, let's go to the Audiences tab and click *Create Audience*.

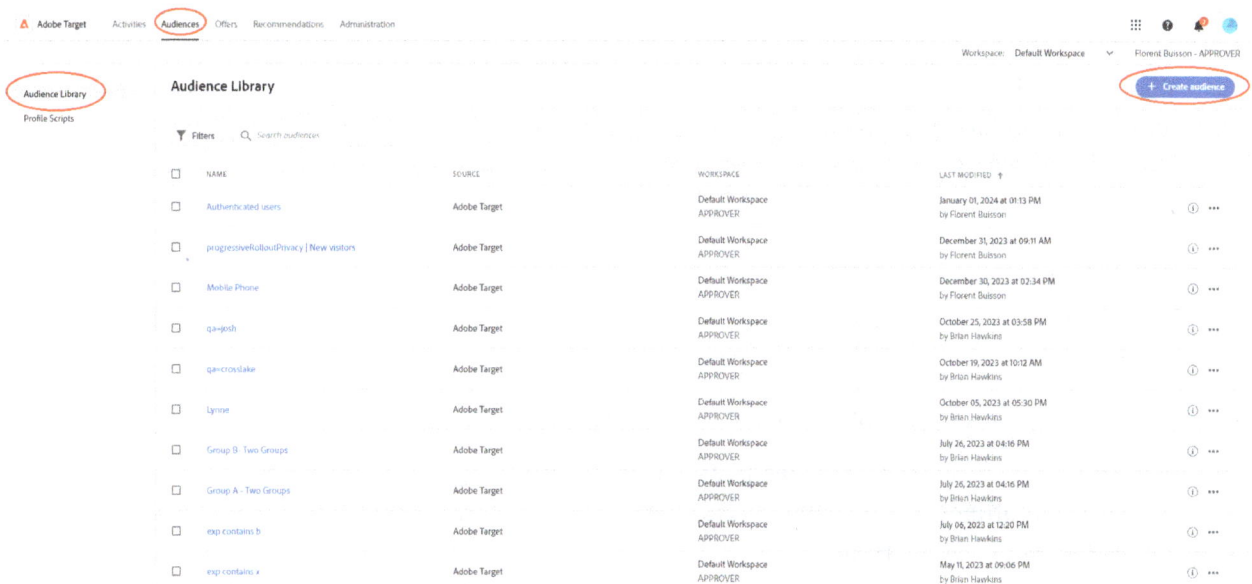

99

This opens the Create Audience screen, where we can see profile parameters under the Attributes header.

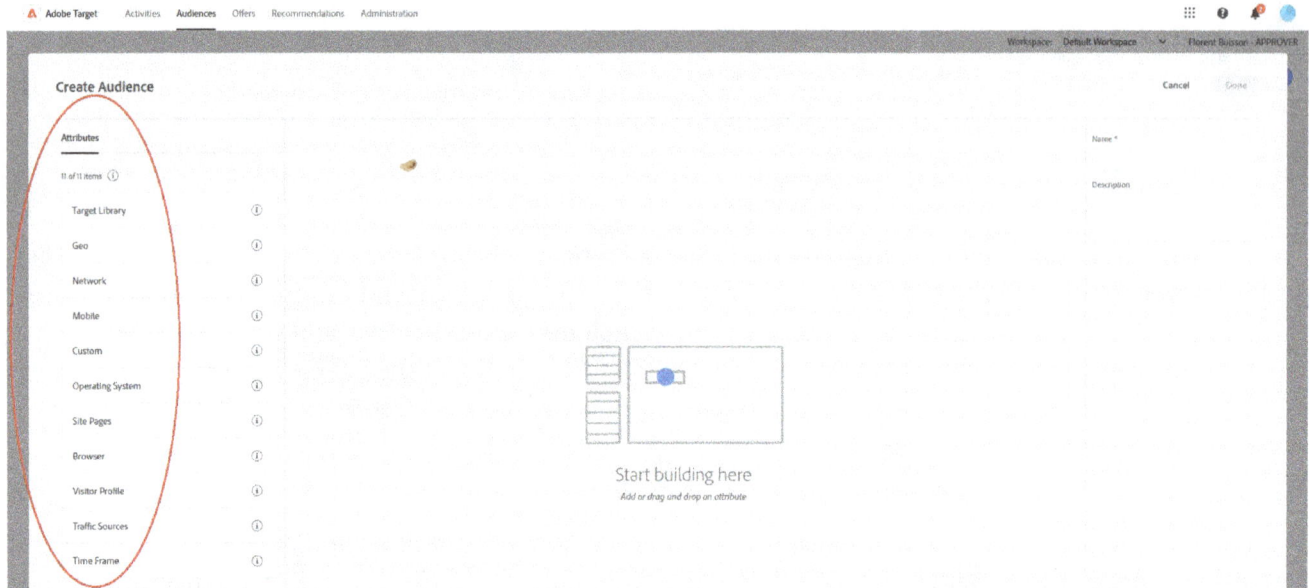

Here's a synthetic view of the main attributes by category:

- **Target Library** (target users based on pre-built targeting rules): Firefox Browser, Referred from Google, Mac OS Operating System, Windows Operating System, New Visitors, Internet Explorer, Safari Browser, Chrome Browser, Referred from Bing, Returning Visitors, Tablet Device, Referred from Yahoo, Linux Operating System.
- **Geo** (target activities and experiences based on a visitor's geographical location): Country/Region, State, City, Zip code, Longitude, Latitude, DMA (Designated Marketing Areas), Mobile Carrier
- **Network** (create audiences based on network details): ISP, Domain Name, Connection Speed
- **Mobile** (target mobile devices based on parameters such as mobile device (Y/N), type of device, device vendor, screen dimensions by pixels, and more): Device Marketing Name, Device Model, Device Vendor, Is Mobile Device, Is Mobile Phone, Is Tablet, OS, Screen Height (px), Screen Width (px)
- **Operating System** (target visitors who use a certain operating system): Linux, Macintosh, Windows
- **Site Pages** (target visitors who are on a specific page on your site)
- **Browser** (target users who use a specific browser or specific browser options when they visit your page): Type, Language, Version
- **Visitor Profile** (target visitors who meet specific profile parameters): New Visitor, Returning Visitor, In other tests, First page of session, Not in other tests, Not first page of session, Category Affinity (Note: This category is also where profile script return values show up as "user.[scriptname]".)
- **Traffic Sources** (target visitors based on the search engine or landing page that refers them to your site): From Baidu, From Bing, From Google, From Yahoo, Referring Landing Page: Domain, Referring Landing Page: Query, Referring Landing Page: URL
- **Time Frame** (target users who visit your site during a specific time frame using start/end dates; set Week and Day parting options to create recurring patterns for audience targeting)

There are a few caveats and "gotchas" to keep in mind here:

- Per Adobe's website, the variables in the Target Library category are legacy versions of variables appearing in other categories and should not be used for new work. For instance, *New Visitors* also appears under Visitor Profile.

- Profile parameters are not persistent. Their value is reevaluated for each request, and they are deleted at the end of a session. If you need to persist them, you should build the corresponding profile script (more on that later in the chapter).
- In many cases, a designated marketing area (DMA) is a better descriptor than the city, because it better represents the actual urban area. DMAs are recorded by name in Target, so you can type "Chicago" or "San Francisco" and easily pull the corresponding DMA.

Profile scripts

Profile scripts are small pieces (*snippets*) of JavaScript code that are run whenever an mbox makes a request to the Adobe Servers. You may remember that we created our first one for the progressive rollout in chapter 1.3, to keep returning visitors in the same experience as in their first visit. We'll now take a deeper look at them and other use cases.

As a reminder, you can create profile scripts by going into Audiences > Profile Scripts > Create Script.

This opens the Create Profile Script editor, where you can enter JavaScript code.

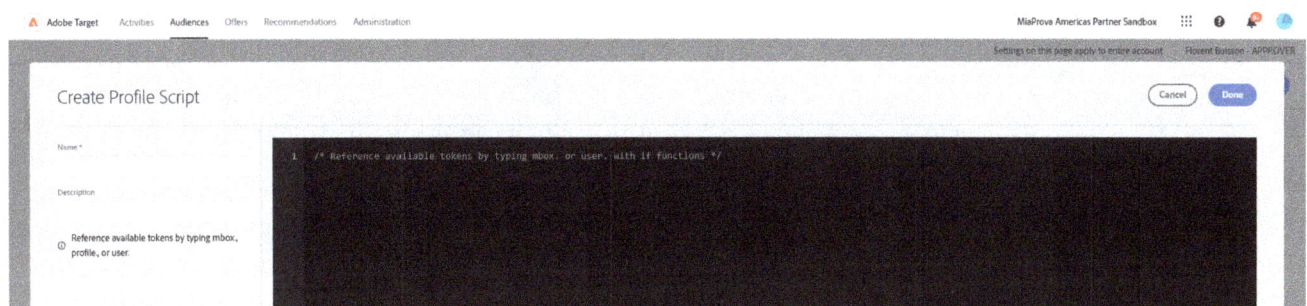

Variables available in profile scripts

The variables a profile script can access are grouped under the following prefixes (a.k.a. *objects*):

- **mbox:** the mbox that made the request to the server
- **profile:** information about the user sent by the client browser
- **user:** information about the user stored in a cookie
- **page:** information about the page the request came from

Mbox variables

The most important parameter of the mbox is its name, which can be used if you want the script to run only for a certain mbox:

```
if(mbox.name == 'privacy'){ … }
```

This instruction would run any commands in the block between brackets only for the privacy mbox. If we have a global mbox, then we can pass to it page-level parameters, which would be stored in *mbox.param*.

Profile variables

The profile object makes available to profile scripts certain of the profile parameters mentioned above. The main ones are:

- **profile.isFirstSession:** equals true if this is a visitor's first visit to your website
- **profile.isNewSession:** equals true if this is the first page of the visit
- **profile.activeActivities:** a list of the activities that a visitor has ever entered in the current or past visits
- **profile.daysSinceLastVisit**
- **profile.tntId:** the primary identifier for a user in Adobe Target.

User variables

When we run a profile script, it generally returns a value. The values of these **Profile Script Attributes** are assigned to the user object, which unfortunately can be confusing. Profile script attributes should not be confused with profile parameters. One key difference is that profile script attributes will persist after the end of a visit and will be stored in a cookie. By default, that cookie has a lifetime of 14 rolling days, meaning that the clock restarts after each visit to our website. (If necessary, that lifetime can be increased to up to 90 days by filing a ticket with Adobe's customer service.)

The important thing to remember is that if we create a profile script named *progressiveRolloutPrivacy*, as we did in chapter 1.3, its value can be accessed with `user.get('progressiveRolloutPrivacy')`. A common use case is to have a script check itself to see if it has already run and sent its value to the user object and if so, stop its execution. This ensures that the script assigns a value to a visitor only once and doesn't overwrite its previous runs.

Page variables

Profile scripts can access some information passed by the mbox about the page it's on, as well as the referrer page (the last external page visited before your website) and the landing page (the first page visited on your website).

One of the main pieces of information about a page is its URL, and profile scripts can access the URL of the current page with `page.url`, like `https://www.miaprova.com/privacy/?source=google&device=mobile`. We rarely need the entire URL though, so we have a few built-in slices:

- **page.domain:** the part of the current URL before the first single slash, i.e., for the previous URL that would be `https://www.miaprova.com/`.
- **page.query:** the part of the current URL after the first (and normally single) question mark '?'. here, that would be `source=google&device=mobile`.
- **page.param('name'):** allows you to pull a single parameter by name from the query. For instance, page.param('source') would return `google`.
- **page.protocol:** returns `http` or `https`, depending on the page's protocol.

One last useful slice is missing from this list, namely the part of the URL before the query. In the previous example, that would be `https://www.miaprova.com/privacy/`. Of course, you could simply use `page.url` and cut the query in the data analysis stage, but URLs can get quite long, to the point of exceeding the number of characters you can handle. A better solution is therefore to use the `.split()` function, which allows us to cut a string in multiple pieces. The syntax is as follows: `page.url.split('?')[0]`.

The function is appended at the end of the variable we want to split, and we pass as an argument to it the character or string at which we want to make the cut(s). Thus, `page.url.split('?')` will cut our page URL on the question mark that marks the beginning of the query and return the two slices as a list. We then select the first element of that list with `[0]`, because in JavaScript indexing starts at 0. For our example above, that would be the way to obtain `https://www.miaprova.com/privacy/`.

We have the same options for the referrer page and the landing page, simply by replacing **page.** with **referrer.** or **landing.**, for example **referrer.domain**, **landing.query**, etc.

Writing profile scripts for typical use cases

With all the variables described above as the building blocks for profile scripts, let's see how to put them together and what to use them for.

Persistent swimlanes on first site-wide call

As the volume of tests run on your website increases, you might feel the need to build mutually exclusive *swimlanes* so that visitors are only made eligible to one of several experiments running at the same time. I'll discuss in chapter 3.4 why I don't think that's a good way to avoid interaction effects, but there are still legitimate use cases for this pattern, including for logistical or technical reasons. Here's the code we'll use:

```
if(!user.get('twoLanes')){
    var random_number=Math.floor(Math.random()*99);
    if (random_number <= 49) {return 'Lane1';}
    else {return 'Lane2';}
    }
```

Let's look at the syntax of the script line by line:

After a visitor has been assigned to a lane, we want them to stay in it, so we'll use the `if (!user.get()) { ... }` block pattern that we've seen before. This way, the script runs only once and its value persists over time.

Because lanes get assigned before activities, we can't directly use Adobe Target's internal randomization system; we have to do it ourselves by hand using JavaScript: `var num = Math.floor(Math.random() * 99);`

In JS, `var` is used at the beginning of a line to declare a new variable. `Math.random()` generates a random decimal number between 0 and 1 which we multiply by 99. We then round it down to the nearest integer with `Math.floor()`. This means that `num` has an equal probability of being any integer between 0 and 99. We split this interval in sub-intervals of equal length; if num is less than 49, the visitor is assigned to the first lane: `if (num <= 49) { return 'Lane1'; }`. Otherwise they get assigned to the second lane.

Let's save our profile script by clicking *Done*.

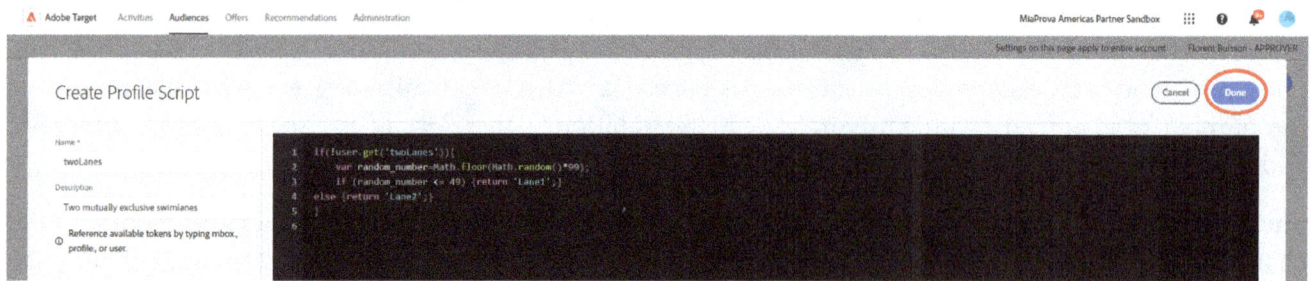

Persistent script on first call for a specific mbox

In the previous example, we wrote a script that would run on the very first call to Adobe Target servers during a visitor's visit and then persist the swimlane assignment permanently. However, we might want to trigger the script only on a specific mbox. We can do so by using the *mbox.name* variable:

```
if(mbox.name == 'privacy' && !user.get('twoLanes')){
    var random_number=Math.floor(Math.random()*99);
    if (random_number <= 49) {return 'Lane1';}
    else {return 'Lane2';}
    }
```

The IF condition in the parenthesis is now a composite of two sub-conditions, where '&&' is the JavaScript syntax for AND. That is, the IF condition will evaluate to 'true' only if the mbox name is 'privacy' *and* the script hasn't run yet.

Validating profile scripts

Profile scripts are a very powerful feature of Adobe Target, but their versatility can also make them error-prone. It's pretty easy to put two nested IF-THEN conditions in the wrong order and not account for rare edge cases.

Our first safety net is Adobe Target's editor itself. If there is a syntax error in your JavaScript code, it will let you know by putting a triangle with an exclamation mark before the corresponding line. Hovering over the warning triangle will open an explanatory message.

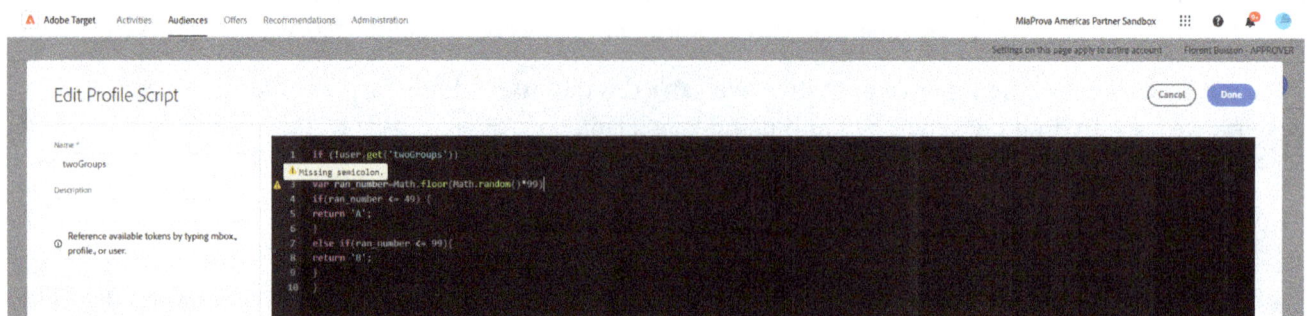

The second tool at our disposal is response tokens, which allow us to check in real life that a profile script does the right calculations and returns the right value, as we'll see in the next section.

Response tokens

Response tokens are the last piece of our trio after profile parameters and profile scripts. As described above, Adobe Target servers define and capture profile parameters and run profile scripts when answering requests from your website. This makes the values available to your activities. But sometimes, it is useful to bypass the activity and directly expose these values. Adobe Target offers this capability through **_response tokens_**.

As an analyst, you'll probably deal with these mainly for debugging purposes. Using A/B traces provides you with a lot of information (such as the return values of all the scripts that ran in response to the mbox request), but you might want to access some profile parameters or other variables that are not available in the profile attributes of the A/B trace of the activity. For instance, you may want to look at the list of activities the visitor has entered in their current visit (which is accessible through the native response token profile.activeActivities, as we'll see below). When in trace mode, you can see not only the A/B traces but also the response tokens in your browser's console.

Managing response tokens

You can manage these by going to the Administration tab and then selecting _Response tokens_ on the left-side menu.

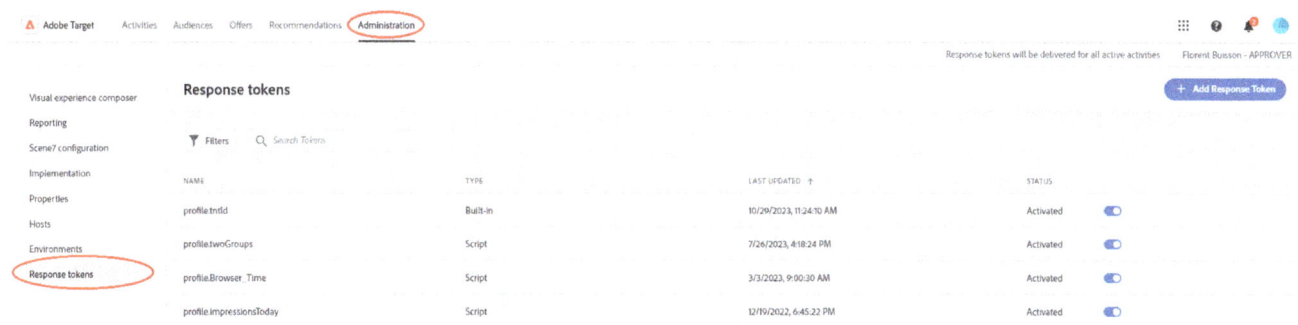

You can use filters for easier navigation.

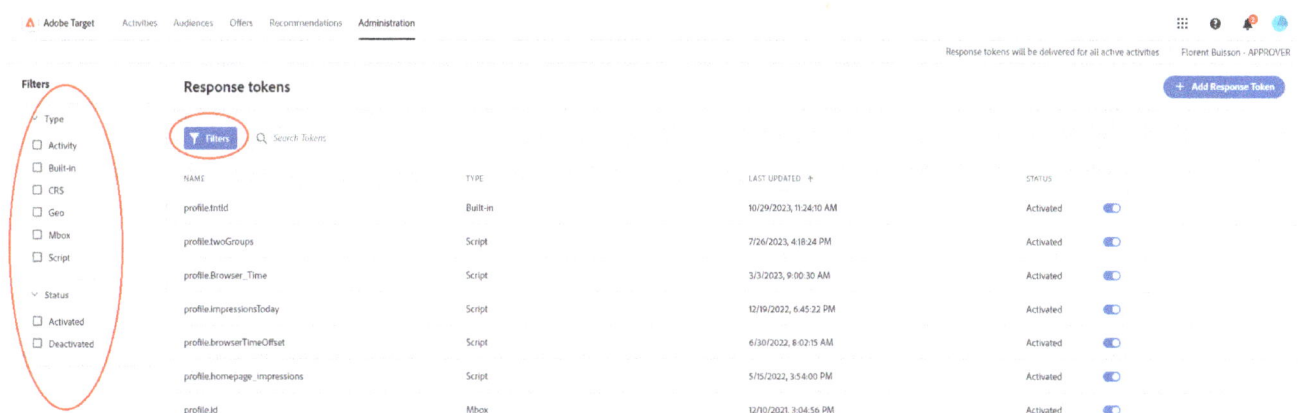

There are different types of response tokens:

- **Activity:** offer.id, experience.trafficAllocationType, option.name, experience.id, experience .name, activity.id, activity.name, offer.name, activity.decisioningMethod, option.id, experience .trafficAllocationId

- **Built-in:** profile.isNewSession, profile.isFirstSession, profile.marketingCloudVisitorId, profile.daysSinceLastVisit, profile.thirdPartyId, profile.tntId, profile.activeActivities, profile.categoryAffinity, profile.categoryAffinities
- **CRS**
- **Geo:** geo.city, geo.country, geo.state, geo.connectionSpeed, geo.ispName, geo.zip, geo.domainName, geo.mobileCarrier, geo.dma
- **Mbox**
- **Script:** the return values of profile scripts, a.k.a profile script attributes

All the response tokens for each type except Script are automatically built in and are deactivated by default; each can be activated using the appropriate toggle on the right side of the screen.

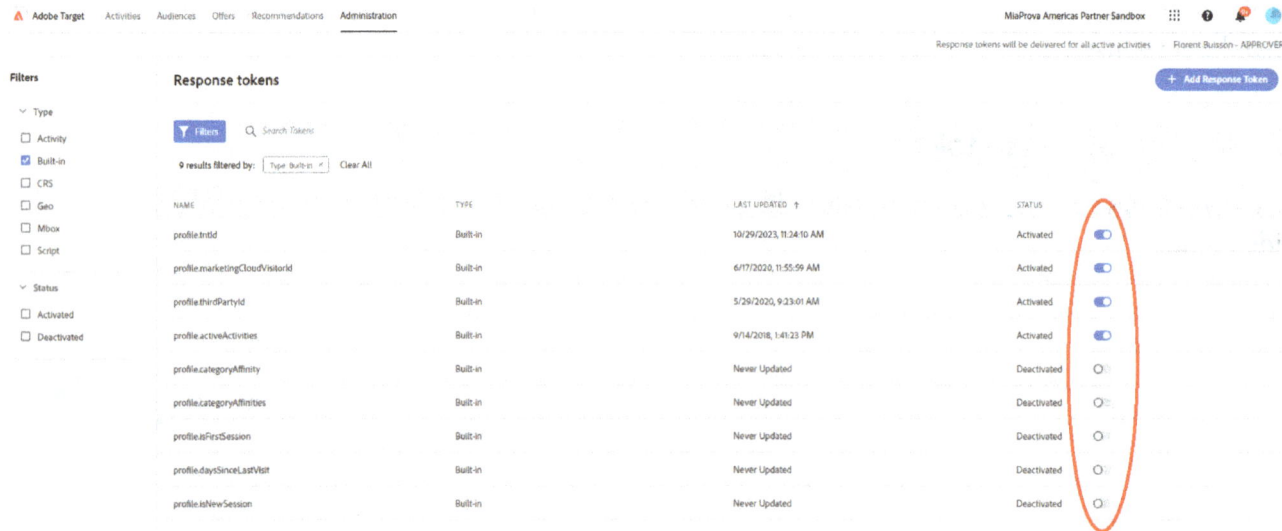

Activating a response token makes it available in trace mode in addition to the A/B traces themselves, as we saw in chapter 1.2.

Response tokens are delivered in the form of key-value pairs, such as `profile.isFirstSession: true` (technically speaking, all the pairs are delivered as part of a JavaScript object).

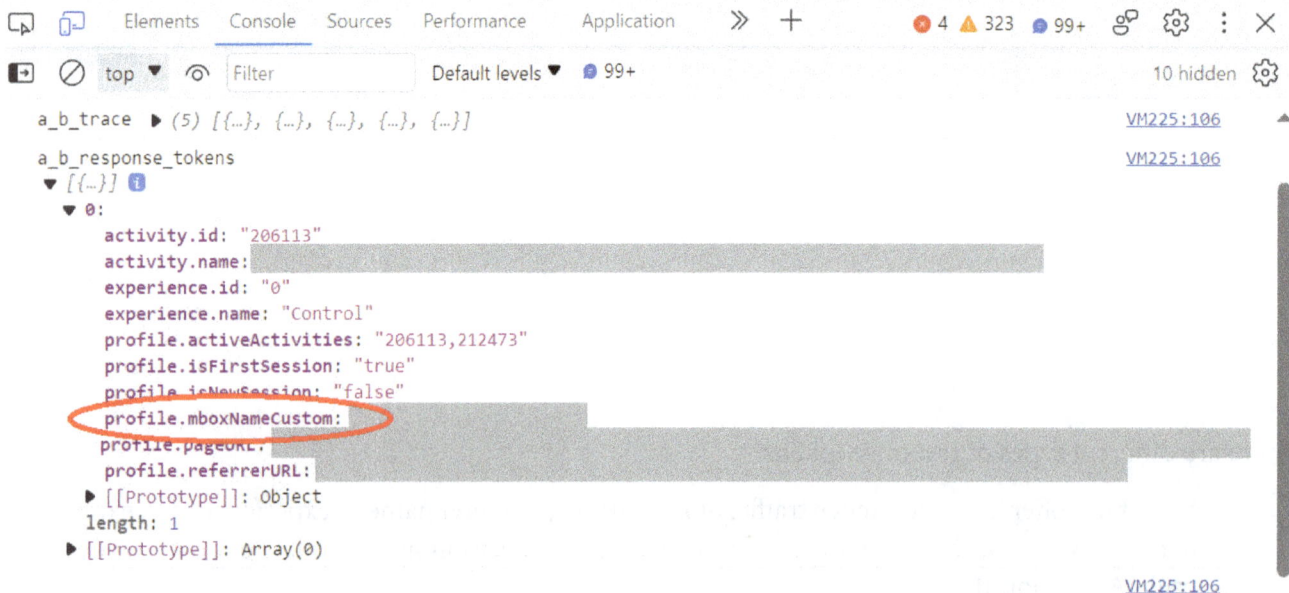

Creating response tokens for profile parameters and profile script attributes

While built-in response tokens already provide a lot of useful information, creating new ones is a great way to access profile parameters and profile script attributes.

Making profile parameters available in this way is a two-step process, so it's worth first going through the built-in response tokens to see if you can already access that information directly. If not, we have to write a profile script that returns the profile parameter we're interested in.

As soon as we've activated the profile script, we'll have to create and activate the corresponding response token—in this case, *profile.mboxNameCustom*.

We can add new response tokens by clicking on + *Add Response Token*.

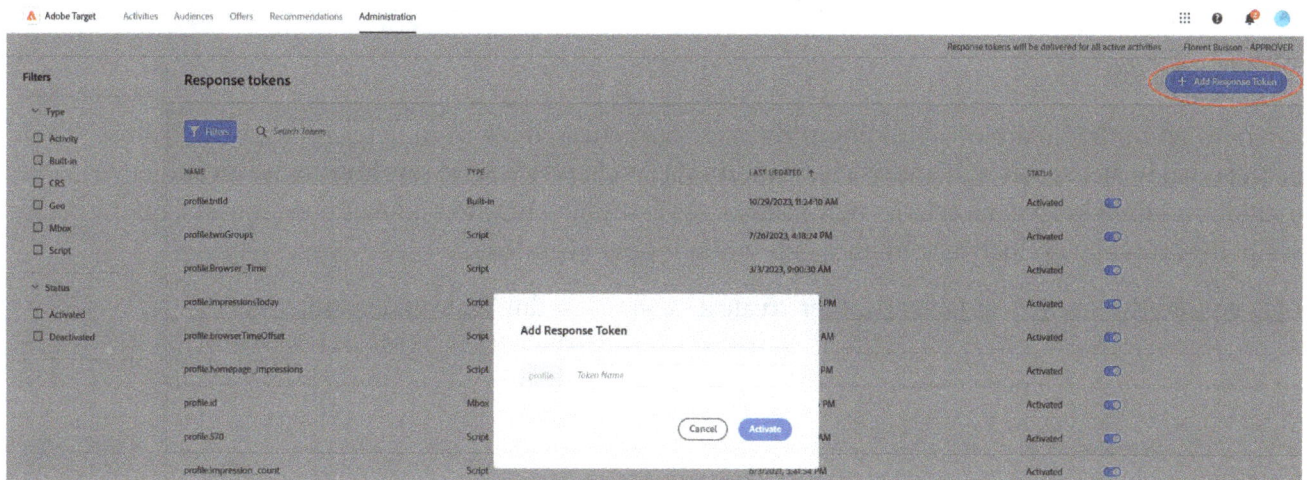

As you can see, the prefix *profile.* is baked in and cannot be modified. Simply adding the name of a profile script in the Token Name bar and clicking *Activate* will make the return value of the corresponding profile script available among the response tokens in trace mode. This will allow us to see whether the profile script works as expected and therefore determine if things are going wrong at either the profile script stage (i.e., it sends the wrong value to the audience) or the audience assessment stage (i.e., the audience receives the correct value but makes the wrong decision based on that value).

Reading response tokens from the page

Another reason to use response tokens is to pass information directly to our website for other purposes. This use case is more targeted towards developers, but it's good to be aware that we can pass information from Adobe Target to other entities this way.

For instance, let's say we've defined an activity with a "West Coast" experience based on the visitor's state. While the experience seen by a given visitor will be captured via our traditional analytics pipeline, the state assigned by Adobe Target won't be. A response token can tell us what state Adobe Target assigned to a visitor so we can confirm that it matches with our other data sources.

This ability can also be helpful if we are using another third-party tool (such as Google Analytics) and want to make it aware of the experience assigned by Target. By using response tokens, we can deliver a JavaScript object that other tools can read through JavaScript *event listeners*. The exact process depends on whether we are using the Platform Web SDK or the at.js script.

In the latter case, the corresponding code is a very straightforward addition to our page html head:

```
<head>
....
<script src="at.js"></script>
<script>
document.addEventListener(adobe.target.event.REQUEST_SUCCEEDED,
function(e) {
 console.log("Request succeeded", e.detail);
});
</script>
<head>
```

Audiences

We now get to the final piece, building audiences. Audiences allow us to determine which visitors should be included in an activity and under what conditions. In chapter 1.3, we saw how to use an audience to only include and then keep in an activity new visitors. We'll see here how to build audiences based on the profile script for mutually exclusive swimlanes, one audience per swimlane.

Let's go into the Audiences tab and either create a new one or duplicate an existing one.

Clicking *Create audience* opens the audience editor. Our profile script was called twoLanes, so after selecting *Visitor Profile* in Attributes we'll type "user.twoLanes," then select *Equals (case insensitive)* and *static value*.

Finally, we'll name our audience "twoLanes: Lane1" by typing "Lane1" into the Values box.

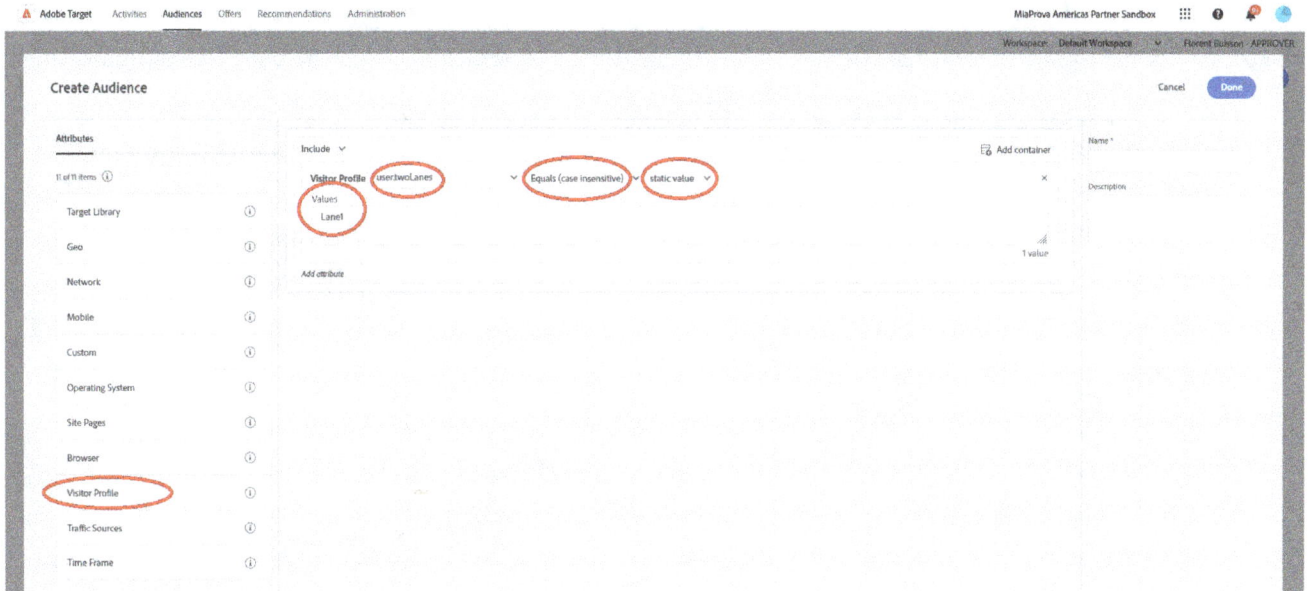

Creating an audience for the second lane would follow the same process; as you might guess, we'll call this audience "twoLanes: Lane2". We can then use an audience with a specific activity to ensure that the activity is restricted to the correct swimlane.

Let's go back to the progressive rollout activity we defined in chapter 1.3 and replace its audience.

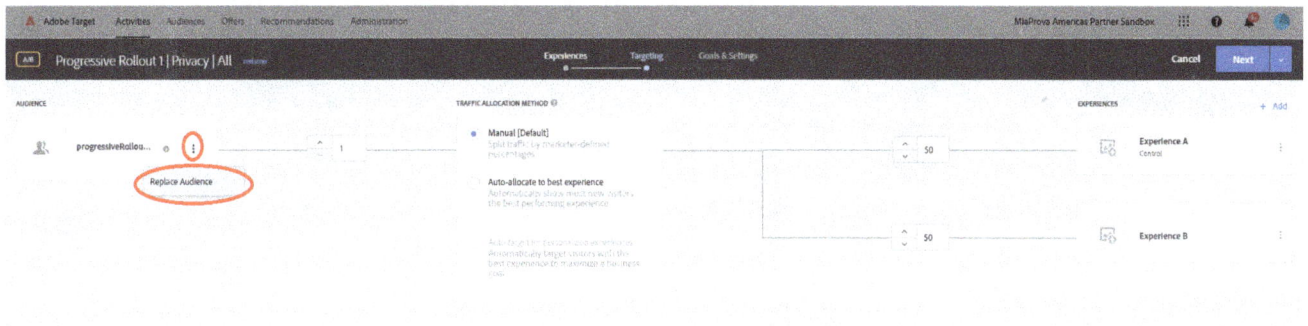

What we'll do this time is combine our new audience (twoLanes: Lane1) with the prior one (progressiveRolloutPrivacy | New Visitors).

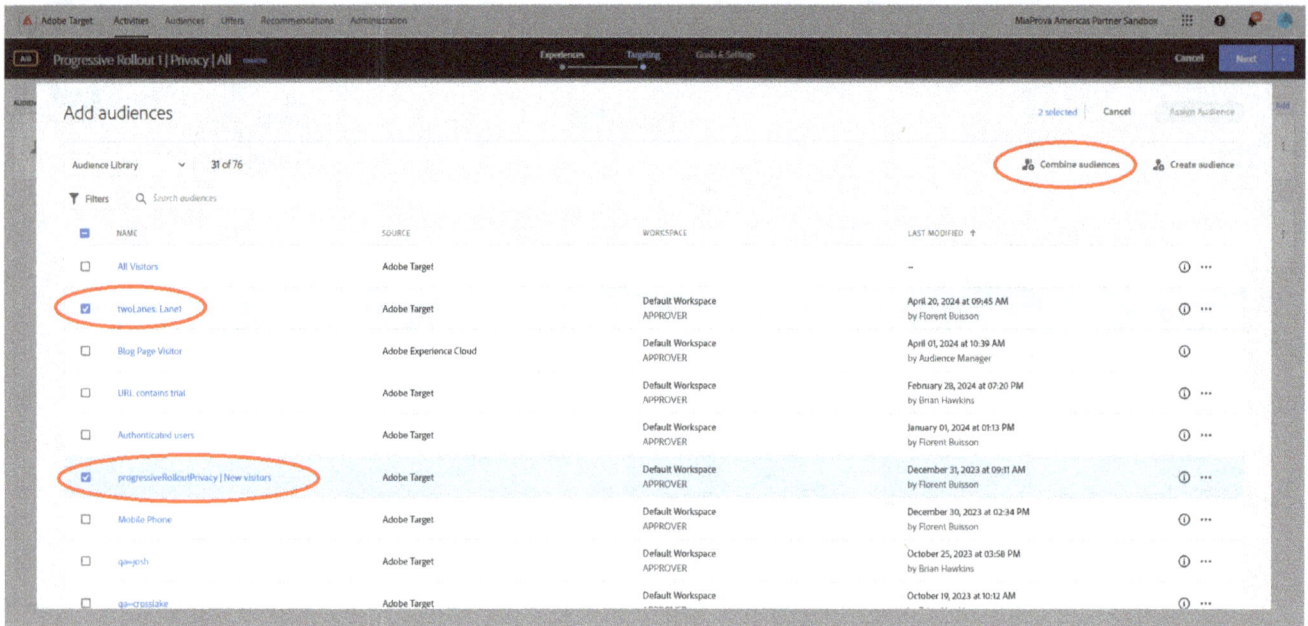

As you can see in the following screen, this new combined audience will be specific to this activity. It will not become available in the general list of audiences. Let's update the name of the combined audience by joining the names of the two audiences that it combines: "progressiveRolloutPrivacy | New visitors | Lane 1".

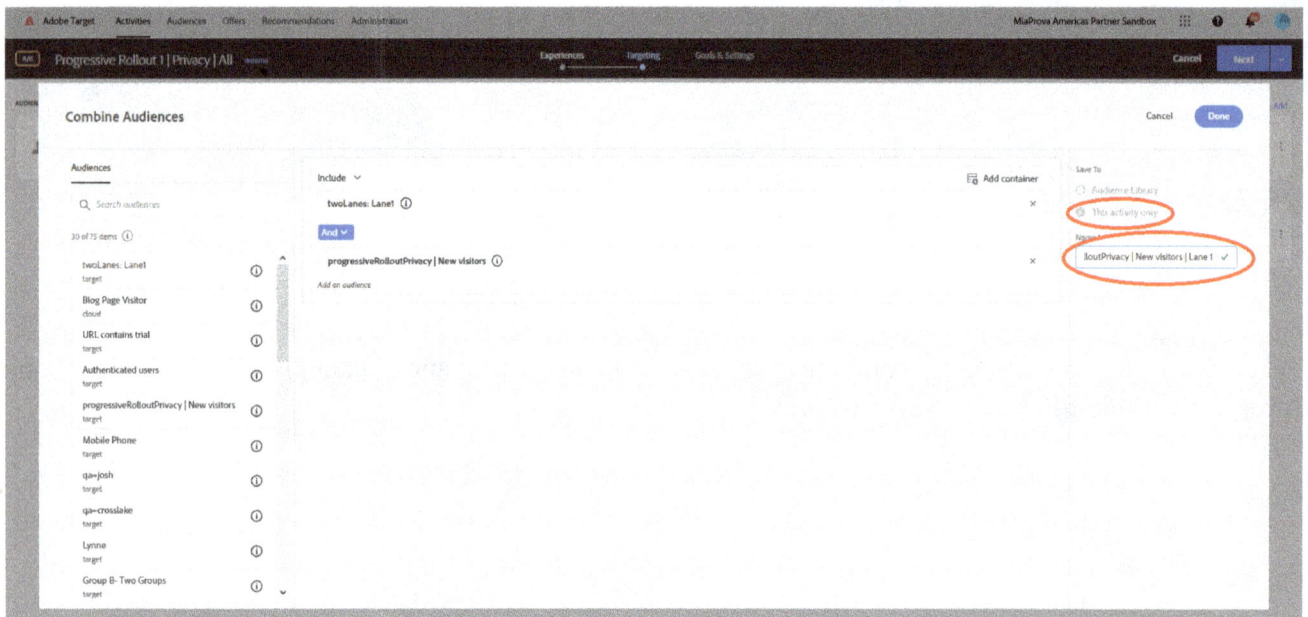

After we click *Done*, the new audience becomes available, and we can assign it to our activity.

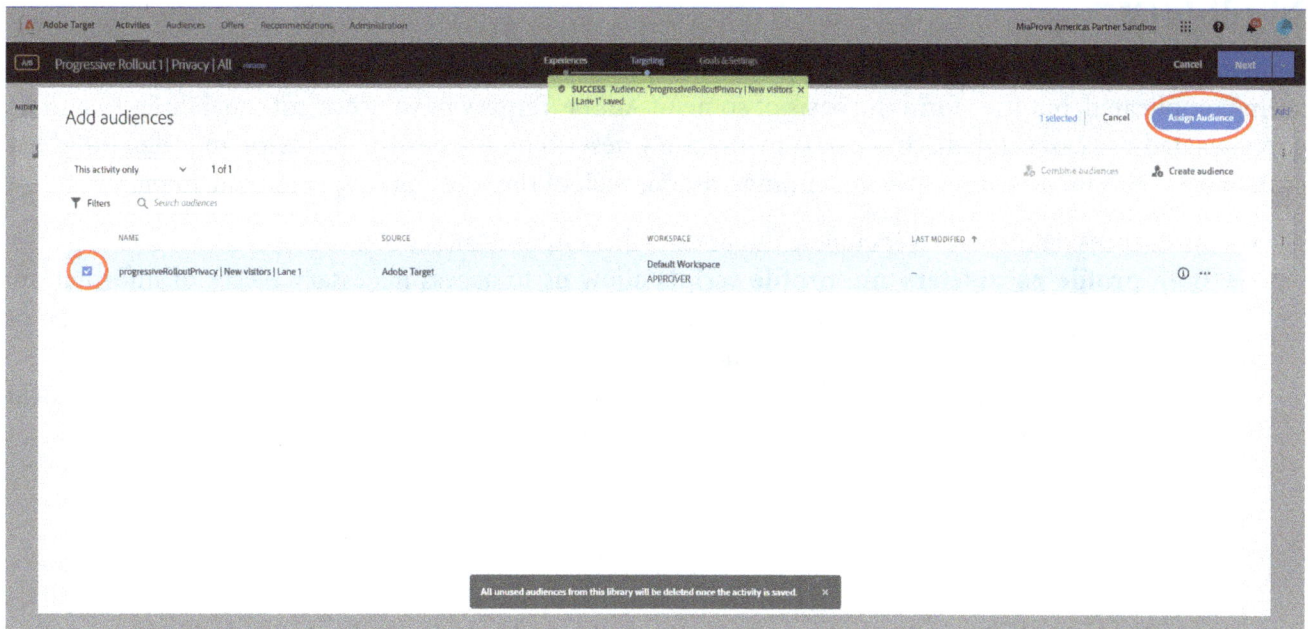

We can confirm that our audience has been correctly updated by going back to the activity summary page and selecting the information button to the right of its name.

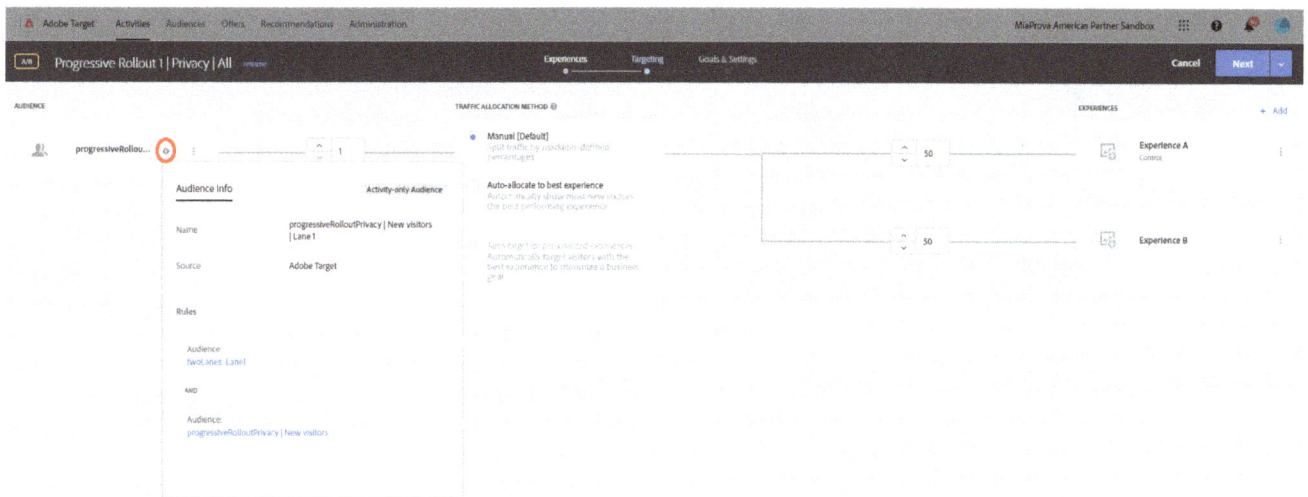

When building swimlanes, I prefer to combine audiences into temporary, activity-specific audiences rather than to build a single, large profile script. I find the former option more robust for the following reasons:

- Once the profile scripts for each of the lanes have been created, they can be reused without any need to edit them. If the logic is valid, it will remain so the next time we use them.
- Combining audiences is done by dragging and dropping elements in the Adobe Target user interface, which means we can't really make a typo at that stage.
- Each profile script returns its own separate value. This makes debugging easier if anything goes wrong, because you can quickly determine whether the swimlane script returned an incorrect value, the return visitor script returned an incorrect value, or the two values were combined incorrectly.

Summary

Audiences, profile parameters, profile scripts, and response tokens combine into a system that at times can seem complicated, but they form the basis of some of Adobe Target's most powerful capabilities to handle sophisticated use cases. It helps if we start by precisely describing the desired behavior and then build the system one criterion at a time. When defining criteria, each of the tools has a specific role to play:

- **Audiences** define who is included and under what circumstances.
- Both **profile parameters** and **profile scripts** allow us to access necessary pieces of information. Profile scripts also allow us to create rules that are more complex than include/exclude, such as maintaining a user's assignment after their first visit.
- **Response tokens** allow us to validate these building blocks during debugging. We'll see in the next chapter how these tools come together in a concrete example.

Chapter 3.2: Case Study in Audiences and Visitor Profiles: Filtering out Paid Traffic in E-Commerce

On a surface level, using visitor profiles and audiences is pretty straightforward, but there are quite a few "gotchas" to keep in mind. In this chapter, we'll walk through a full example: We'll learn how to filter out paid traffic so that experiments run only on organic traffic.

However, I will not just show you how to do this very specific thing; I will walk you through the steps I took to figure out how to do it. This will give you a solid foundation for approaching any novel situation in which you're unsure how to build the desired audience. The three-step process we'll use is as follows:

1. Try things out (bottom-up exploration)
2. Formalize the desired audience (top-down construction)
3. Iterate

Bottom-up exploration, a.k.a. fumbling around

When approaching a situation with novel audience criteria, we must remember that we don't know what we don't know. Even when there are built-in profile variables or audiences that seem to be a perfect fit, there might be edge cases that fall through the cracks. There are also probably several ways to represent the desired audience, with differing pros and cons in terms of covering all possible scenarios. Situations like this call for agile, iterative development. Therefore, instead of reading through Adobe's documentation and forums on how to filter out paid traffic, I took a shot in the dark in the safest possible manner to see what would happen.

I asked around in my company to learn how we defined paid and organic traffic, and I was told that paid traffic represented visitors landing on our site from a sponsored link in a search engine's results. These could be identified, for instance, by the presence of `utm_medium=cpc` (cost-per-click campaign) in the URL of the landing page:

```
www.example.com/?utm_medium=cpc&campaign_id=1
```

I built the corresponding audience in Adobe Target by selecting *Site Pages* on the left-side menu, then in the central container *Landing Page*, *Query*, and *Does not contain*. Finally, I entered `utm_medium=cpc`.

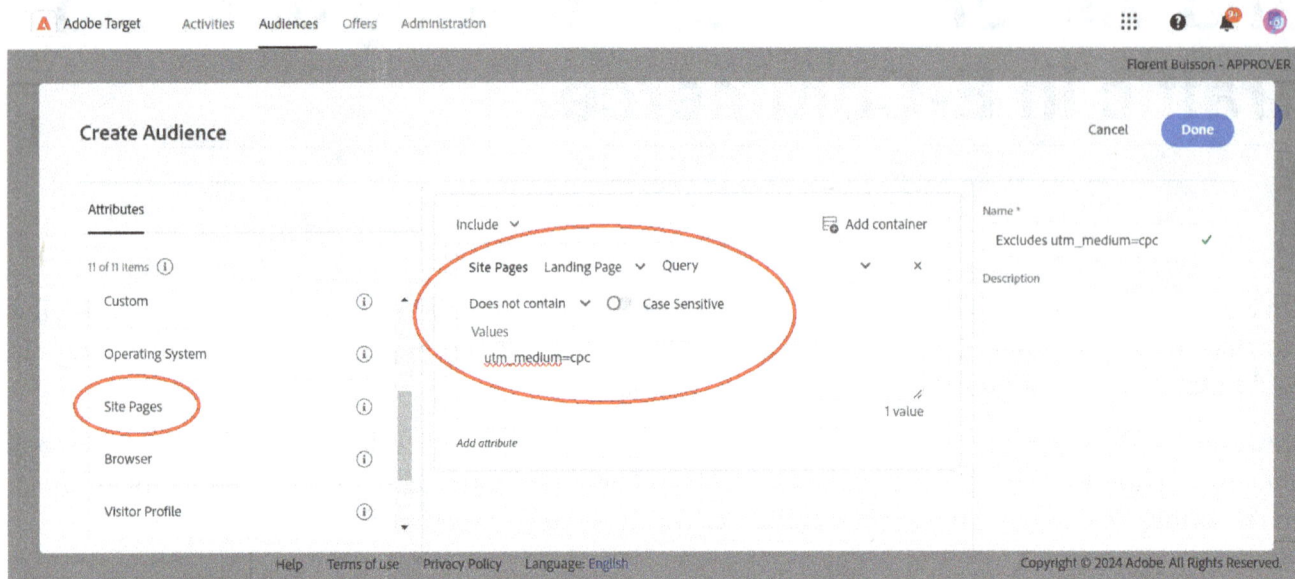

Once I had built that audience, I tried it on with a stealth A/A test using an activity that had just concluded. I built a new activity with the same mbox, assigned to it the newly-built audience, and routed 100% of the traffic to the control experience for a couple of hours. This way I was able to track after the fact which visitors had been routed through the activity without actually altering anybody's experience of the website. (Note that I created a new activity instead of simply reactivating the old activity so that my new data wouldn't inadvertently be included in later analyses of the old activity). The next day, I pulled the data for the visitors who had been entered in the experiment to confirm that everything happened as expected.

At first glance, I found that the assignment *mostly* worked: about 90% of visits in the activity had been initiated from organic traffic, as demonstrated by the absence of the `utm_medium=cpc` string in the landing page query. This answered the most basic question about syntax: did the way I wrote my audience criterion match the trigger in user behavior I was interested in? When a visitor entered the website coming from paid traffic, was it correctly recognized by Adobe Target? Or was it, to paraphrase Inigo Montoya in *The Princess Bride*, "utm_medium, you keep using that parameter, but Adobe Target doesn't think it means what you think it means"?

The question was then: what's going on with the other 10% of visits? Why are they being routed to the activity? By exploring the data further, I quickly realized that the criterion above was not persisting correctly at the visitor level: a visitor's first visit may come from paid traffic, but their second visit the next day may come from organic traffic—i.e., they browsed back to our website by themselves. Even adding our usual *New & Returning visitors in the activity* script wouldn't do the trick here, because the visitor was not entered in the experiment on their first visit, but only on their second one.

Having clarified this issue and marked it for later resolution, I then restricted myself to each visitor's first visit. Even there, a small percentage of the visits routed to the activity had the `utm_medium=cpc` string in the landing page query. To determine why, I zoomed in further, pulling all the data for just one of these visits to look at what the visitor was doing page by page, hit by hit.

This surfaced a second issue that is a variant of the one above: the assignment might change not only between visits but even within a single visit. If a visitor started a visit on our website from paid traffic, then navigated to a search engine (such as DuckDuckGo) and clicked on an organic link back to our website within 30 minutes of their last interaction with our site, that would traditionally be counted as a single visit. However, there would be two different entries in that visit. On their first entry at the beginning of the visit, the visitor is not eligible for the activity, but they become eligible on their second entry. If this happened with a real activity instead of a stealth validation run, the activity might then kick off and modify the user experience within a single visit. Not good.

Top-down construction

Audience definition

By playing around with a stealth activity, I had been able to confirm that the syntax I used in defining my audience was correct. However, I also identified issues with the persistence of the assignment.

To better understand the challenge and how to solve it, let's first review how we would persist the assignment for an activity on mobile devices only. We would use a script that returns TRUE if the visitor is new or was previously in the activity, in conjunction with a criterion for mobile devices: ((NEW VISITOR) OR (PREVIOUSLY IN ACTIVITY)) AND (MOBILE DEVICE). Let's see how that plays out over time:

VISIT NUMBER	NEW VISITOR	PREVIOUSLY IN ACTIVITY	MOBILE DEVICE	((NEW VISITOR) OR (PREVIOUSLY IN ACTIVITY)) AND (MOBILE DEVICE)
1	TRUE	FALSE	TRUE	TRUE
2	FALSE	TRUE	TRUE	TRUE

This sort of table, known as a **truth table**, allows us to determine when a complex expression will be true based on its components. As you can see, the overall condition for the visitor to be included in the activity is always true:

- The *New Visitor* condition is true during the entire first visit, even if *Previously in activity* is false, and in later visits, their values are swapped, but the expression (*New Visitor* OR *Previously in activity*) as a whole is always true.
- Given that a user is actually defined as a device, the "Mobile Device" condition remains true across all visits.

Now let's go back to the problem with ((NEW VISITOR) OR (PREVIOUSLY IN ACTIVITY)) AND (ORGANIC TRAFFIC) when the visitor enters on organic traffic on the first visit and paid traffic on the second one.

VISIT NUMBER	NEW VISITOR	PREVIOUSLY IN ACTIVITY	ORGANIC TRAFFIC	((NEW VISITOR) OR (PREVIOUSLY IN ACTIVITY)) AND (ORGANIC TRAFFIC)
1	TRUE	FALSE	TRUE	TRUE
2	FALSE	TRUE	FALSE	FALSE

The (ORGANIC TRAFFIC) condition may not be continuously true for a given visitor, and therefore the overall composed condition may also not be true if it's built as above. Now that we see the problem, let's build the correct conditions. For the first visit, we want the visitor to be entered in the experiment if they are a new visitor and they come from organic traffic, i.e., ((NEW VISITOR) AND (ORGANIC TRAFFIC)). For the later visits, we want the visitor to be entered in the activity if they were previously entered in it, regardless of their current channel of entry, i.e., (PREVIOUSLY IN ACTIVITY). Our correct audience definition is therefore ((NEW VISITOR) AND (ORGANIC TRAFFIC)) OR (PREVIOUSLY IN ACTIVITY). We can confirm that by building the corresponding table.

VISIT NUMBER	NEW VISITOR	ORGANIC TRAFFIC	PREVIOUSLY IN ACTIVITY	((NEW VISITOR) AND (ORGANIC TRAFFIC)) OR (PREVIOUSLY IN ACTIVITY)
1	TRUE	TRUE	FALSE	TRUE
2	FALSE	FALSE	TRUE	TRUE

Building truth tables can feel a bit cumbersome, but it can be really helpful when we want to ensure that your audience works the way you want it to in all scenarios.

Audience construction

Once we have defined our audience, we need to think about how we're going to build it.

As we've seen above, our first challenge is that a single visit may have multiple entries, and therefore the built-in *landing page* variable isn't precise enough in itself.

I decided to use a profile script instead, as I felt it would be easier to validate its behavior with trace mode.

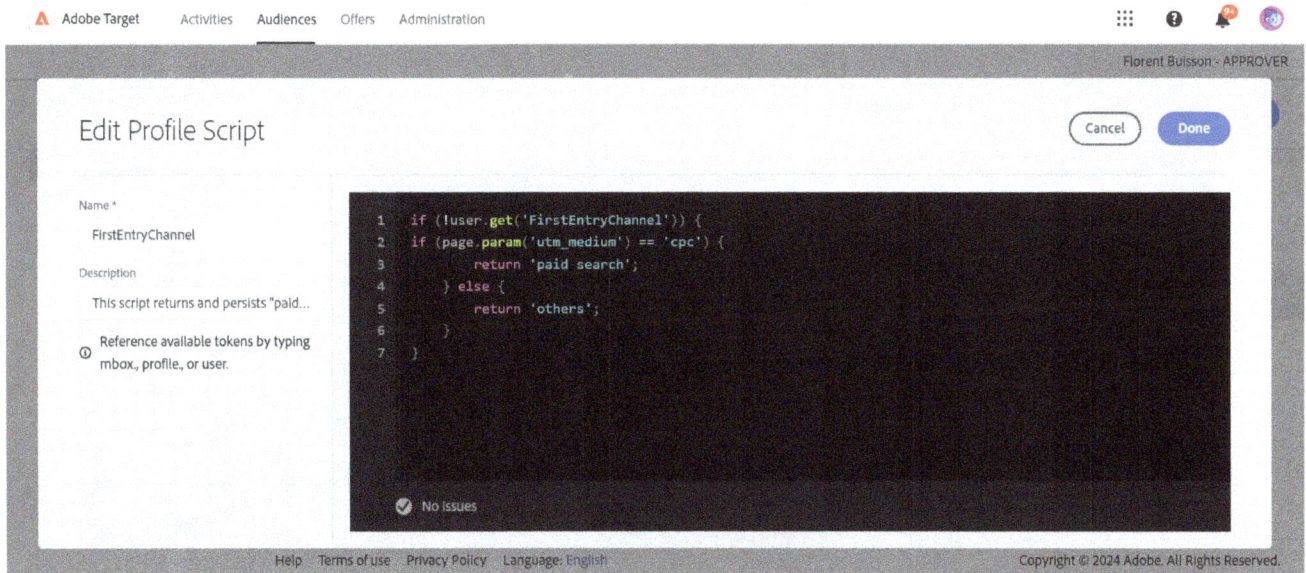

Working from the inside out, the innermost expression is pretty self-explanatory; it simply returns `paid search` whenever the page query includes the parameter *utm_medium* with the value `cpc`:

```
If (page.param('utm_medium') == 'cpc') {
    return 'paid search';
} else {
    return 'others';
}
```

One thing to note, though, is that I used the phrase 'others' instead of 'organic'. I prefer to use meaningful terms for specific, explicit conditions (such as `utm_medium=cpc`), and more vague or opposite terms (e.g., `not paid search`) for residual conditions like *else*. Here, we may *believe* that what's not paid search is organic, but we haven't actually confirmed that or defined it through an explicit enumeration. For instance, if the company later introduced social media ads, the 'organic' label would become misleading, whereas 'not paid search' or 'others' would remain accurate.

The outer expression is a variation of the pattern we've seen to persist activity assignment:

```
if (!user.get('FirstEntryChannel')) { … }
```

The way it works is that it only evaluates the page query condition if the FirstEntryChannel script doesn't exist, i.e., on the very first visit's landing page. After that, user.get('FirstEntryChannel') will return either 'paid search' or 'others', which convert to 'true' when evaluated as a boolean (true/false variable). This way, the value will never change, even if the visitor exits and then reenter the website.

I then built the script for returning visitors, to keep visitors in the experiment after they have entered it once.

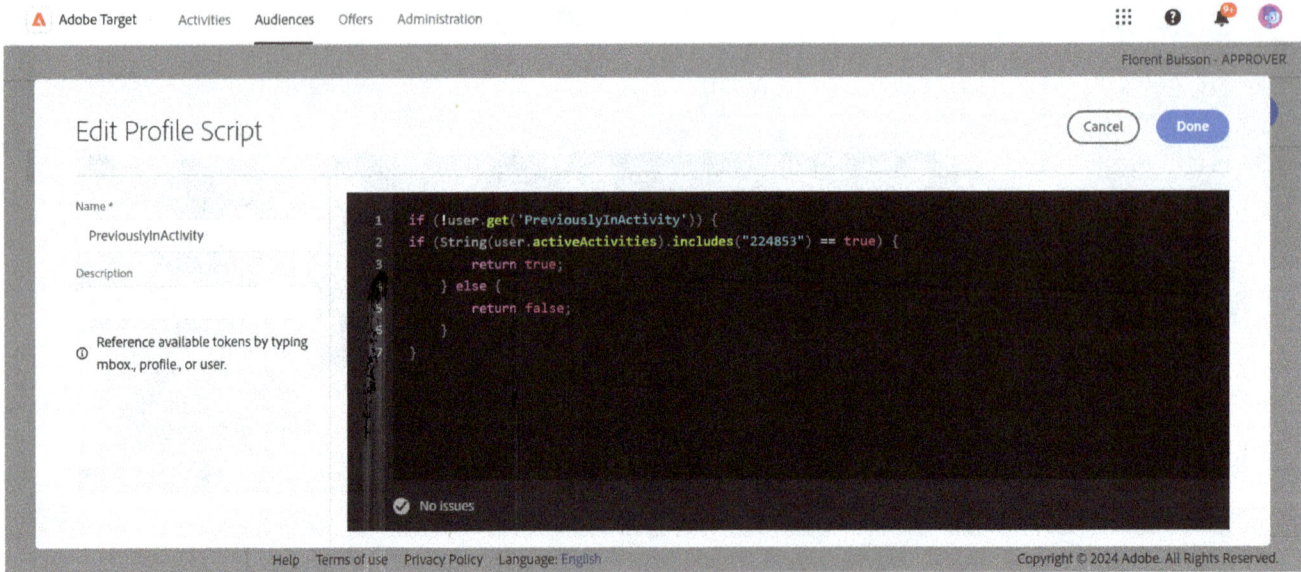

There's nothing special here; it's identical to what we've used in the past.

Once I had the two dedicated scripts, the final challenge was to get the right logical structure for the combined audience, ((NEW VISITOR) AND (ORGANIC TRAFFIC)) OR (PREVIOUSLY IN ACTIVITY). Let's work through this together.

Note that there are parentheses around the first two criteria, because otherwise the order of operations between AND and OR would be ambiguous. Parentheses can be represented by using a **container** when building the audience. As soon as we drag one of the attributes from the left menu to the central area, the *Add container* button appears.

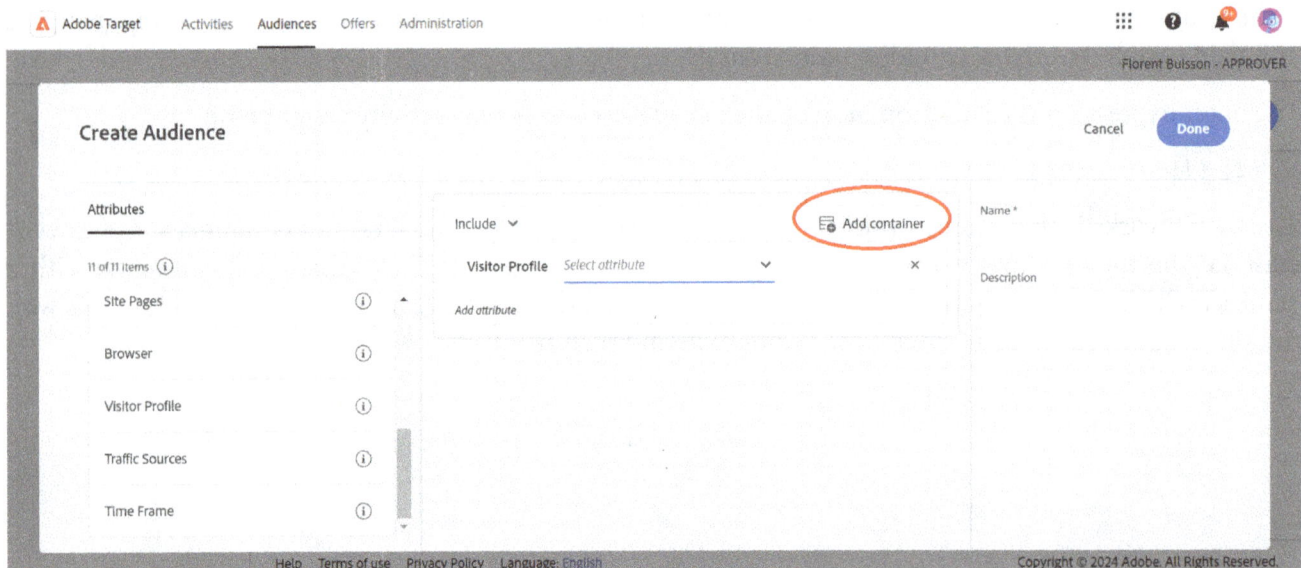

Clicking *Add container* creates a box into which attributes can be added.

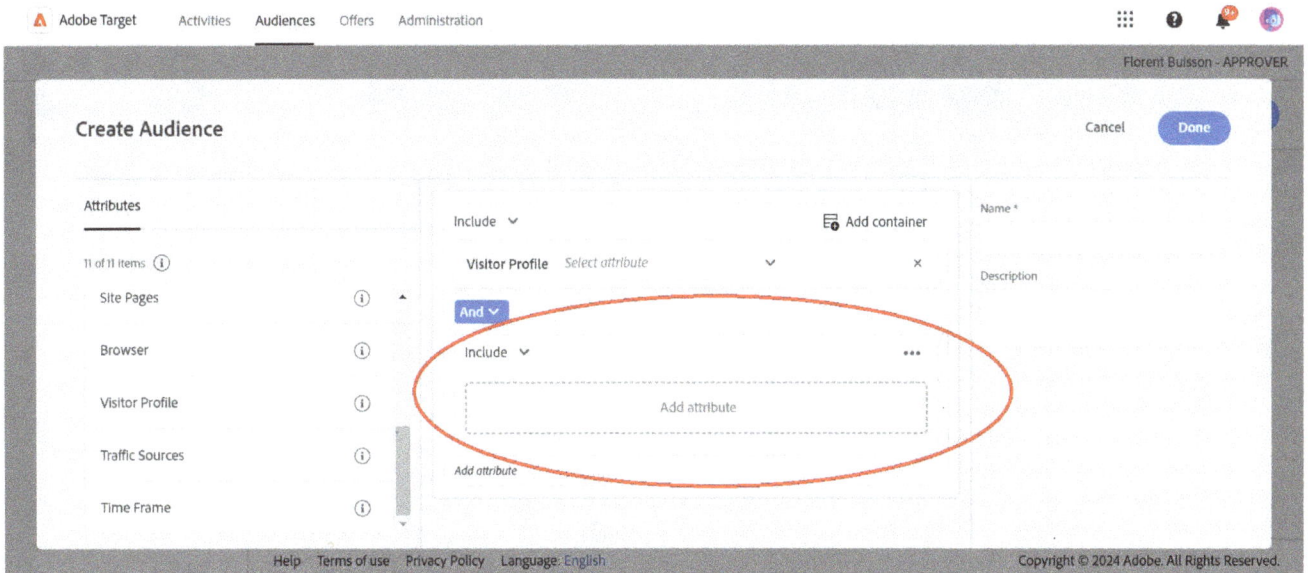

For clarity, let's delete the *Visitor Profile* attribute above the container at this point, then drag *Visitor Profile* from the left menu into that new box. We'll then select *New Visitor*, then drag in *Visitor Profile* a second time, this time selecting *user.FirstEntryChannel* and filling in the corresponding fields.

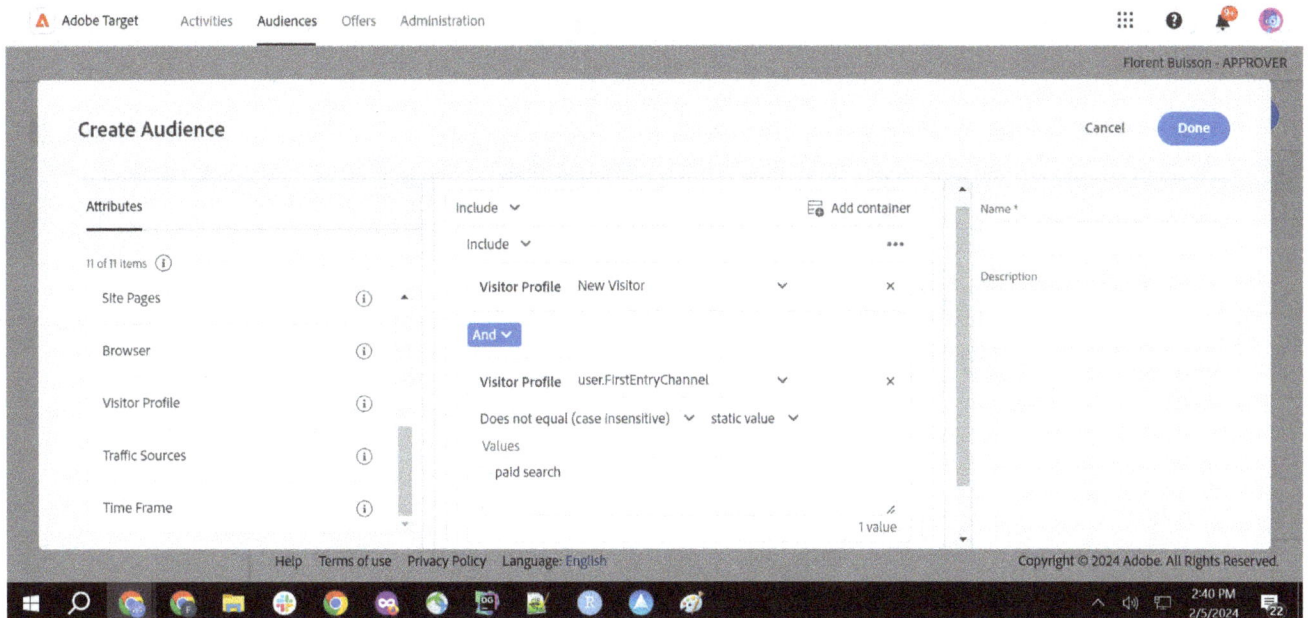

At this point, the audience comprises only New Visitors, excluding those from paid search. We then drag *Visitor Profile* one last time, dropping it *under and outside of* the container.

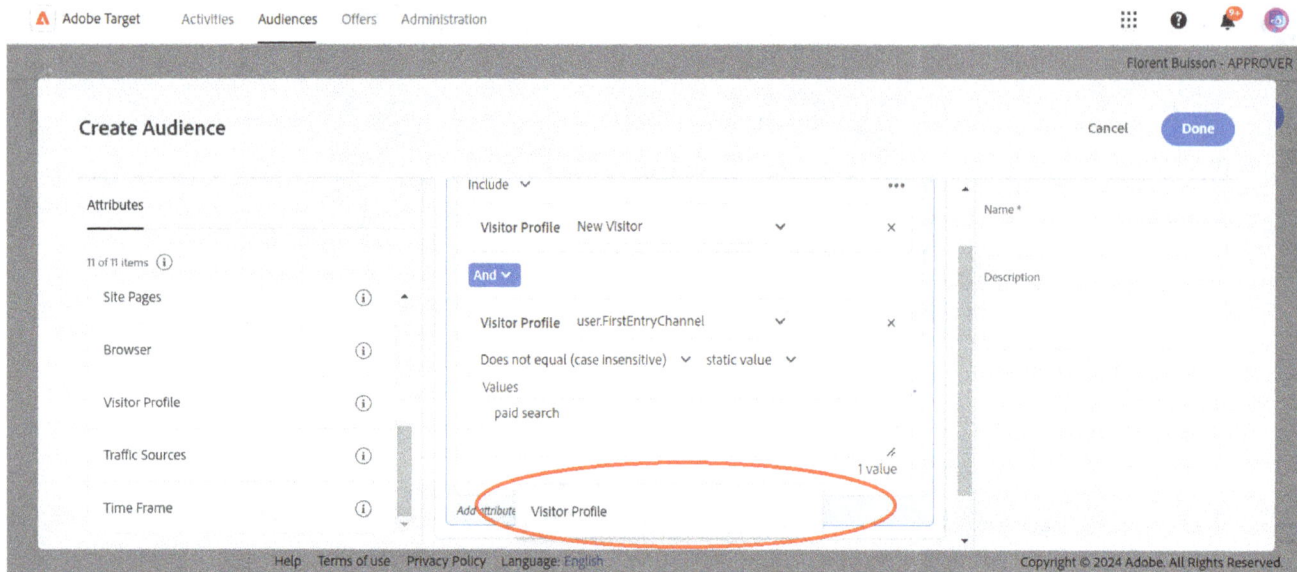

Note that while we're dragging an attribute, the area where it will go becomes pale blue to help us get it in the right spot.

Finally, we'll add the *user.PreviouslyInActivity* script and the corresponding fields, remembering to switch the *And* connector to *Or*.

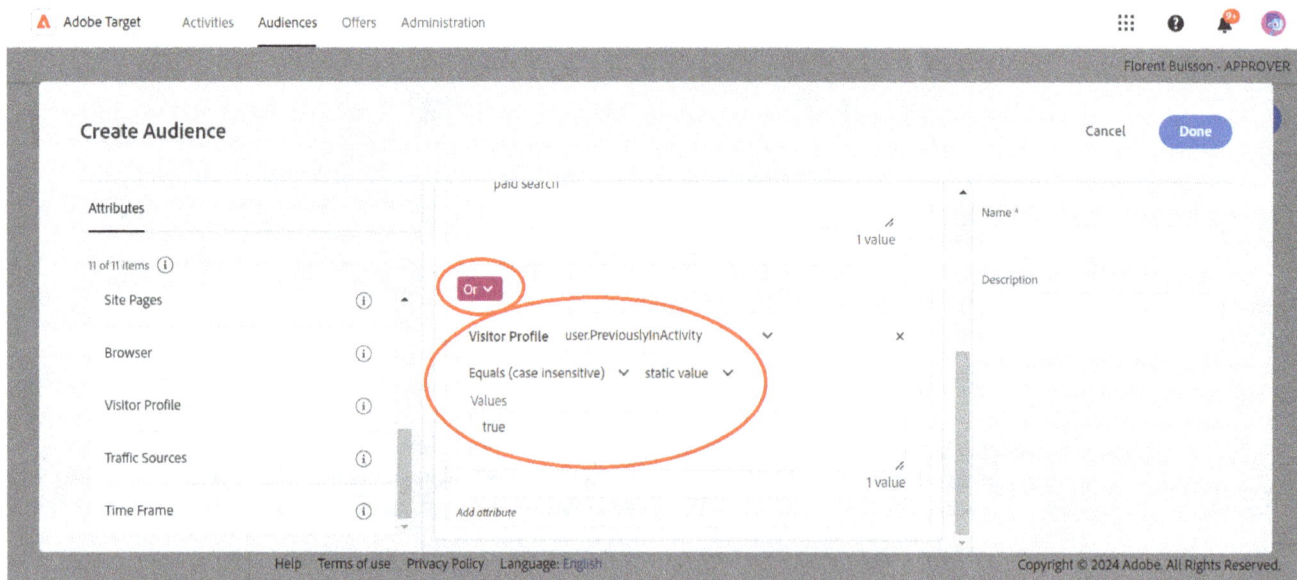

After naming and saving the audience, we'll open its definition from the list of audiences—and voilà, the parentheses are in the right places!

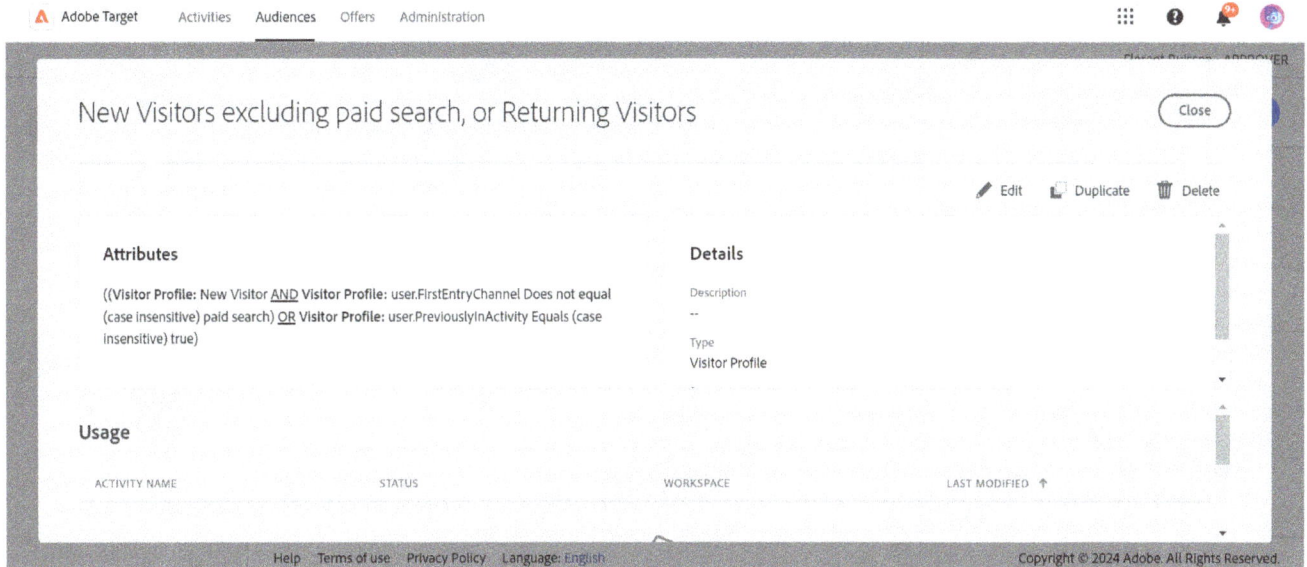

Summary

In this chapter, we saw that:

- When dealing with new or complex criteria in audiences, it's best to confirm that the audience behaves appropriately through a **stealth activity** where 100% of the traffic goes to the control group.
- Even the best built-in Target variable may not correspond exactly to what you want, depending on your data model and use cases. **Validate** and **iterate**!
- When you have a complex combination of criteria and AND/OR connectors, you can use **truth tables** to "debug" an expression and **containers** to express parentheses in the audience builder.

Chapter 3.3: Debugging from the Browser

The Adobe Experience Cloud Debugger is a browser extension that allows us to access rich context data in real time while browsing our website. It offers a complementary approach to the processes we looked at in chapter 1.2.

Installing the debugger

It can be installed from the extension store of any browser, such as Chrome.

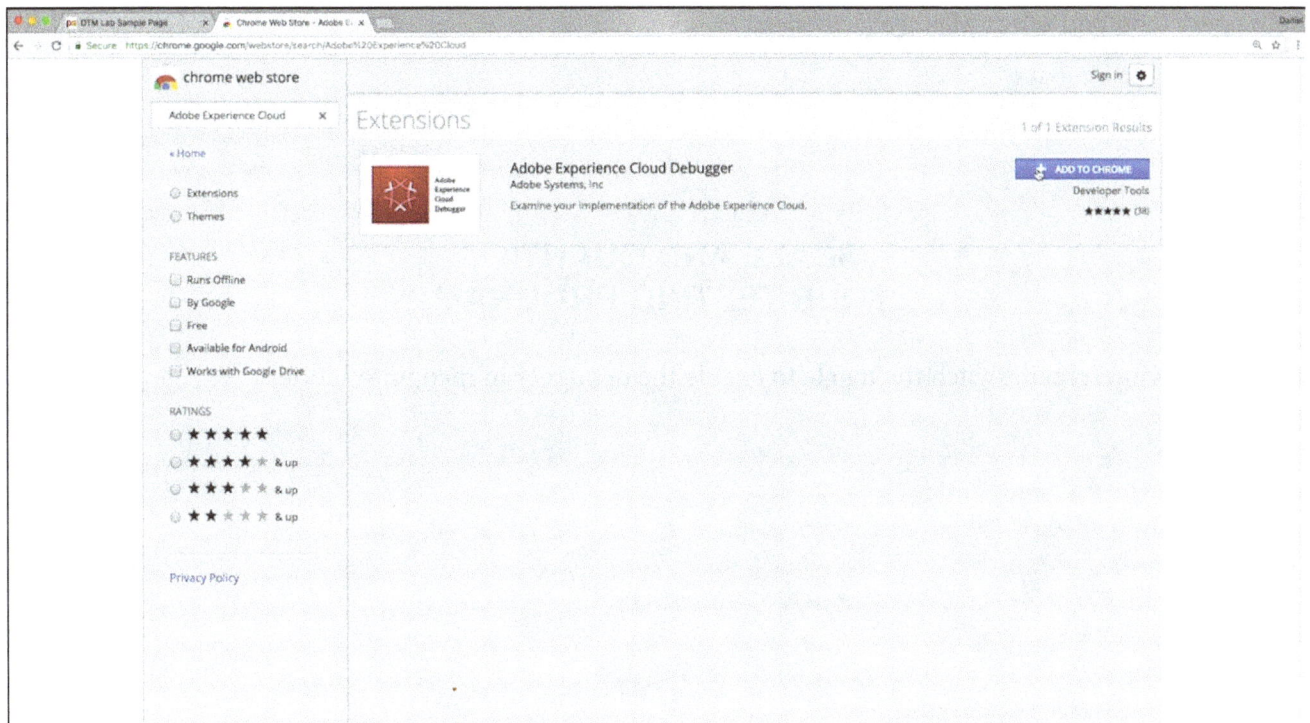

The extension should then appear in your browser's toolbar; if it doesn't, you can pin it there by going into the browser's extension manager.

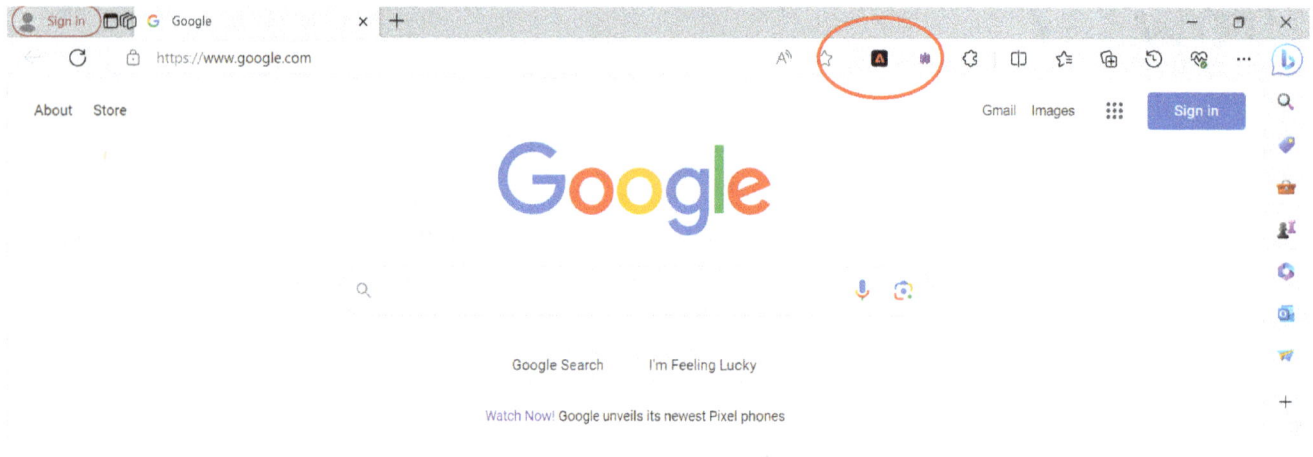

As web analysts, we often use a browser's incognito mode to simulate the experience of a new visitor; therefore, we'll want to make sure that the debugger is enabled for that purpose. Let's right-click on the debugger's icon and select *Manage Extension*.

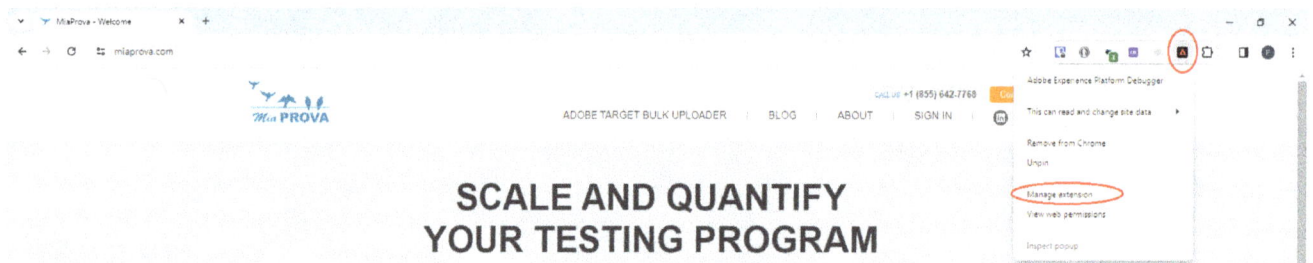

In the following screen, switch the toggle to enable the debugger in incognito mode.

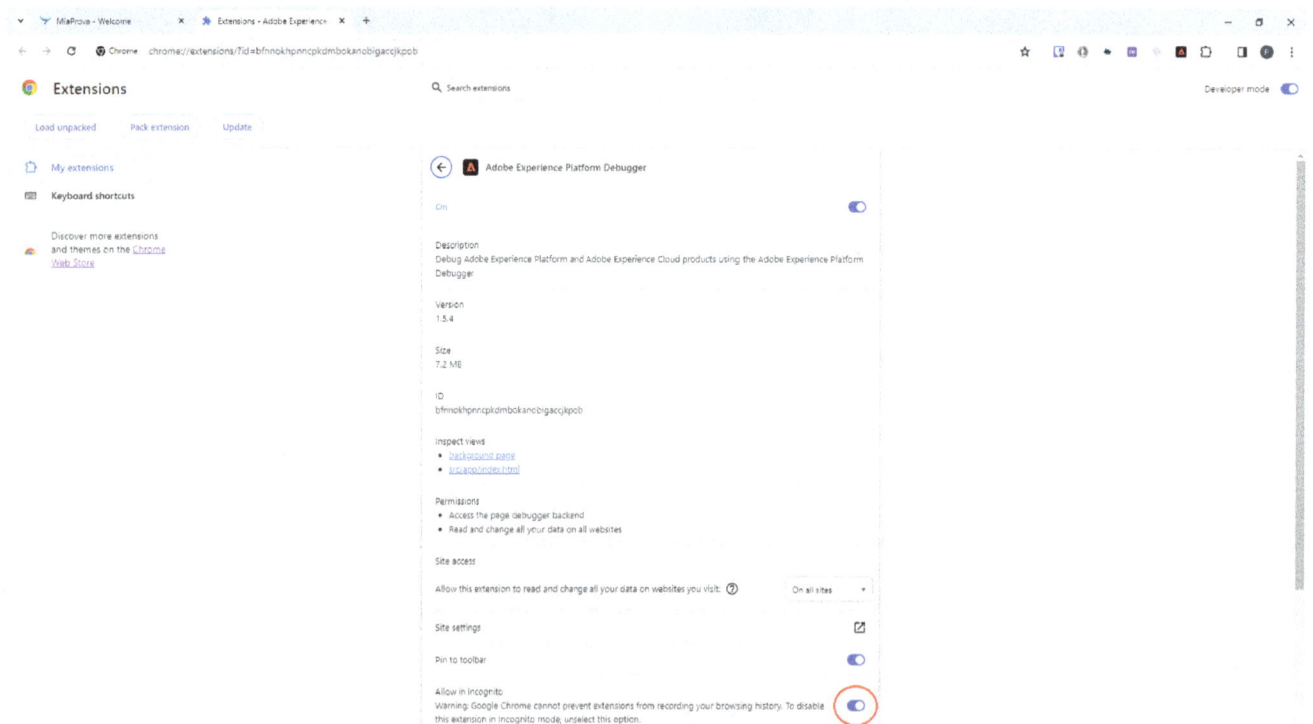

Launching the debugger

It's best to launch the debugger *before* navigating to our website so that we can capture all the initial requests that happen at the beginning of a session. Once we've installed the debugger, we'll click on the extension's icon to open the extension's pop-up; then we'll select *Sign In*.

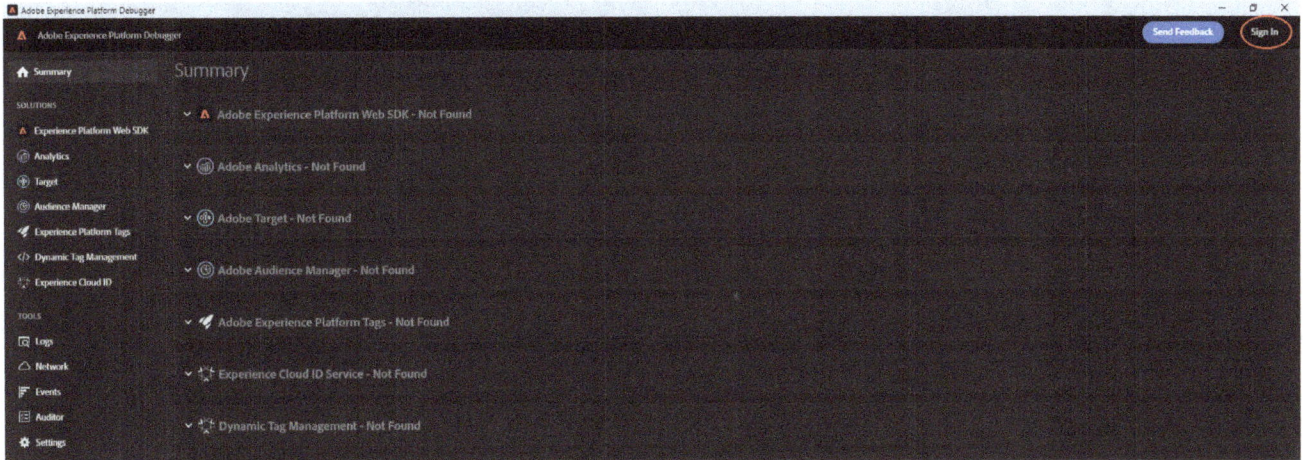

After signing in, navigate in the browser to your site. The debugger will then show the Adobe products that are implemented on the website.

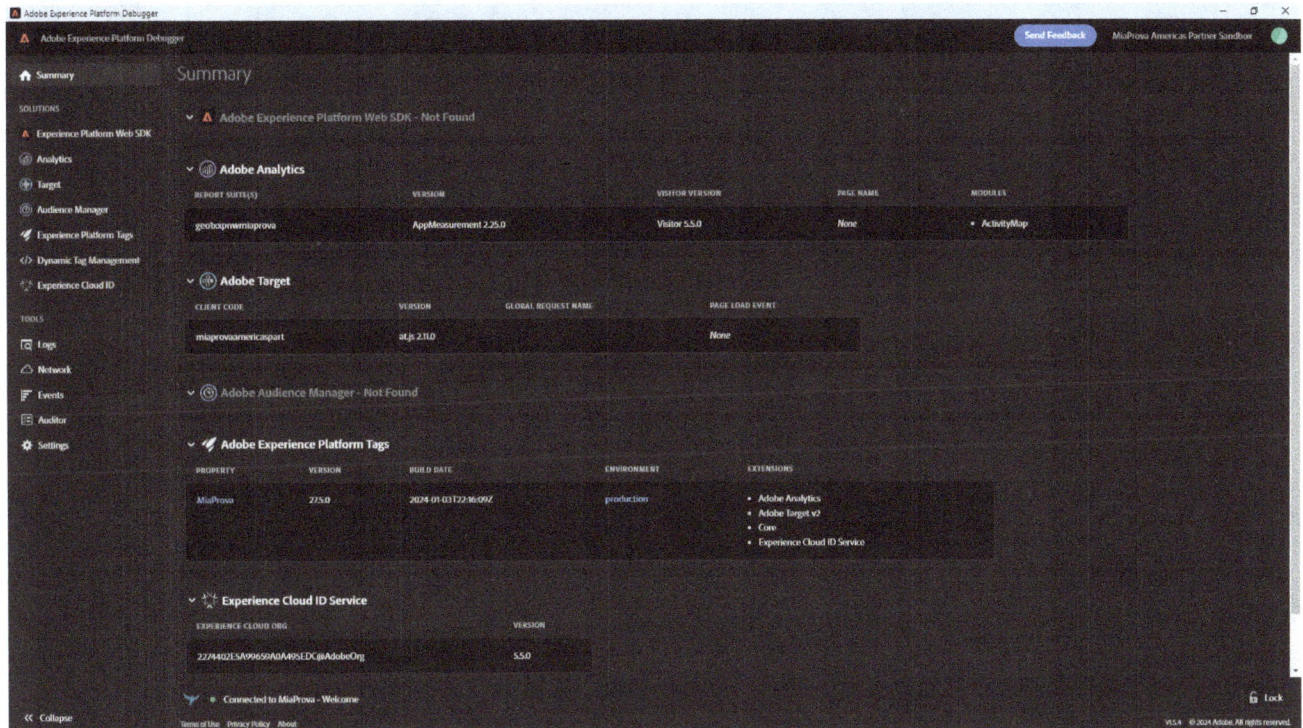

By default, the debugger will focus on the active tab in the browser. This means that if we open a different tab, it will change focus automatically. If we want it to stay focused on a specific tab, we can select *Lock* in the bottom right corner of the debugger window.

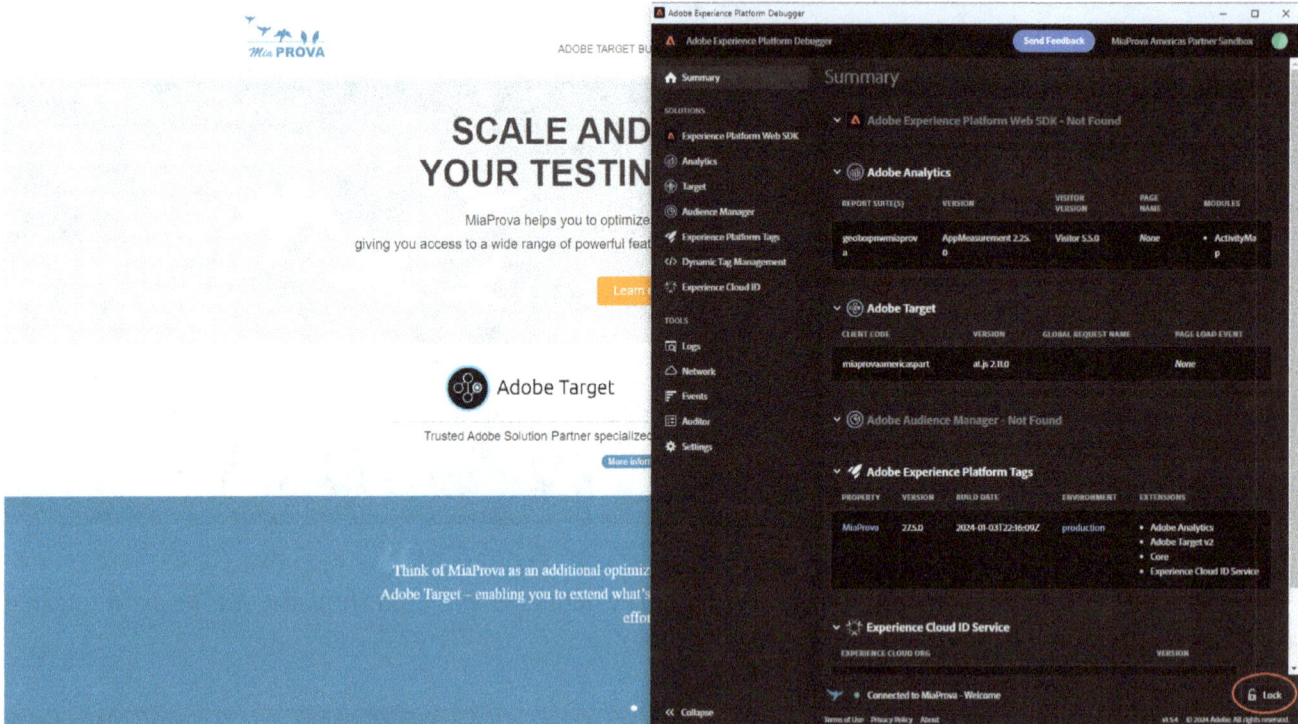

Debugger tools

Let's look at the left-side menu. We'll come back to the top section, but first let's look at the one just below it: Tools.

First on this list of transversal tools is the Logs tab, which allows us to visualize all the console logs emitted by the applications.

Next, the Network tab lets us visualize all the network requests emitted by the applications. This can be especially handy if we need to confirm the order of operations.

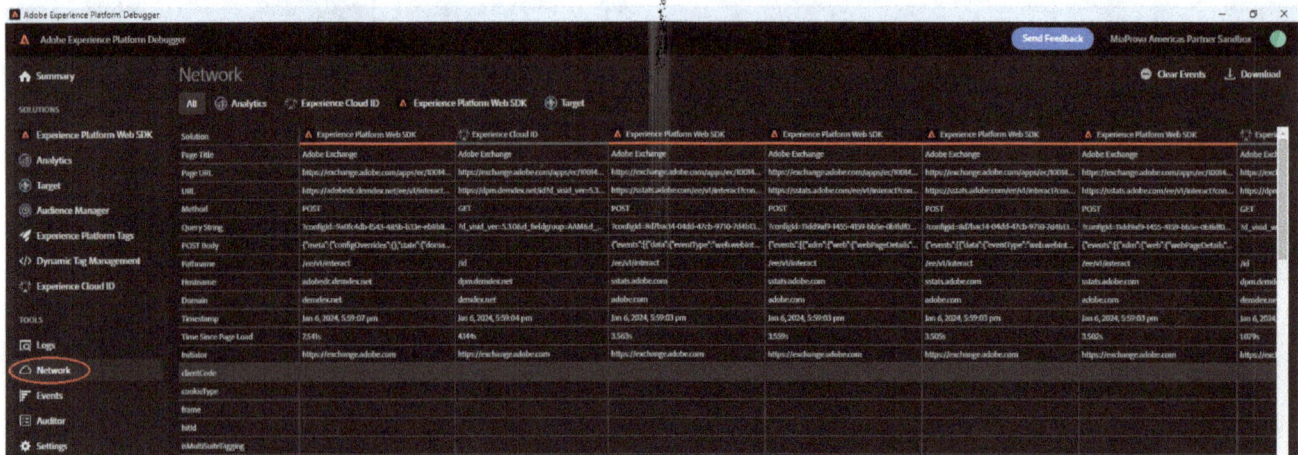

The Events tab offers a similar but more synthetic view of the events triggered by Adobe applications.

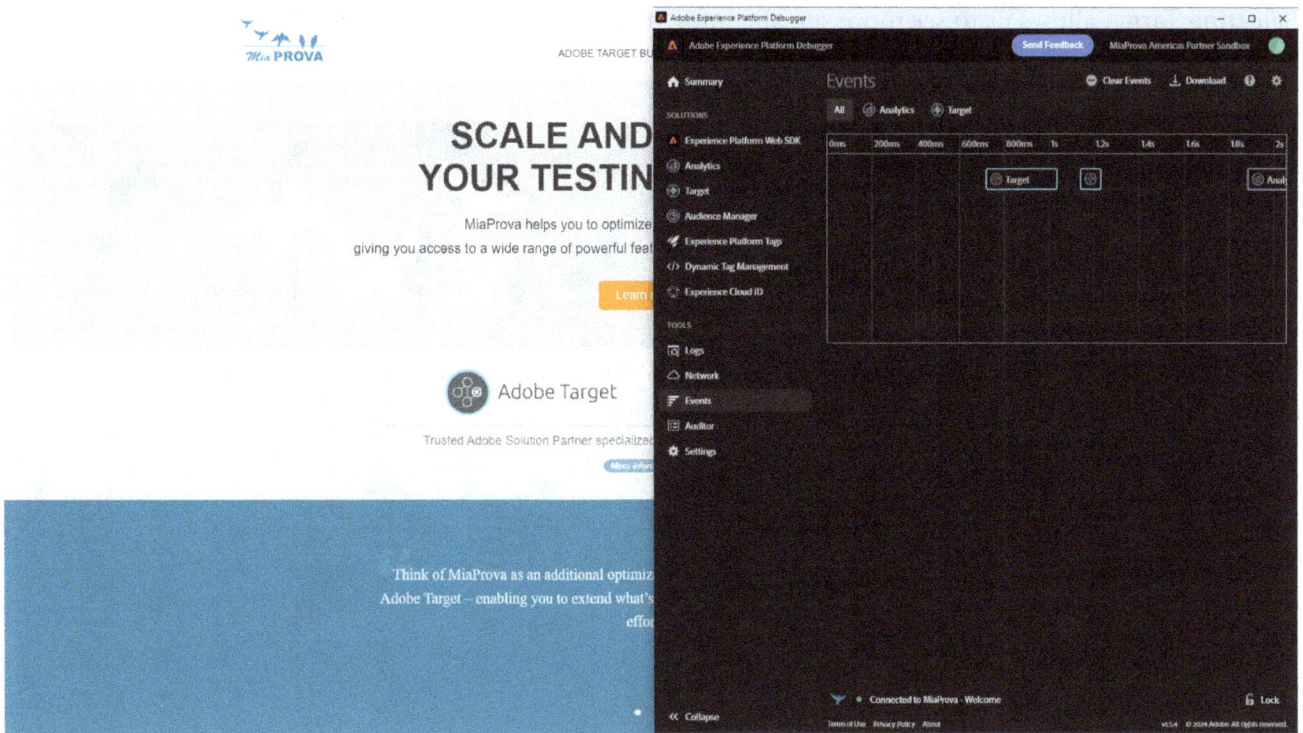

The Auditor tab enables us to run auditor tests, to detect any potential issues with the applications.

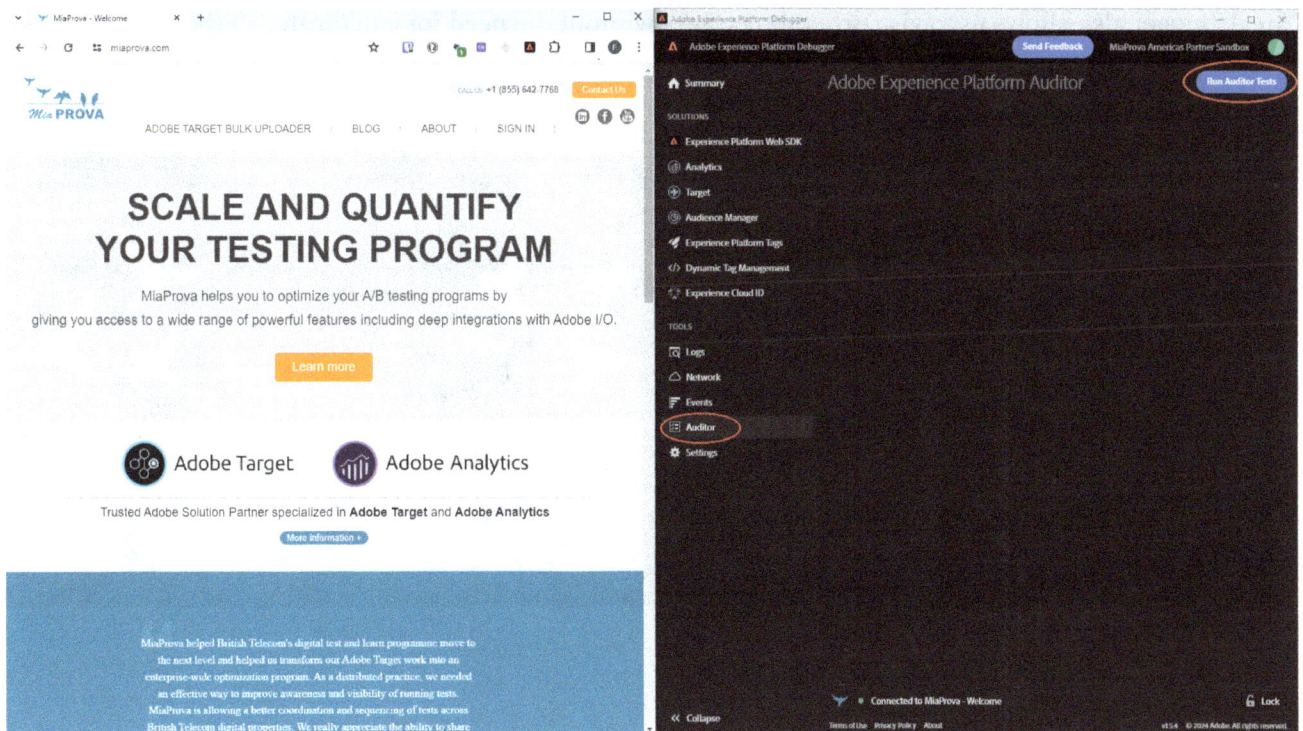

Target tab

Now we'll go back to the top section on the left-side menu, the list of applications (also called **Solutions**). Selecting Target allows us to see more specific information. By default, the network requests are displayed.

The debugger also allows us to visualize mbox traces without the need for a dedicated authorization token. Go into Configuration and turn on the toggle for *Target Trace*.

This enables the Target Traces tab under Adobe Target, with a list of the mboxes that have been triggered on the page. (Note that the "list" may consist solely of Target's global mbox.)

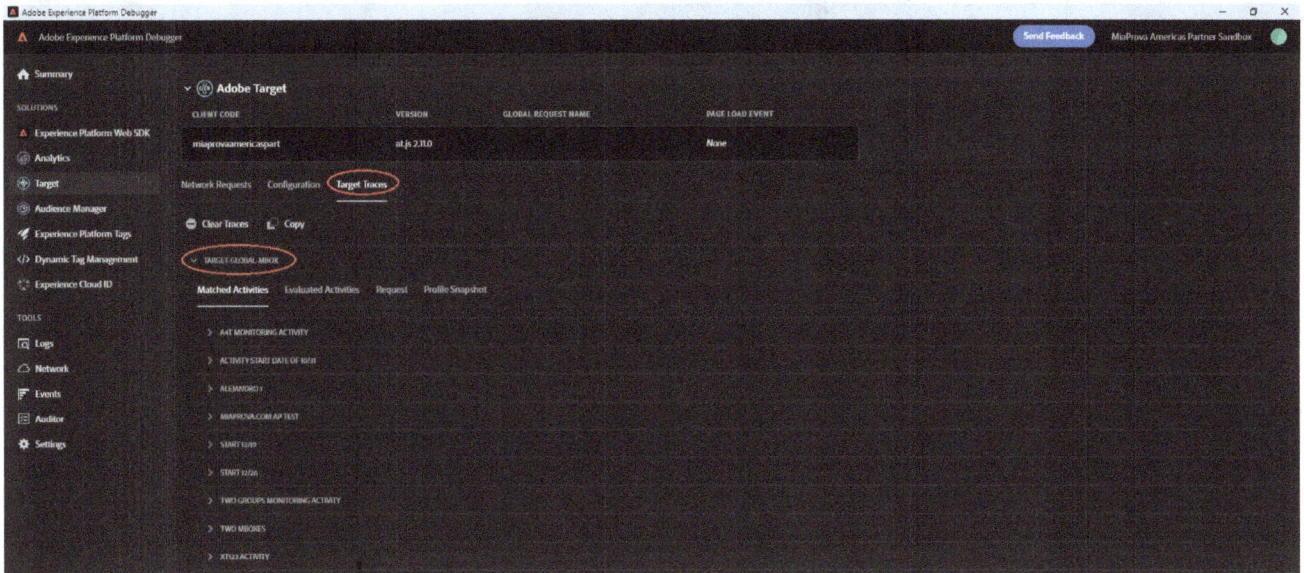

Under each mbox's name, we can see the following sub-tabs:

- Matched Activities
- Evaluated Activities
- Request
- Profile Snapshot

Matched Activities shows *only* the activities that we, as visitors, were entered into (because we met the conditions), whereas **Evaluated Activities** shows the list of *all* active activities on that mbox. For example, remember that our canary release in chapter 1.2 targeted only mobile visitors. So if we used a desktop browser, the activity would show up in the Evaluated Activities list but not in the Matched Activities list. Furthermore, if we select an activity under Evaluated Activities that we haven't been entered in, we can see which condition was not fulfilled.

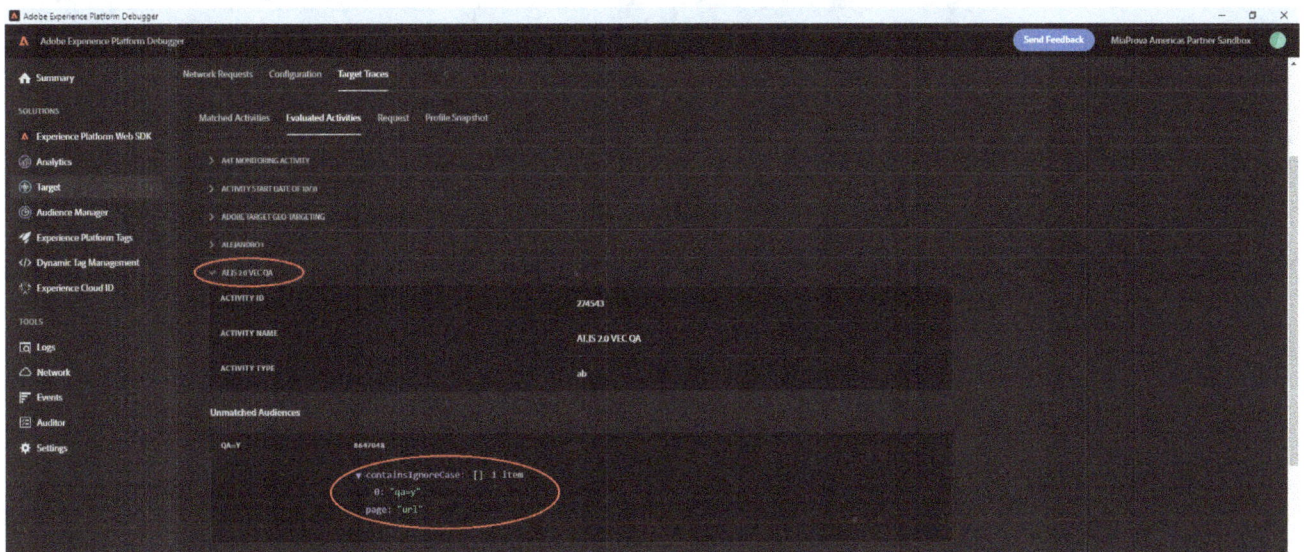

Request shows some details of the mbox request that we may need to access, such as mbox parameters.

Finally, **Profile Snapshot** displays some visitor-level information, such as the *tntId*, which you might use to find in your database the record for your visit. It also displays under the Profile Snapshot sub-tab a list of profile parameters before and after the mbox evaluates all the relevant scripts.

This allows you to much more easily see which parameters were modified and the values involved.

Chapter 3.4: Interactions Between Activities

Once we have run a few activities, the question arises: how do we handle or avoid interactions between them?

No interactions: exclusive sequential activities

The first and most conservative approach is to run one activity at a time and make sure that no visitor is part of two activities. If we have only one activity active at a time, the only potential issue is returning visitors—for instance, visitors who entered A/B test #6 on their first visit to the website and then come back later when test #6 has ended but test #7 is now running.

In the chapter on audiences, I suggested not including in a test returning visitors who were not part of that test on their first visit. Following this recommendation will normally ensure that a visitor can be part of at most one test when we have only one test active at a time (of course, there are always exceptions caused by visitors clearing out their cookies, bugs, etc.).

For an extra layer of safety, we can also add to the audience for tests the criterion *Not in other tests*, which is a native variable created by Adobe Target in the Visitor Profile.

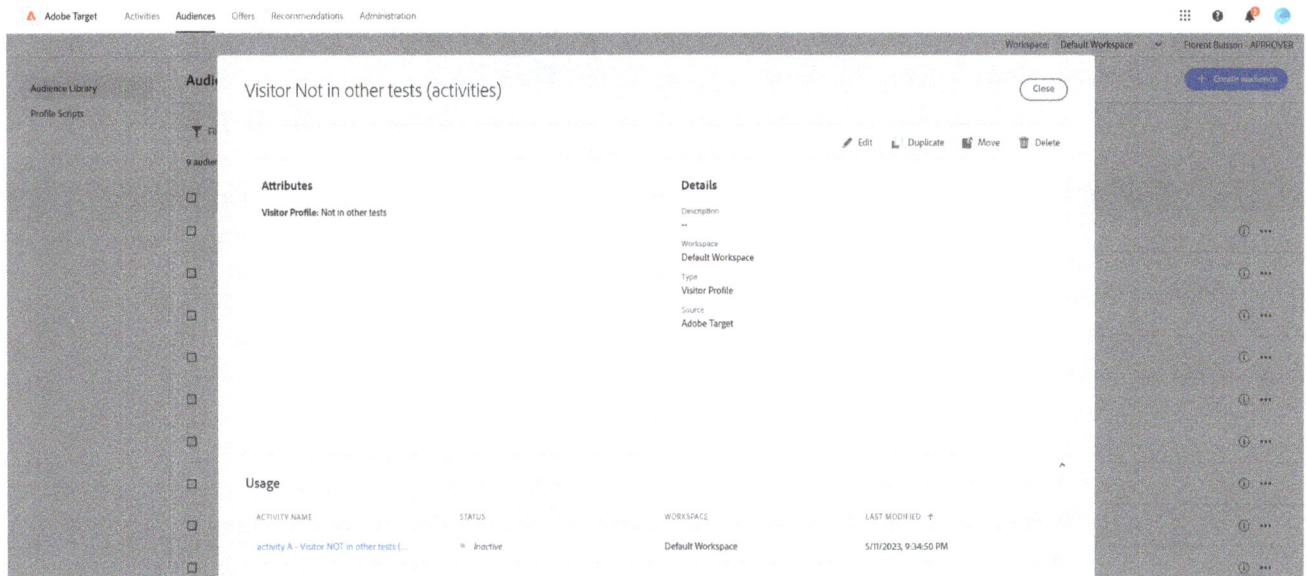

Since running a single activity at a time on a website is obviously very restrictive, we'll soon need to figure out how to deal with multiple activities at once. Let's look at how to prioritize activities.

Solving local interactions with prioritization

Starting at the most granular level, we might have multiple activities that are available at the same time on a single element of a page—for example, on a button. We could have defined these activities in the VEC, in which case the button is identified by its CSS selector, or we could have defined them in the Form Composer, in which case the button is wrapped in an mbox. Either way, we have two activities that may be triggered when a visitor enters the page.

We can determine whether there's any conflict by going into the Collisions tab of an activity's summary page.

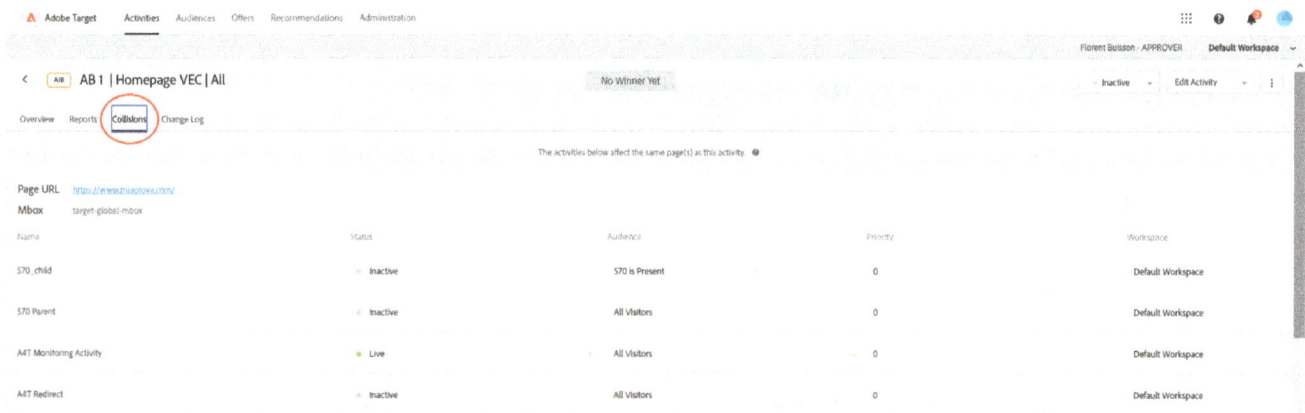

Any activity affecting a selector or mbox on the same page as the current activity will show up in this tab.

How we should handle a conflict or interaction really depends on the nature of the activities involved: are these permanent personalization activities or temporary A/B tests used to pick a winner or for measurement purposes?

In the case of permanent personalization activities, it makes sense to use prioritization. When creating an activity, we can assign it a Priority in the Goals & Settings step.

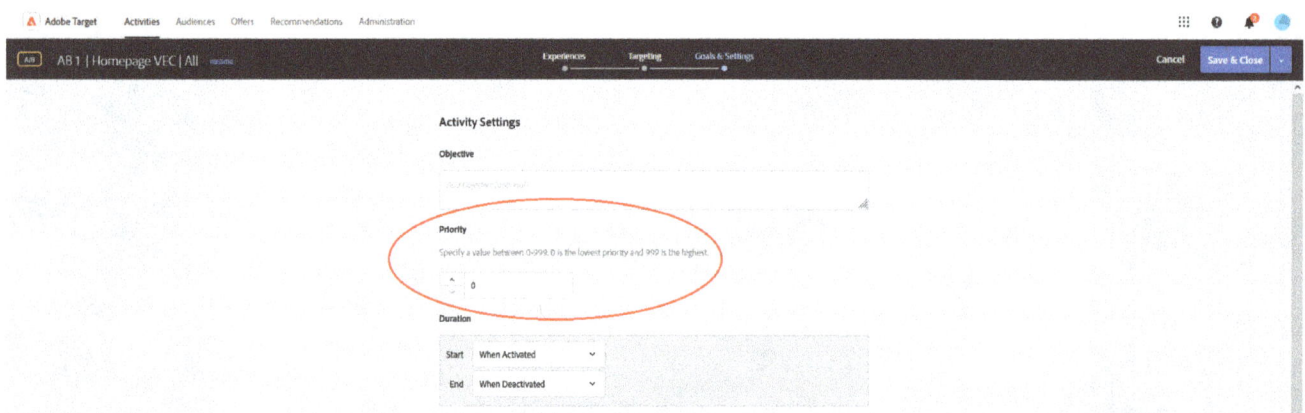

This way, higher-priority activities will take precedence. For instance, the preference-based campaign may be preferable when the relevant information is available, but otherwise the page should display the geo-based campaign.

Note: By default, the priority slider only has three levels—low, medium, and high. If we anticipate that we might have more than three activities running in the same place, we can enable a scale from 0 to 999 (which would theoretically allow us to prioritize up to a thousand activities in the same place!) by going into the Administration > Reporting tab.

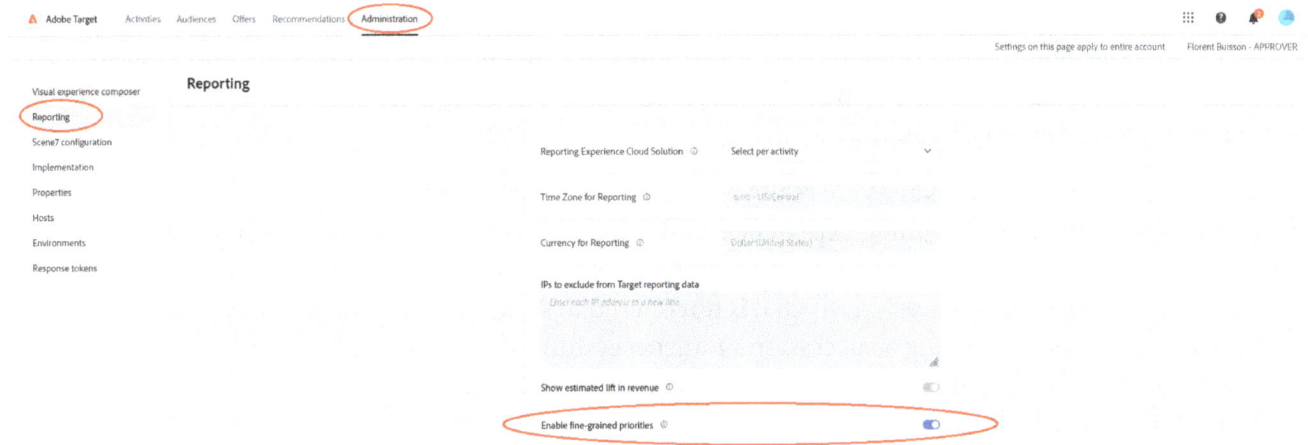

However, prioritization is not the correct approach with A/B tests, except in very specific cases. It can be unpredictable and lead to unreliable results because of the way it interacts with user segmentation and randomization. Let's say, for instance, that we have the following two A/B tests:

- Test #1 is targeted only to users on a mobile device and uses 40% of relevant traffic (20% in control group and 20% in treatment group). We give this test higher priority.
- Test #2 is targeted to users on all devices and uses 100% of relevant traffic (50% in control group and 50% in treatment group). We give this test lower priority.

All visitors on non-mobile devices such as laptops will be entered in Test #2, but only 60% of visitors on a mobile device will, due to the priority given to Test #1. This will bias the average result of Test #2.

Device type is not the only factor that could bias the result of a test by interacting with prioritization. The locations of the tests can have a similar impact. For instance, if Test #1 is triggered on the Home Page (HP) and Test #2 is triggered on Product Detail Pages (PDPs), prioritization would work correctly for visitors who go through the HP before seeing a PDP, but not for visitors who enter a PDP through a different journey.

Therefore, when conducting A/B tests (regardless of whether they use the same location), it is better to use a different approach, such as mutually exclusive swimlanes.

Mutually exclusive swimlanes

As we saw in chapter 3.1, another approach is to use profile scripts to split our traffic into separate groups and then run an activity on only one of them. For instance, we might split our traffic equally into Group 1 and Group 2 and run an A/B test on Group 2. While the A/B test is active, all visitors in Group 2 would be split between a control group and a treatment group. Yes, that means groups within groups, which can be very confusing. Two pieces of advice to make life easier:

- Use different words for the overarching groups that include activities and the groups within an activity. Going along with the analogy of lanes in a swimming pool, let's call the overarching groups *lanes*.

- Use a different indexing system for the overarching groups (lanes) that include activities and the groups within an activity. If, as is customary, the groups within an activity are indexed by alphabet letters (Group A, Group B, and so on), then use numerals for the overarching groups (Lane 1, Lane 2, and so on).

Going back to the hypothetical situation above, our traffic is now split into Lane 1 and Lane 2, with an A/B test running on Lane 2. While the A/B test is active, all visitors in Lane 2 are split between a control group (Group A) and a treatment group (Group B). Much less confusing!

The main use case where swimlanes are really helpful is with exploratory/discovery tests. With most tests, the goal is to implement the winning experience, and measurement is only a step in that process. However, sometimes the measurement is the point. For instance, if we want to precisely determine the value of a specific feature, we might run a test in which it is not offered to some users. Lukas Vermeer (of Booking.com fame) tells a story about running a succession of unsuccessful tests to improve the display of hotels on the landing page, then finding out that removing that display had no impact whatsoever on user engagement. He had been trying to optimize a feature that was entirely superfluous.

My preferred alternative to swimlanes

On the face of it, swimlanes offer a neat solution to the problem of interactions. Let's take a classic example: a button is failing to catch the visitors' attention, so one team runs an A/B test in which the button is colored in red, while another team tests having the text of the button in red. Having both the button and its text be the same color would be problematic because the text would be invisible. With the use of swimlanes, no visitor is exposed to both treatments while the tests are running.

Unfortunately, this only pushes the problem further down the pipeline: if both tests are successful and both teams decide to implement their solution, the problematic interaction is now pushed directly into production and shown to 100% of visitors! In such a contrived situation, one might argue that someone will probably realize along the way that the treatments are incompatible, but in other cases the interaction effects might be more subtle and never actually be detected. Thus swimlanes can temporarily avert problems but don't actually solve them.

Therefore, my general recommendation is to let A/B tests overlap naturally. If anyone raises a concern about interaction, or if some numbers look suspicious, you'll be able to look at the visitors who were exposed to both treatments through sheer randomness and check to see what happened to them.

Sometimes however, you may want to have more control than that over the process—for instance, when you have strong concerns about the potential interaction between the treatments of two upcoming tests. This is especially relevant if only a small fraction of traffic is exposed to the treatment in one or both of these tests. In such a situation a very small percentage of visitors would naturally be exposed to both treatments, leaving us uncertain about interaction effects. A better solution in such cases is to merge these two tests into a single one.

For instance, if we want no more than 10% of our traffic to be exposed to each treatment, we'd still allocate 20% of our traffic to the test as a whole, split as follows:

- 5% of traffic gets the current version of the website (overall control group)
- 5% gets only the first treatment (Treatment 1 group)
- 5% gets only the second treatment (Treatment 2 group)
- 5% gets both treatments (interaction group)

The beauty of this approach is that if we don't see an interaction effect, we can simply pool the two groups that were exposed to the first treatment and the two groups that were not exposed to it to measure the effect of that first treatment (and do likewise for the second treatment). We're not sacrificing statistical power on the individual treatments just because we wanted to account for interaction effects. Nonetheless, we'll have enough visitors exposed to both treatments to be reasonably confident about the size of the interaction effect.

Of course, "reasonably confident" is not the same as properly statistically significant. If we want to ensure a truly stat sig comparison between the interaction group and the overall control group right from the get-go, we'll need to increase our sample size.

The annoying truth is that interaction effects are not that frequent, but they do sometimes happen. In my opinion, the best compromise overall is to combine the general policy of looking after the fact at the interaction between independently run tests with the special policy of merging tests for treatments presenting a higher risk of interaction. And remember: if we have run two independent tests, and both treatments are promising but the interaction measured after the fact is worrisome, we can always implement the most promising of the two treatments as the new default. We can then run a follow-up test to determine whether or not we should also implement the second treatment.

Summary

As soon as you're running more than one activity at a time on your website, you'll need to think about **interactions**, if only because stakeholders often worry and inquire about them. My preferred course of action in general is to let activities interact freely and check for any evidence of interaction after the fact, running a follow-up test focused on the interaction if necessary.

When there are strong concerns about potential interactions between upcoming tests, you can alleviate these concerns by **combining the tests**. This requires a bit more legwork but allows us to avoid sacrificing statistical power.

Finally, despite the popularity of **swimlanes**, I recommend using them only for exploratory tests, where you want to get the cleanest possible measurement, or in the early stages of iterative testing, when you can postpone thinking about interactions until the feature is ready to ship.

Chapter 3.5: Server-Side and Hybrid Implementation

Adobe Target was initially centered around client-side implementation, i.e., JavaScript code running on a visitor's browser and contacting the Adobe servers without the need to go through the website's server. However, server-side rendering of websites—namely, doing more of the computation on the website's server instead of on the visitor's browser—has been gaining popularity for a while now. Therefore, Adobe Target now offers a server-side implementation as well as a hybrid implementation that blends elements of both client-side and server-side.

Server-side implementation

Let's first contrast how server-side implementation works in comparison to client-side implementation. As mentioned, in the client-side option the visitor's browser sends requests directly to Adobe's server as well as to our website's.

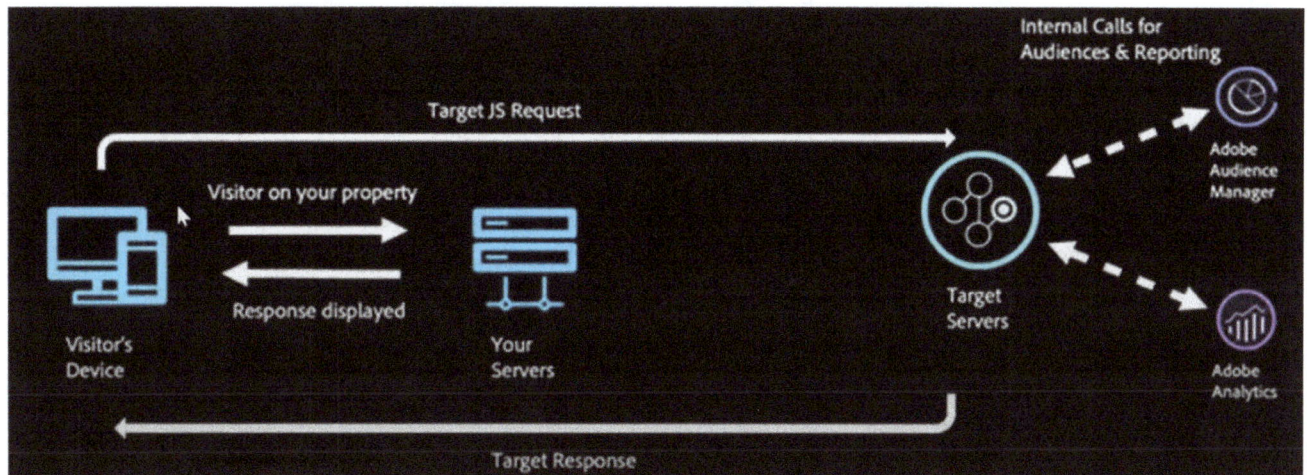

(Source: Adobe blog)

On the other hand, with server-side implementation the visitor's browser only sends requests to our website's server; our server, in turn, sends requests to Adobe's server in order to determine what content it should serve to the visitor.

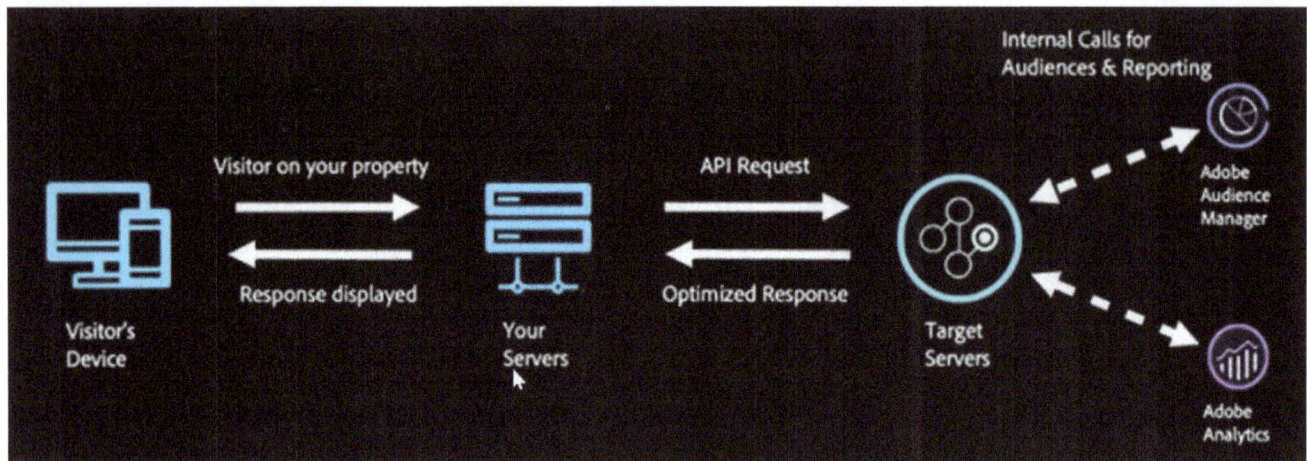

(Source: Adobe blog)

One of the main advantages of server-side implementation is that it avoids the flickering that occurs when the visitor's browser displays some content, sends a request to the Target servers, retrieves the relevant content, and replaces it in the browser. With server-side implementation, our website's server retrieves all the necessary information from the Target server before sending any content to the visitor's browser, so there is no flickering.

The distinction between client-side and server-side is mostly relevant for the software engineers who have to deal with it when adding new features to the website that will be tested. However, it also has some implications for us, the analysts.

For instance, because the requests to the Target servers are sent from our website's server and not the browser, we will not be able to see the requests in the Adobe debugger browser extension; we'll have to use trace mode instead.

We also won't be able to use the Visual Experience Composer, which relies on client-side implementation; instead we'll have to use the Form Composer with named mboxes.

Hybrid implementation

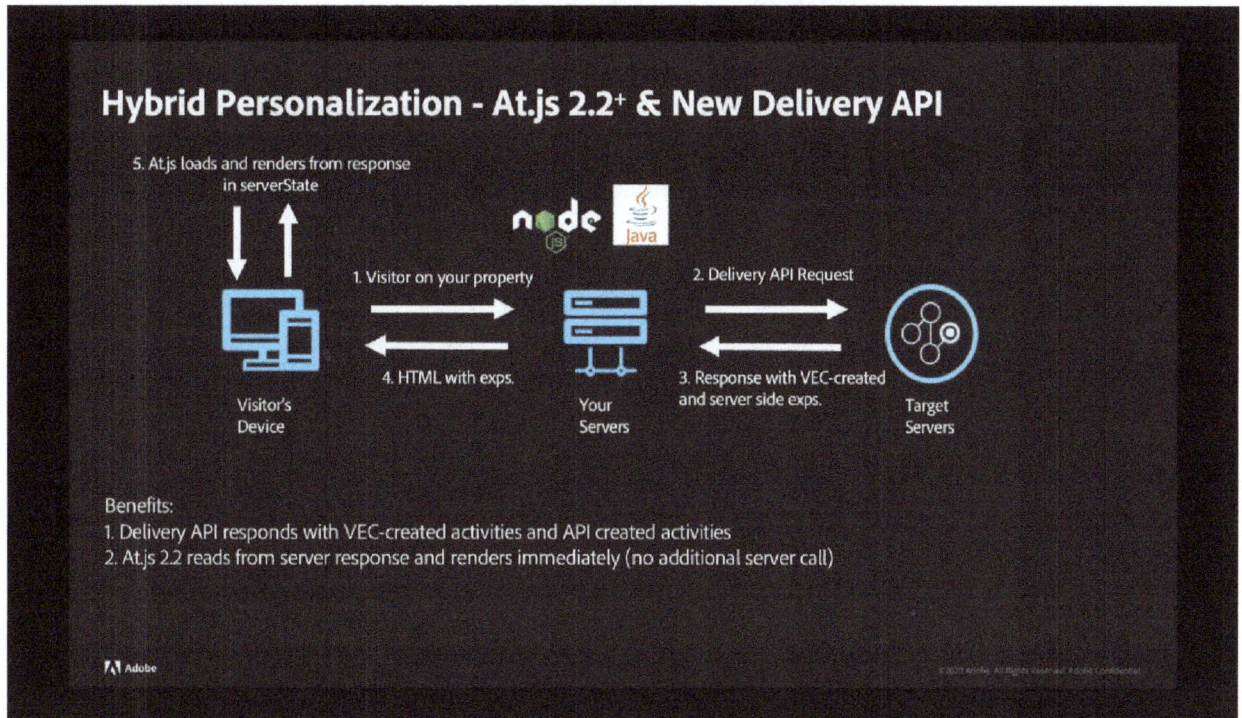

(Source: Adobe Target documentation)

The hybrid implementation offers a middle ground between client-side and server-side: we can use the VEC and reduce flickering (this is good), but because the fetching is done from our server, the requests won't show up in the Adobe debugger browser extension (this is not so good).

Summary

The topic of **client-side versus server-side implementation** is an odd one. On the one hand, it is an engineering architectural decision that will have been resolved well before your arrival, and most of its implications will only affect software engineers. On the other hand, it has vast ramifications in terms of what you can or cannot do as an analyst. If your Adobe Target implementation is client-side, you can basically disregard this chapter. But if your implementation is server-side or hybrid, you'll need to remember that it precludes using the Adobe debugger browser extension (in both cases) or the VEC (unavailable in server-side only).

Chapter 3.6: Single-Page Applications (SPAs)

Single-page applications (SPAs) can often provide a more fluid experience for visitors, which has been a strong factor in their success. But they also create specific challenges in using Adobe Target: historically, Target would fire whenever a page (re)loaded, but there is no page refresh or loading with an SPA.

Adobe Target Views

Adobe Target version 2.0 (at.js 2.x) addresses this issue by introducing the concept of *views*. Adobe defines a view as "a logical group of visual elements that together make up an SPA experience"—i.e., a unit of visual content that can be used to mimic and replace pages for the purpose of testing. For instance, we might define the *home view* as the content that is displayed when a visitor enters our site URL in a browser, regardless of any changes in various subsections of the display, such as entering preferences in a form. Then we might define as *product detail view* all situations in which a product's details are displayed in the central area, regardless of what's happening in the side bars. As such, a single view can include several transitions that would cause a page (re)load in a traditional website. Conversely, we can define different views conditionally based on a visitor's stated preferences or journey—e.g., have different billing views for visitors who selected pickup versus delivery.

Basic implementation

The developer's part

This is a book for web analysts, not developers, but I find that it often helps to have at least a basic understanding of what's happening under the hood. Here, the developers will create a function that captures the name of the current view (either from the URL or your site's router, depending on the implementation) and fires `adobe.target.triggerView(viewName, options)` whenever it changes. This allows marketers to use the VEC to design and run the A/B and XT tests for the defined views.

On the other hand, once at.js has been configured and set up on the site, it will send a request to the Adobe server to get the offers only when the site loads initially, and it will then store all the relevant offers in cache.

Thus, when the view name changes, `triggerView()` will access the relevant offers for the current view from the cache and serve them without needing to get them from the server. (It will still send a notification to the server for reference, but that will not impede the delivery of the content.)

The web analyst's part

Once the developers have set up at.js and configured `triggerView()` to fire at the right place and the right time, we can develop tests on views in the Visual Experience Composer. That is, view names are automatically recognized by the VEC and provided to us the same way as page names. Let's see what it looks like in practice, with an SPA that I created for that purpose.

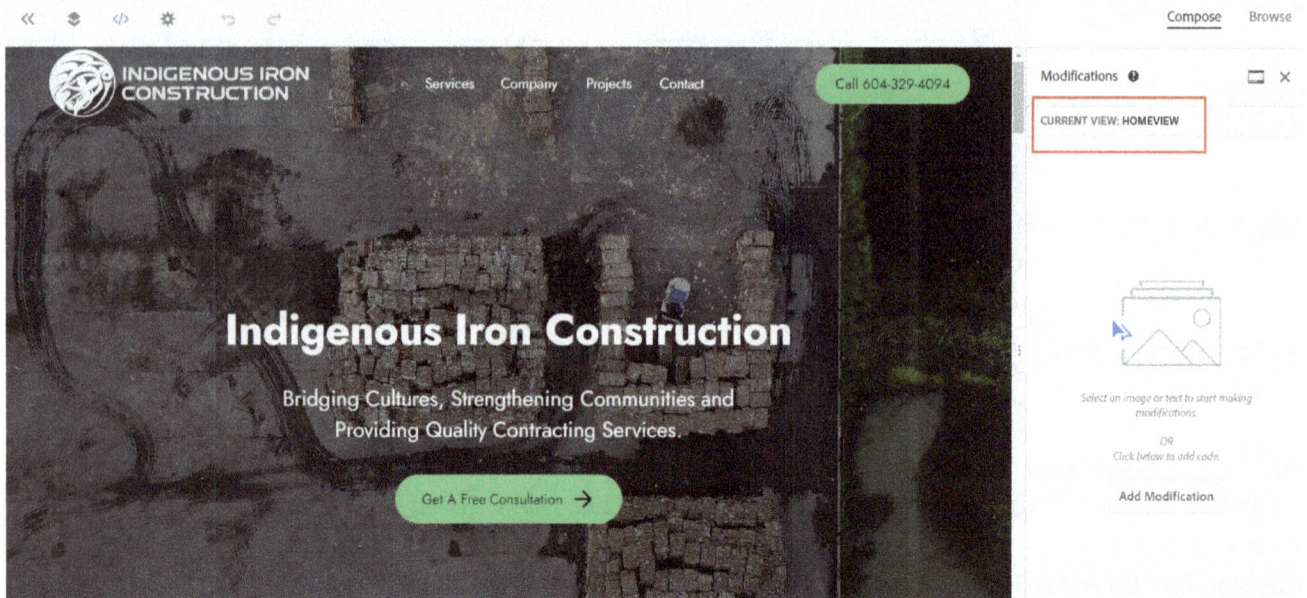

One of the main differences when using the SPA version of the VEC is that when we need to make changes in several places that fall under different views, we don't need to use the multi-page feature anymore. We can simply click on a link and select *Navigate to this link* to go to a different view.

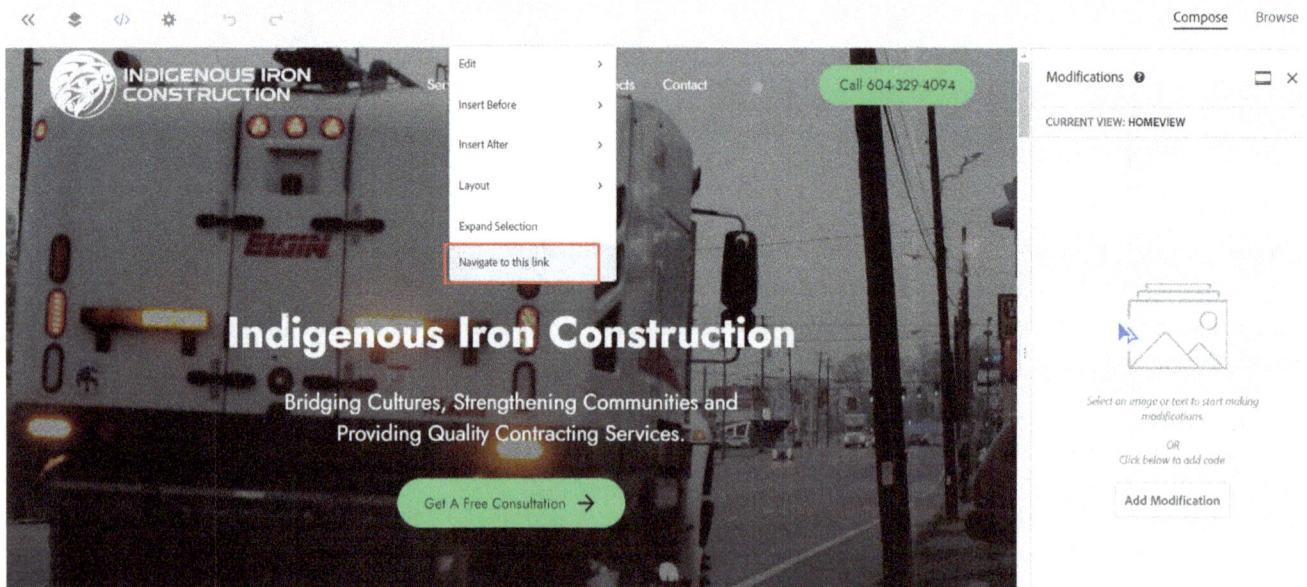

The Current View setting on the right updates automatically to the new view, but the changes to the previous view are preserved.

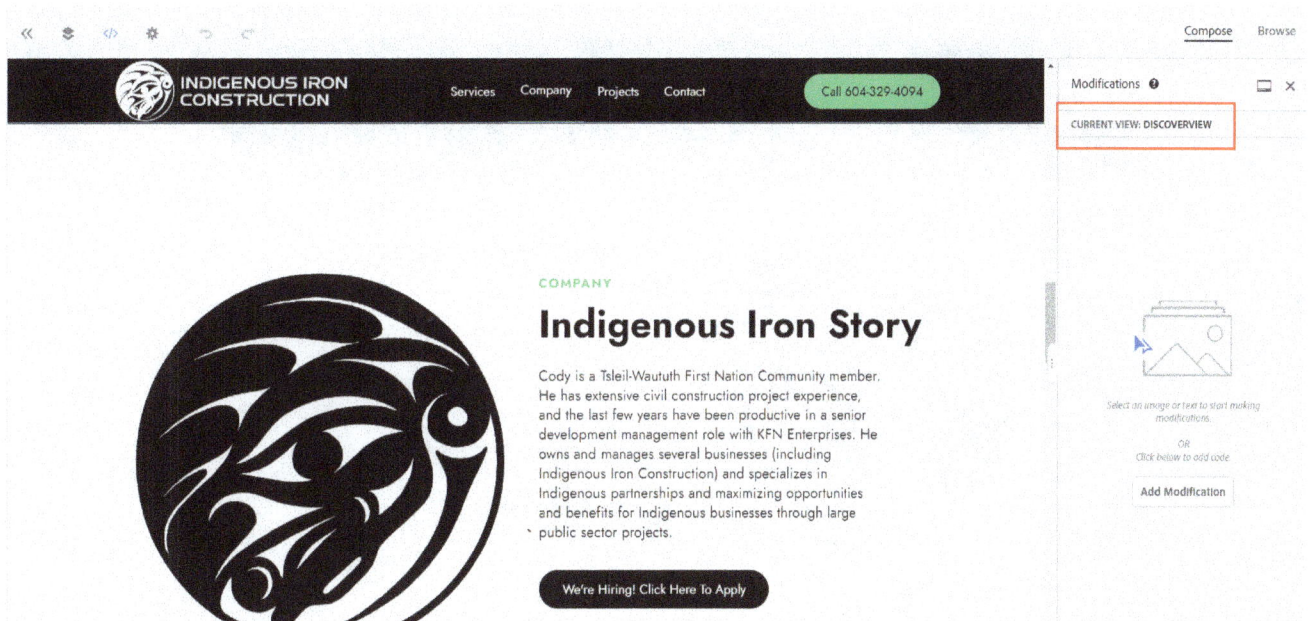

One of the big advantages of using SPAs is the ability to keep some parts of the display, such as menus and sidebars, unchanged even as some other sections are modified. The upside to this is that we don't have to reload them again and again. The downside is that creating an activity that affects durable menus and sidebars requires an extra step.

After modifying the desired element, we'll need to click on the *Move* button that appears when we hover over that change in the right-side menu.

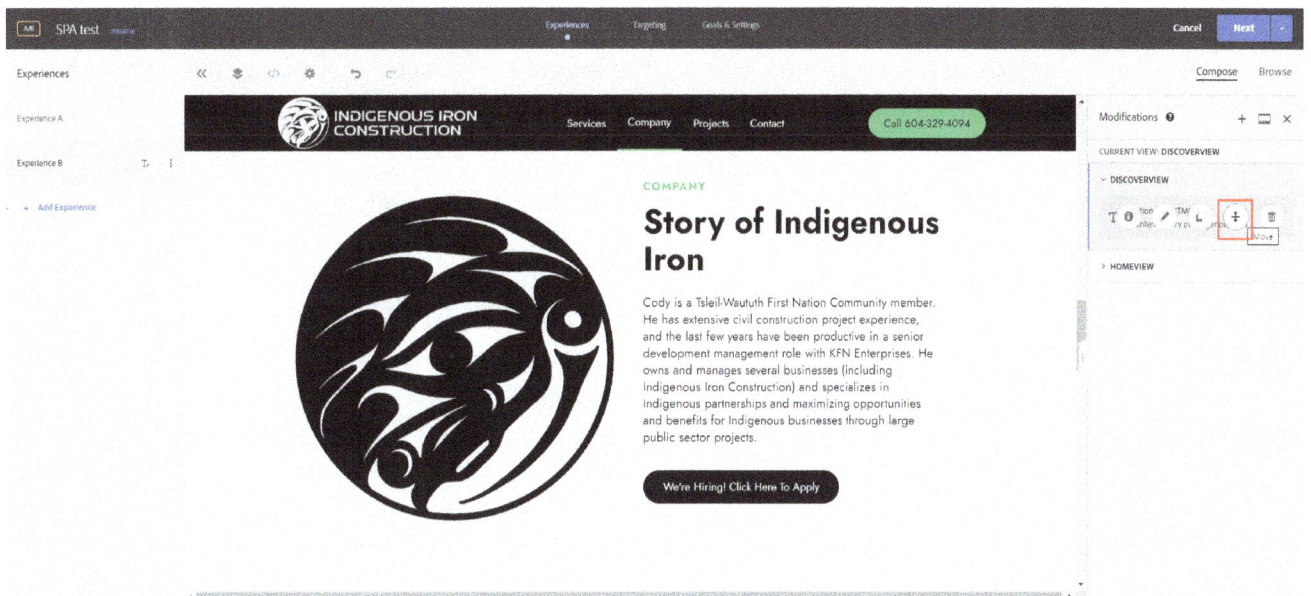

This will move "up" the change to the page load event within the current view, so that it applies to all applicable views. (Here, "up" means both higher in the right-side menu and higher in the logical hierarchy of the SPA architecture.)

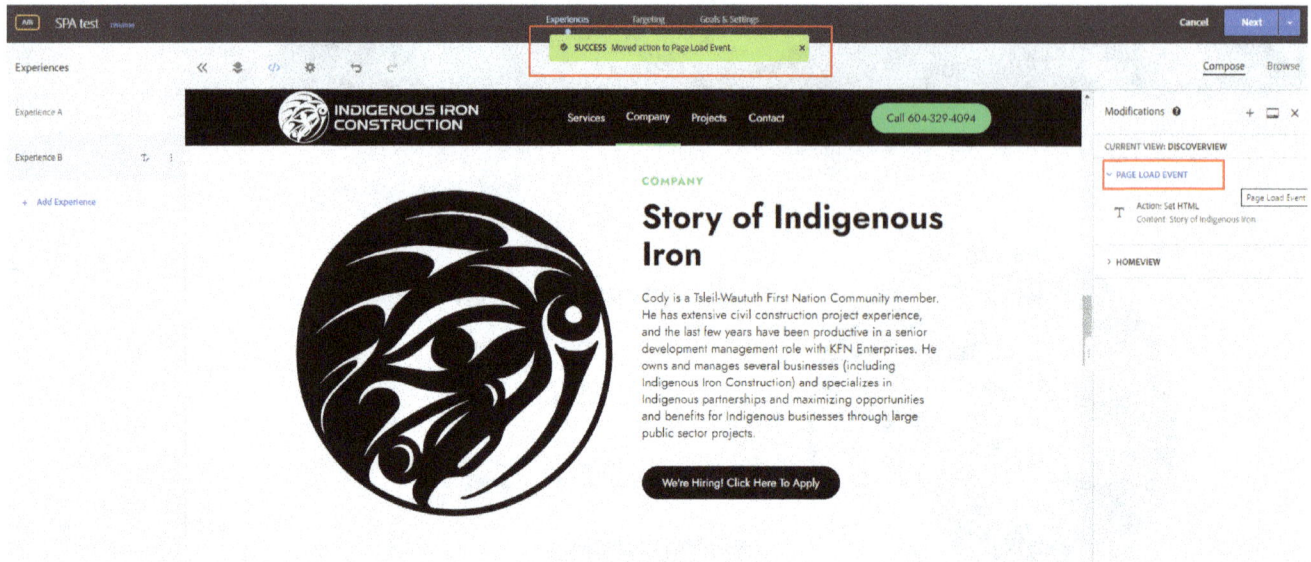

A note regarding SPAs: At the moment, at.js 2.x supports A/B tests with a fixed allocation or Auto-Allocate, as well as Experience Targeting, but it doesn't support multivariate tests, Auto-Target, or Automated Personalization. Moreover, the VEC is the only approach that is supported for SPAs; we can't use the Form-based Experience Composer.

Updating audience criteria based on customer behavior

As I mentioned earlier, at.js will normally only send a request to the Adobe server for the relevant offers once, on the initial loading of the website. "Relevant" is the operative word here: only offers whose audience criteria are currently fulfilled by the visitor will be sent. But obviously, these criteria can change as the visitor browses through the site and takes actions such as logging in. If some of the activities on the site are defined only for logged-in visitors, the corresponding content will not have been loaded in the initial call to the Adobe server.

Fortunately, Adobe Target provides a solution to fetch offers after the initial load: the developers only need to call the function `adobe.target.getOffers()`, and then pass its response to `adobe.target.applyOffers()`. In other words: as web analysts, we're not limited to creating activities on an SPA website based only on the initial audience criteria available when the site initially loads; we also can use audience criteria that gets updated based on the visitor's behavior. The only (unfortunate) difference is that we can't do it all alone in Adobe Target anymore, we'll need the developers to add the relevant functions in the site's code.

Summary

As with the client-side versus server-side chapter, this one will also be relevant only to a small subset of readers. If you're working on an **SPA**, you'll need to remember the slight differences this causes in the use of the VEC. The use of the function triggerView() also means more opportunities for bugs to be introduced in the code, so you'll have to watch out for that.

Chapter 3.7: Administration

While most of our time as analysts will be spent creating and running activities, we'll sometimes have to deal with the administration of Adobe Target—for instance, managing users and other settings. As you can see below, the Adobe Target interface offers a dedicated tab with several sections:

- Visual Experience Composer
- Reporting
- Scene7 configuration
- Implementation
- Hosts
- Environments
- Response tokens
- Users

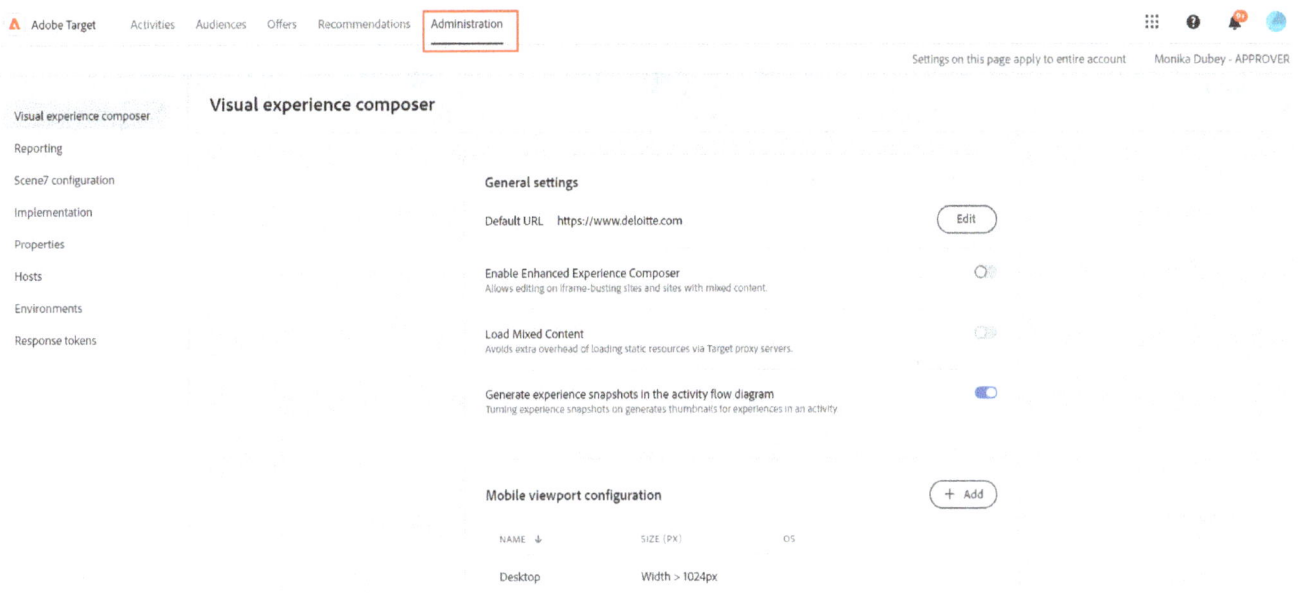

You may never need to deal with some of these sections, so I won't do an exhaustive walkthrough; they are called out in various places in the rest of the book where relevant. I'll only cover user management below, as it is the section you're most likely to have a need for.

User management

No one is an island in themselves, and experimentation is a team effort. This means that you'll probably need other people to have access to Adobe Target; for instance, software engineering managers might request access so that they can deactivate an activity that is wreaking havoc on the website while you're unreachable. In this section, we'll see how you can add and remove users as needed.

Note that in this section, **user** will refer to internal users of Adobe Target, such as other analysts or members of the product teams, not to consumers visiting your website.

Let's go into Administration > Users, where we can see a list of current users. Clicking on *Users Management* will open a new tab to Adobe's Admin console.

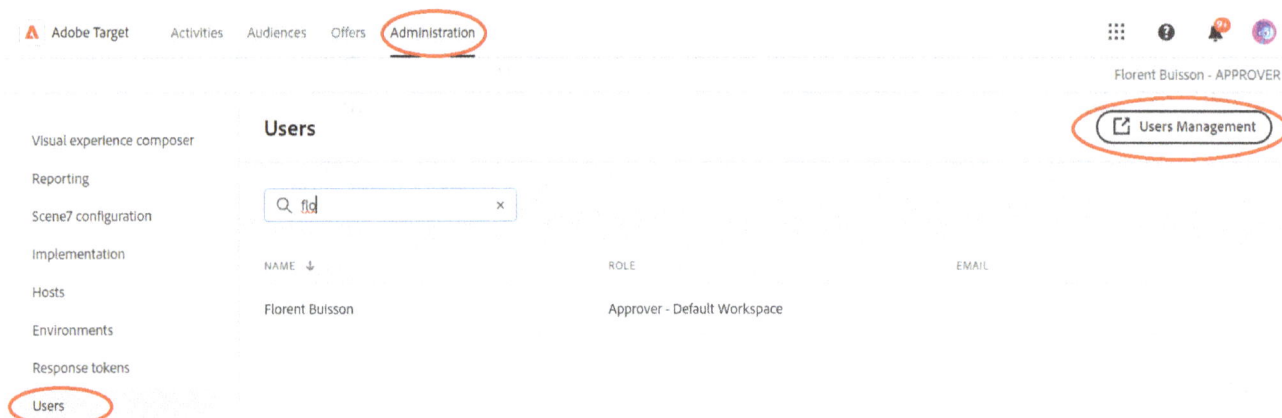

The Admin console automatically opens on the Product profiles section of the Adobe Target page.

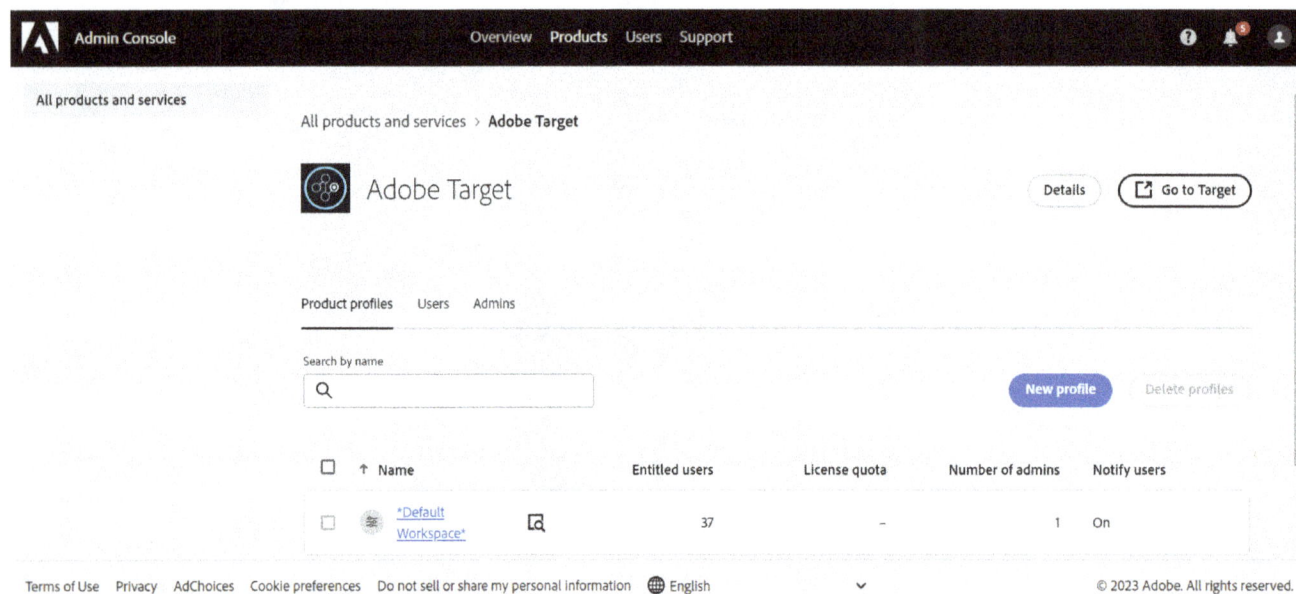

Product profiles (a.k.a **workspaces**) determine which products and features a user has access to. Only people in your organization with **product admin** status can create or modify product profiles. I'll assume that as an analyst you don't have that status; if you need to learn more about this topic, please refer to "Manage product profiles for enterprise users" on the Adobe documentation website. Just note that users in **Default Workspace** will have access to all features and all activities on all properties.

Let's click on the name of the product profile for Adobe Target, which opens the Default Workspace screen.

Note that in the previous screen, the three tabs displayed were Product profiles, Users, and Admin, whereas now we have Users, Admins and Permissions. Unfortunately, the Users tabs in the two cases are different and display different information. Make sure that you're in the Adobe Target > [product profile name] section if you need to visualize or edit users' product roles under the Users tab.

In the Users tab, which is the one open by default, we can see a list of current users and their Product roles. There are four possible roles, with decreasing levels of permissions:

- **Approver:** can create, edit, and activate or stop activities
- **Editor:** can create and edit activities before they are live, but cannot approve the launch of an activity
- **Publisher:** can view and activate activities, but cannot create or edit them
- **Observer:** can only view activities

We can add users by selecting the *Add users* button. This opens a pop-up window where we can enter the information of the new user we want to add.

Once Adobe has recognized the user, we can determine which product role they should be assigned.

For practical purposes, anyone who needs to be able to stop an activity must get the Approver role. I feel that the distinctions between the other roles don't matter much in practice, but your company might have strict policies you must follow in that regard.

A1. Glossary

The field of experimentation and optimization is full of concepts that are complex, vague, or both. People (including me!) often use different terms interchangeably to mean the same thing. In this book, I have tried to be consistent, so you can be sure that if I use one of the following terms, its meaning is the definition given here.

This problem is further compounded by Adobe's rich history of product development and acquisition of other companies, which has led to a succession of different technical terms over the years. I have tried to make this glossary a go-to reference that will allow you to become fluent in Adobe jargon.

If you don't find what you need here, you might try your luck with Adobe's own glossary for Target at experienceleague.adobe.com/en/docs/target/using/introduction/glossary.

A4T: Acronym for *Analytics for Target*, the integration of Adobe Analytics and Adobe Target, which enables the use of richer data in Target—e.g., using conversion metrics defined in Adobe Analytics as success metrics for Adobe Target activities.

A/A test: An **A/B test** in which two groups of visitors are served the same version of the website but are tracked separately, to confirm that visitors are effectively assigned to a group at random and behave in similar ways, and that all necessary tracking works as expected.

A/B test: A project in which several different versions of the website are delivered at random to external visitors according to a predetermined allocation. In the most common version, half of the visitors are served the current version of the website (the **control** or version A), and half of the visitors are served a version with a change that we're considering implementing (the **treatment** or version B). Because of the random nature of the assignment, any average difference in outcomes between the visitors who have been served one version and the visitors who have been served the other version(s) can be attributed fully to the difference between versions.

active/inactive: Status of an activity in Adobe Target. An **activity** that is *active* is being delivered to external visitors to your website. An activity that is *inactive* might be accessed by internal users (i.e., company employees) for QA purposes but is not delivered to external visitors.

activity: The implementation of a single project in Adobe Target, whether an **A/A test**, a **canary release**, a **progressive rollout**, an **A/B test**, or a **multivariate test**. This is a term specific to Adobe Target. In the past, *activities* were called "campaigns."

Adobe Experience Cloud: Adobe's suite of tools dedicated to digital experiences (typically websites and mobile apps). It includes solutions such as Adobe Analytics, Adobe Target, **Adobe Experience Manager**, and Adobe Campaign. It was previously named the Adobe Marketing Cloud.

Adobe Experience Manager (AEM): An Adobe product combining digital asset management and a content management system, allowing companies to source, adapt, and deliver assets in a consistent and personalized manner.

Adobe Experience Platform (AEP): Adobe's centralized data foundation, underpinning many other products such as Target.

Adobe Marketing Cloud: see **Adobe Experience Cloud**.

AEM: see **Adobe Experience Manager**.

AEP: see **Adobe Experience Platform**.

alloy.js: The JavaScript file corresponding to *Alloy*, the name code of the **Adobe Experience Platform (AEP)** Web SDK. alloy.js must be loaded on your site to use the AEP SDK.

authorization token: A string of characters used in a browser URL to enter Target **trace mode** and access debugging information such as **response tokens**. It is generated in the Administration > Implementation tab of the Adobe Target console and is valid for only six hours.

campaign: see **activity**.

canary release: A release of a new feature or experience that is targeted to a small group of users–e.g., only internal users-, in order to confirm that things work as expected.

cohort: All the visitors who visit the website for the first time during a certain period of time—e.g., *the January cohort* or *the January 2nd cohort*. Cohorts are generally aggregated retrospectively for the purpose of consistent reporting, e.g., "the January cohort had a probability of purchase of 5%."

control/treatment: Lingo derived from academic and medical research, for which randomized experimentation was initially developed. When investigating a medical treatment, researchers would measure its effectiveness by assigning it at random to some patients in their study, while the other patients in the study, who did not receive the treatment, served as a baseline to control for other phenomena such as the placebo effect. By extension, in applied experimentation & optimization for business, we sometimes call the new feature or version of the website under consideration the *treatment* and the current, preexisting version of the website the *control*.

debugger: A browser extension that allows you to visualize in real time information about the Adobe applications implemented on your site (e.g., console logs, network requests) as you navigate the site. Officially called the *Adobe Experience Cloud Debugger*.

DTM: see **Tags**.

ECID: Acronym for *Experience Cloud ID*, a unique identifier assigned when a new visitor enters your website and then stored in a cookie to be retrieved during later visits.

environment: In software development lingo, a version of a software or website with a specific use and audience. Typically, new features are implemented first in a *development* or *non-production environment* restricted to internal users for validation before being implemented in the *production environment* used by the normal users.

experience: A particular version of a website, e.g., the existing version seen by most users or the test version with the new feature under consideration. Also called a *variant*. An experience can be based on multiple **offers**.

Experience Cloud ID: see **ECID**.

Experience Data Model (XDM): Unified data model for the **Adobe Experience Platform**. It offers out-of-the-box, standardized data definitions for common business concepts such as orders. Watch this Adobe summit video for more information.

experiment: Another term for **A/B test**.

global mbox: Updated version of the traditional **mbox**, or *marketing box*. In the traditional approach, an mbox was created for each activity, wrapping the code for the corresponding content on the page. This resulted in one server call for each mbox, with a potential for "flicker" when the visitor reached the content and the corresponding server call had to be made. Now, a single *global mbox* is initiated at the top of the page, generating a single server call for all activities on the page and reducing flicker.

group: All the visitors in an activity who have been randomly assigned to be served the same version of the website. In an **A/B test**, for instance, the *control group* (or *group A*) refers to all the visitors who have been served the current version of the website, whereas the *treatment group* (or *group B*) refers to all the visitors who have been served the tentative version of the website with the new feature that is being tested.

host: Web domain (i.e., example.com) or server that contains a site.

inactive: See **active**.

Launch: See **Tags**.

location: Area on a page, typically corresponding to a single <div> element, where different pieces of content can be served in an **activity**. It can be wrapped in a local **mbox** or referred to from the **global mbox**.

mbox: Initially the acronym for *marketing box*, a JavaScript reference indicating a piece of the website code that can be modified by Adobe Target. Traditionally, one mbox corresponded to one **location**, but this approach has been replaced by the use of a single **global mbox**.

MCID: Acronym for *Marketing Cloud ID*, an Adobe unique identifier that was a precursor to the current **ECID**.

multivariate test (MVT): a test that combines multiple **offers** in multiple **locations** to determine the best combination overall.

offer: In Adobe Target, a piece of content displayed within an **mbox** or **location** on the website during an **activity**. For instance, an **A/B test** in a single **location** on the site would have two different offers (**control** and **treatment**).

page parameter: A snapshot at a point in time. It can be generated by JS with the targetPageParams() function or by a tag management system. Also known as a *request parameter*.

profile parameter: Persistent variable generated/captured by the Adobe Target servers and stored in a cookie.

profile script: Small pieces ("snippets") of JavaScript code that are run whenever an **mbox** makes a request to the Adobe Servers.

profile script attribute: The value returned by a profile script.

progressive rollout: Experimentation & optimization process in which a new feature is rolled out to an increasing percentage of customers or visitors—e.g., 10% of new visitors on day one, 20% of new visitors on day two, and so on.

property: Generic term for all of an organization's websites, mobile apps, kiosks, and gaming devices where Adobe Target is being implemented.

QA mode: Short for *Quality Assurance mode*. A mode in Adobe Target that allows the user to visit their website and experience a certain variant of a selected **activity**, bypassing the random allocation and regardless of the status of the activity. It is typically used to validate that a new experience works correctly before activating the activity on visitor traffic. It is triggered by adding specific query parameters to the URL.

request parameter: See **page parameter**.

response token: Any one of a variety of values created or captured by Adobe Target when it answers a request from your website, such as **profile parameters** or the output of **profile scripts**. The user can mark these values as *response tokens* in Adobe Target's configuration so that they are made available in the browser's console in **trace mode**.

SDID: Acronym for *Supplemental Data ID*, an identifier for unique pageviews that is used by both Adobe Analytics and Adobe Target. It enables **A4T** by providing a mechanism to join the data generated in the two tools.

session: Standard definition for a visit in web analytics. A visitor may come to a website, leave it open while opening a different tab, and then get back to the original website a few minutes or several days later, which creates the need for a standard definition of a visit. A *session* is defined by a period of continuous activity on a site followed by a certain duration of inactivity, typically 30 minutes (i.e., if a visitor goes to a different tab but then returns to the tab with the original site within less than 30mn, this is considered a single session).

Tags: The new name for the client-side implementation of the Launch product within the **Adobe Experience Platform**. Launch was formerly known as Adobe *Dynamic Tag Management (DTM)*.

test: See **A/B test**.

tntId: The acronym for Test 'N' Target ID, the primary identifier for a user in Adobe Target. If it is not provided by your site, it will be auto-generated by Adobe Target.

token: See **authorization token** or **response token**.

trace mode: A browser mode that enables debugging information to be printed in the browser's console when navigating on the website.

treatment: see **control**.

variant: see **experience**.

Visual Experience Composer (VEC): A what-you-see-is-what-you-get interface in Adobe Target to create activities. It allows the user to make modifications to a website as it appears in a browser instead of having to modify its code.

XDM: See **experience data model**.

A2. Index

www.ingramcontent.com/pod-product-compliance
Lightning Source LLC
Chambersburg PA
CBHW080554220326
41599CB00032B/6473